W9-BSZ-373

Theatre Arts

Consultants

Laurence Binder
Cypress Fairbanks Independent School District
Houston, Texas

Diane Brewer
Hill Country Middle School
Austin, Texas

Nita Buell
Powell High School
Powell, Tennessee

Cindy Dunn
Coral Springs High School
Coral Springs, Florida

Krin Perry
Austin, Texas

Theatre Arts

The Dynamics of Acting

Fourth Edition

Dennis Caltagirone

National Textbook Company
a division of *NTC Publishing Group* • Lincolnwood, Illinois USA

Acknowledgments

Special thanks to Lee Caltagirone, Frank T. Wisniewski (Fashoo the Clown), Mary Booth Johnson (Tickles the Clown), Frank W. Springstead High School, Spring Hill, Florida, Parkway Middle School, Kissimmee, Florida, and Mowat Middle School, Lynn Haven, Florida.

Photo credits begin on page 319, which should be considered an extension of this copyright page.

Development: Word Management, Inc.
Interior and cover design: Ellen Pettengill

Library of Congress Cataloging-in-Publication Data

Caltagirone, Dennis, 1944–
    Theatre arts : the dynamics of acting / Dennis Caltagirone.—4th ed.
      p.   cm.
    Rev. ed. of: The dynamics of acting / Joan Snyder. 3rd ed. c1989.
    Includes index.
    Summary: Provides an overview of the theatrical production process with a focus on practical acting skills.
    ISBN 0-8442-5165-8 (hardcover)
    1. Acting—Juvenile literature.   [1. Acting.]   I. Snyder, Joan. Dynamics of acting. II. Title.
    PN2061.S617   1996
    792'.028—dc20   95-51220
                                      CIP
                                      AC

Published by National Textbook Company, a division of NTC Publishing Group.
© 1997 NTC Publishing Group, 4255 West Touhy Avenue
Lincolnwood (Chicago), Illinois 60646-1975 U.S.A.
All rights reserved. No part of this book may be reproduced, stored
in a retrieval system, or transmitted in any form or by any means,
electronic, mechanical, photocopying, recording, or otherwise, without
prior permission of NTC Publishing Group.

Manufactured in the United States of America

67890 QB 0987654321

CONTENTS

PART ONE Acting Skills 1

Chapter Two Characters for the Stage 20

Chapter Three The Stage Environment 38

Chapter Four Actors Using Pantomime and Clowning 58

Chapter Eight Imagination   **138**

PART THREE Theatre Production 157

Chapter Eleven   Behind the Scenes   198

PART FOUR Modern Theatre   237

Acting Skills

CHAPTER ONE

Setting the Stage

EXPECTATIONS

After reading this chapter, you will be able to

1.1 define and use basic theatre terms explained in this chapter

1.2 demonstrate active participation in individual and team theatre activities

1.3 display skills in basic acting techniques for body awareness and relaxation

1.4 participate in simple story dramatization

1.5 appreciate theatre experiences through the application of audience etiquette guidelines

verybody has a story to tell. Our stories are funny, sad, frightening, puzzling, mysterious. There are stories for every mood, for every age, for every people, for every occasion. Not only do we all have personal stories, we all enjoy hearing, watching, or listening to the stories of others. Somehow in the stories of others, we learn more about ourselves.

Stories for Theatre

Telling a story, listening to a song, watching a television program, movie, or video, or participating in a play all involve at least three important things:

1. the *story* as presented in a book, song, play, movie, video, or television show;
2. the *performer* who is the writer, singer, actor, or television personality; and
3. the *audience* that is responding internally to the story and the performers.

In the context of the theatre, the story is called the **play.**

Play: A story told in dialogue form by actors on stage for an audience.

Types of Plays: Tragedy

There are many kinds of stories, and there are many types of plays. Long ago, actors relied on two basic kinds of masks to help tell their stories: the mask of tragedy and the mask of comedy. Even today, plays are basically a variation of one or the other. A **tragedy** is a serious play that ends unhappily because the main character has a serious flaw or is caught in a perilous circumstance that must be overcome.

Tragedy invites a thoughtful response that takes the audience beyond the confines of its own time and place. Tragedy has universal appeal because it involves strong emotions that cause conflict and move the audience to sympathize with the main character. We all know the power and problems created by love, anger, hate, ambition, or revenge. A tragedy tells the

Tragedy: A play in which the main character has a major flaw or is caught in circumstances that must be overcome, or the flaw or circumstances will destroy the character's life.

story of a character caught in the power of one or more of these strong emotions and analyzes the consequences for that character and others.

Tragedy Is Psychological. Great tragedies help us understand great heroes. We learn that the main character is caught up in powerful emotions or situations. This hero can be a better-than-average person, as Aristotle suggests, or a common person trapped in a conflict because of lack of good judgment or circumstances beyond personal responsibility.

The main character usually suffers much in a tragedy. But through the conflict, pain, and suffering, the main character usually gains a greater sense of purpose or knowledge of self or others. The character either becomes a better person or is wounded or destroyed by the internal, or psychological, conflict.

Tragedy Is Emotional. When an audience experiences the story of a tragic hero, it usually feels sympathy or pity. The audience

An actor's role in a tragedy is to evoke strong sympathy from the audience.

realizes that the great qualities of the main character will not protect him or her from the struggle or fall. There is a sense of doom, the sense that what is going to happen is inevitable.

The Tragic Hero. The main character, or **protagonist,** in a tragedy usually has a strong personality with distinct principles and goals, for which he or she will have to make many sacrifices to achieve. The main character in a tragedy stands above the other characters because of noble birth, high rank, great virtues or vices, or unusual circumstances. The protagonist is a person of principle or dreams, which are often in conflict with the values of society or the common laws of the time. Sometimes the conflict is internal, and a protagonist is caught in difficult choices.

Almost always, a tragic hero is ready and willing to sacrifice all for a dream or goal. A protagonist never asks another to do what must be done. He or she seems willing to pay the personal price for the pursuit of the goal.

Protagonist: The main character in a play.

Types of Tragedies

In the description of tragedies, you probably recognized features of some of your favorite movies or television programs. Think of some examples of programs that ended unhappily because of a character flaw or circumstances that caused the protagonist to struggle.

Classical Tragedy. The Greeks and Romans had a host of gods and heroes, and the opportunity for conflict, struggle, and sacrifice was great. In the play *Antigone,* by Sophocles, the tragic hero, Antigone, disobeys the ruler's order that her brother be denied a proper and honorable burial. When she gives her brother a token burial by placing dust on the body, she pays for her devotion with her life.

Modern Tragedy. Many of the themes of the traditional tragedies of Shakespeare or the classical tragedies of the Greeks and Roman find modern expressions. People of all ages and countries have enjoyed Shakespeare's *Romeo and Juliet* for instance. This same tragic theme is played out in *West Side Story*, an updated tragedy about star-crossed lovers caught in a war between two New York City gangs.

Types of Plays: Comedy

Comedy: A play with a happy ending and humorous treatment of characters and situations.

In contrast to tragedies with their unhappy endings, **comedies** resolve funny situations with charm, wit, and laughter. Comedies are peopled with amusing characters who find themselves in amusing situations that usually have a happy ending.

Comedy has universal appeal because, through clever dialogue and silly misunderstandings, we learn about ourselves. We gain insight into the charming or annoying aspects of human nature.

The Role of Laughter. Not all comedies will make all audiences laugh out loud. Because laughter is so unpredictable, comedies are more difficult to perform than tragedies or other kinds of dramatic plays.

THE DIFFERENCES BETWEEN TRAGEDY AND COMEDY

	Tragedy	*Comedy*
Story	Universal themes	Specific time and place
Ending	Unhappy, inevitable	Happy, unpredictable
Protagonist	Average or noble	Average or less than average
Goals	Failure to achieve	Successful resolution
Audience	Emotional appeal	Physical, romantic, intellectual appeal

Types of Comedy. There are comedies that appeal to physical humor, those that appeal to the heart, and those that require real thought. Those that use slapstick or sight gags make us laugh.

In comedies that appeal to the heart, the audience feels tenderness toward and compassion for the protagonist. Many of Shakespeare's comedies, such as *A Midsummer Night's Dream* and *As You Like It,* are enjoyed for the romantic elements and witty dialogue.

Other Types of Stories

Drama captures the attention of the audience by featuring serious characters who portray a serious story. Dramatic actors can deliver both serious and humorous lines and use the strength of their character to bring realism to what are frequently difficult situations.

Drama: A play that considers serious issues and suggests solutions.

Musicals are another type of play that can be either humorous or serious in nature. Americans have long enjoyed musicals presented on both stage and screen. In 1993, the musical *Oklahoma!* received a special award in recognition of its fiftieth anniversary. Modern musicals like *Les Miserables* or *Phantom of the Opera* continue to draw large audiences. Actors in musicals need singing and dancing skills as well as acting ability.

Musical: A type of play that contains both song and dance.

Mysteries are a long-time favorite of audiences. These plays can be either serious or comic, and some invite audience participation. Audiences generally enjoy trying to figure out the complex motives of various characters. The twists and turns of the story create suspense and emotional involvement on the part of the audience.

Mystery: A type of play that focuses on a crime or situation that requires the use of clues to figure out the solution.

Summary

The theatre involves at least three important parts—the story, the actors, and the audience. The stories for theatre are called plays and there are many types. Tragedies and comedies are the main types of plays performed on stage. They can be compared in terms of qualities of the protagonist, ending, and emotional appeal. Other types of plays include dramas, musicals, and mysteries.

Almost any story can become a comedy, or tragedy, or musical, or mystery, or drama. It all depends on your imagination, skills, and resources. Take this opportunity to convert a well-known story into a fun play. Here's what you do.

Step One
The Play. Use the story of Cinderella (or any fairy tale) and change it into a play. Decide which kind of play you want it to be. Work in a group that wants to do the same type of play.

Step Two
The Plan. Make a list of characters for your play and decide who will play each part. Choose a director to help the actors with their lines and gestures. Talk about how to make your story into the type of play you have chosen. Discuss how each actor can help make the play into a comedy or whichever type of play you have selected. Make a list of scenes you will

need for your play. If you can, make a simple costume or mask for each character. Make a simple sign or poster to identify each scene.

Step Three
The Practice. The director works with the actors to tell the story, plan lines to say, develop gestures, and create costumes, scenery, masks, or signs. Practice at least twice before your final "dress rehearsal." You might also want to make a program for your play.

Step Four
The Performance. Each group will perform its play for the rest of the class. If there is time and interest, your class might invite another class to be the audience for the performances.

Step Five
The Ratings. After your group has performed, take some time to think about what you think you did well. Find something to compliment, or praise, each other about. Then think of the things you would want to do better. You might start a section in your logbook to record the plays you have participated in. Make a chart and list the date, title of the play, your role, memorable moments, a positive comment about your role, and an area you would like to target for skill development the next time. Share those ideas with your group.

Actors for the Stage

Chances are you are one or more of the following: child, grand-child, brother or sister, friend, student, baby-sitter, dreamer. Think about the difference between the roles you play every day and an actor's role on stage. You both perfect your roles with experience. But learning to be an actor takes work. Perhaps the first lesson an actor learns is how to tame stage fright.

Taming Stage Fright

Every actor experiences some sort of nervousness, or **stage fright,** before a performance. This is natural and creative energy. You can make this nervous energy work for you with self-awareness, relaxation techniques, and practice.

Stage fright: The feeling of nervousness before a theatre performance.

Self-Awareness. Facing the fact that you are nervous before a performance is a major part of taming stage fright. Trying to understand the causes for the nervousness is another.

You would have plenty to be nervous about if you did not come to the stage prepared. The confidence you gain when you know you are prepared is the best defense against stage fright. You may want to make a checklist for yourself to review your cues, costumes, props, or lighting.

Overcoming stage fright depends on physical fitness as well. Reasonable diet, rest, and exercise will also help reduce the physical symptoms of stage fight. When Marianne Hyatt played the lead in *Texas,* she kept a demanding schedule to stay physically fit. She spent two hours working out with weights in the gym. Then she did aerobic training for breath control and vocal projection. After lunch, she took two dancelessons! Like many other actors, Marianne knows the value of physican prepartion to control stage fright.

Keeping yourself physically fit will help you to control stage fright.

A third cause of stage fright is the memory of a bad experience, such as forgetting a line or cue. One young high school actor learned to tame stage fright after she spoke the wrong line in response to a question asked by another actor in a stage performance. The other actor simply asked the question again. This time, she gave the right response, and the play went on. Knowing that every mistake has a solution helps tame stage fright.

Finally, another cause of stage fright relates to unrealistic expectations. Young actors are learning their skills and gaining experience. They cannot expect to give perfect performances. Even professional actors make major mistakes. The popular "blooper" shows demonstrate this.

Relaxation Techniques. Learning how to relax will improve both your health and your acting. Some simple things, such as smiling five quick smiles, can help relax your face. A yawn or a stretch can also relax tight muscles. Taking five deep, slow breaths can help reduce tension.

To develop relaxation skills, try the following:

1. Lie flat on your back on the floor away from anyone else. Concentrate on relaxing one toe at a time. Then focus on your feet. Relax one, then the other. Move up your body, with total concentration on relaxing one part at a time.

2. Now try the reverse process. Start with your toes and tighten each muscle throughout your body. Be aware of how your body feels as your muscles tighten. Then, when all muscles are taut, make a conscious effort to release and relax those tight muscles.

3. Select a monitor to clap every three seconds. At the sound of the clap, tighten all your body muscles, then relax them. Do this ten times.

Practice Makes Perfect. The more practice you give to a performance in theatre, the more experience you have. The more experience you have, the more control you will have over stage fright. Practice lines and movement so they become automatic and natural.

Get in character before you practice your lines. Chapter Two will explain how actors develop their characters. Visualize your character and focus on the character's personality and personal history. Imagine how the body of your character feels, especially if you are playing an older or younger person. When your body and mind feel like your character, concentrate on your lines.

Learning your lines involves several steps. Don't expect to memorize your lines right away. First, read your lines to yourself. Pay attention to what comes before and after what you say.

Second, read your lines out loud by yourself. The first time you do this, you might want to read all your lines for the entire play. Then concentrate on one act or scene at a time. Read the lines out loud until you can almost say the lines with your eyes closed.

Your practice will eventually involve saying your lines with a friend or partner. Learn to give positive feedback. Offer suggestions and swap tips. You will soon feel ready to work on stage.

The more you practice your lines, the sooner they will become automatic and natural.

Training for Actors

Getting started in acting can be easier than you think. You are already participating in an acting class; that is a start. The important thing is to expose your acting skills to an audience.

You may start small like Robby McNeill. When Robby was in kindergarten, he was cast as Papa Bear in *Goldilocks*. But when the costumes arrived, the Papa Bear suit was too large for him. He was quickly reassigned to a lesser role.

Throughout elementary school, Robby put on puppet shows in his backyard. When he was twelve, Robby saw an ad in the local paper for an audition. The county fair wanted variety acts, and Robby had perfected a magic act, so he called to set up an audition without telling anyone. On the day of the appointment, he asked his surprised mother for a ride to the audition. He was a big hit at the county fair. Soon he was hired to perform at birthday parties and company picnics. With training, he went on to become a professional actor.

Summary

Actors need to face the stage fright that attacks almost everyone. There are several successful ways to control nervousness. Being prepared, practicing relaxation techniques, having a positive attitude, and being realistic about your expectations will help control stage fright. Actors receive training and gain experience in a variety of ways. Like many other actors, you can create your own opportunities to perform.

We Need an Audience

At some time or another, we have all been in an audience. Sometimes we seem to have no choice about being in an audience, such as when attendance at a school assembly is required. Sometimes we choose to be in an audience to experience a performance that stretches our mind and imagination. Just as gaining experience as an actor is important, so is gaining experience as a member of an audience.

Active Listening

One of the most important skills a member of the audience brings to a live performance is active listening. When the lights are dimmed and the performance begins, the audience makes a mental transition to focus its concentration on the stage. The audience members stop what they are doing, look carefully at the stage, and listen attentively.

Stop. As a member of an audience, you should stop other activities once the lights are dimmed and the curtain goes up. All talking and coughing should stop. As an actor, you realize how much preparation and practice go into a live performance on a stage. You want a friendly and courteous audience. When you

Take a Tip from Shakespeare

Theatre critics can make or break an actor's career. After you have worked long and hard on a performance, you naturally want the audience, and the critics, to appreciate what you have done. The "Critic's Choice" feature in each chapter will help clarify standards for good performances. You will develop skills in evaluating performances and acting skills.

Let's start with the master. The great William Shakespeare offered sound advice to actors in his famous play *Hamlet*. Compare the original language with a modern version and answer the questions that follow.

Original

"Speak the speech I pray you as I pronounced it to you, trippingly on the tongue; but if you mouth as many of our players do, I had as lief the town crier spoke my lines. Nor do not saw the air too much with your hand thus, but use all gently; for in the very torrent, tempest, and as I may say, whirlwind of your passion, you must acquire and beget a temperance that may give it smoothness. Oh it offends me to the soul, to hear a robustious periwig-pated fellow tear a passion to tatters, to very rags, to split the ears of groundlings, who for the most part are capable of nothing but inexplicable dumb shows and noise. I would have such a fellow whipped . . . ."

Modern

Let me show you how to speak your lines. Take care to speak distinctly with an understanding of your part. Do not use wild or artificial gestures but develop a presence and talent to convey every emotion with style and grace. Never resort to overacting to gain the attention or admiration of fools in the audience.

1. What words or phrases would you substitute for the following: trippingly on the tongue; robustious periwig-pated fellow; ears of groundlings?

2. Read Hamlet's advice out loud. Then try to put that advice in your own words. Write those words in your logbook.

3. Listen to a professional Shakespearean actor recite those words by listening to a recording or tape. Memorize these lines and recite them for yourself or in front of the class. You won't go wrong if you follow Shakespeare's advice.

4. Based on this excerpt from *Hamlet*, make a list of three to five qualities an actor should have. Discuss how a theatre critic might use these qualities to write a review of an actor's performance.

are in an audience, remember how you would like the audience to be if you were on stage. Your courtesy and attention will help those around you become better members of the audience through your example.

Look. Give the stage or screen your full attention. Let your eyes adjust to the change in lighting. Take in the details of the opening scene. Make a mental note of the number and position of the props on stage. Then close your eyes and try to remember exactly where things are.

Look carefully at the costumes, scenery, and makeup. Notice how the colors used help create a mood for the audience. Look at the initial positions of the actors on stage and identify where each one is. Observe as many details as possible and develop a keen eye for the details of the set.

Listen. Most plays have many layers of meaning. The meaning is revealed through words, gestures, double meanings, and symbolism. You must give the performance your full attention.

At the end of each scene or act, you might stop and make a mental summary of the action and describe your impressions of each of the main characters. If you apply some of these listening techniques when you watch a play, your enjoyment will increase.

During the intermission, talk with a friend about what you have seen and heard. Share your impressions of the actors, the scenery, the costumes. Ask your friend to describe his or her views on the performance. In the exchange of comments and impressions, you will be better prepared to listen carefully during the remainder of the performance.

Active Imagination

You enjoy a play more when you participate. Even as a member of the audience, you can become an active partner in the performance. You bring your own experiences, imagination, and emotions to the theatre.

Experience. Watching a play links our own private thoughts and experiences to human emotions and experiences we all

AUDIENCE ETIQUETTE

1. **Dress for the occasion.** Attending a live theatre performance is often a special occasion. It costs money and takes special plans. Dress up to celebrate the special occasion.

2. **Be prompt.** Give yourself plenty of time to arrive at the theatre and be seated. Give yourself time to review the program before the performance starts. Most theatres will not seat you if the performance has already started.

3. **Be considerate.** If you have to pass in front of people in your row to get to your seat, face the people already seated and say "Excuse me" or "Pardon me." Do not turn your back to those already seated as you cross them to get to your seat.

4. **Respect property.** Do not spread out your coats, hats, umbrellas, or personal belongings on the seats around you even if they are empty. All hats should be removed when entering the theatre. Never put your feet on the seat ahead of you.

5. **Keep quiet.** Coughing, whispering, or unwrapping gum or candy will disturb your neighbors and the actors. Turn off the beeper on your watch or pager.

6. **Participate.** Bring your active listening and imagination skills to the performance. Let your emotions respond to the message and environment of the theatre

7. **Stay.** Stay and enjoy the entire play. Do not leave once the play has begun except in the case of an emergency

8. **Appreciate.** Applaud at the end of the performance to show that you appreciated the talent and preparation of the theatre group. Give a standing ovation to the truly extraordinary performances.

9. **Reward talent.** If you want to recognize the contributions of the director or a particular actor, arrange to send flowers backstage. Do not send them on stage.

10. **Spread the word.** If you have enjoyed a performance, share the good news with others. The recommendation of a friend or acquaintance can bring greater numbers of people to the theatre.

Antagonist: *The character or situation working against the protagonist.*

have. As a member of the audience, you begin to identify with the emotions and challenges that the protagonist faces. You react to the antics of the **antagonist,** or villain, with fear, distrust, or humor. Somehow the relationships between the characters in the play reflect some aspect of a relationship you have experienced. Your own experiences link you to the stage because most plays tell a universal story.

Imagination. The production you see as a member of an audience is the product of someone's imagination. When the curtain goes up, you are usually impressed with the scenery, costumes, lighting, and staging you see. When you are in the audience, you can have a lot of fun trying to imagine alternate ways of doing things.

Use your imagination to think of a different color scheme for the costumes and lighting. Or you might envision different costumes for the actors. Follow one actor closely and think of how you might want to play that character.

Emotion. Watching a play can be like getting on an emotional roller coaster. You can feel scared, disappointed, suspicious,

An actor can make a performance great by using his or her character to develop an emotional bond with the audience.

amused, fearful, delighted, relieved. And all that in ten minutes! If you are watching a tragedy, the actors will arouse strong feelings in the audience. The audience will feel sorry for the protagonist; they will fear that they could be caught in a similar situation. The audience will experience **pathos.**

By the end of the play, the audience has felt an emotional climax. The play will have either a happy or sad ending. In either case, the audience will be relieved that the situation the main character had to deal with is over. The fear or sadness or happiness the audience feels may linger, but most members of the audience will express their appreciation by clapping. This is an emotional high for both the performers and the audience.

Pathos: The feeling of pity or sympathy the audience has for a character.

Summary

The audience is an essential part of any performance. The bond between actors and audience can make a performance great. Members of the audience can increase their enjoyment of the performance with active listening and imagination skills.

Stage Fright

1. **Balloon Toss.** With a partner, toss an imaginary water-filled balloon to each other. Focus on the feeling of releasing that balloon and feel your muscles relax. Remember that sharing with a partner can help reduce stage fright.
2. **Tug-of-War.** Two groups of students should form a line by standing in front of each other. Half of the people in the line should turn around to face the other half. Play tug-of-war with an imaginary rope. Imagine seeing and feeling the rope. Make it so real that after the game you feel physically tired. Remember that you are part of a team that supports one another.

Active Listening

3. **Dialogue.** Work with a partner. Each of you should pick out a sentence to read from a book. While one is reading the sentence, the other should close his or her eyes to listen. After the sentence is read, the listener will try to repeat the sentence exactly as it was read. Repeat this activity often.
4. **Noises Off.** When listening to music, stop the tape and try to identify all the instruments you hear. Or try to identify the number of singers you think are performing. Repeat this with different kinds of music to get practice in distinguishing sounds.

Active Imagination

5. **Fairy Tales.** Use the fairy tale you worked on in "Take One" and change it to a modern setting. Work with the same group that presented your fairy tale as a comedy, tragedy, mystery, or musical and talk about how you could give the fairy tale a modern twist. Or discuss how your play would work if a character from another fairy tale suddenly appeared in your fairy tale.
6. **Fairy Tale Sequels.** Imagine a sequel to the fairy tale that you have selected. Keep the same characters but introduce one new one. Describe the new character and tell your story.

Acting Out

7. **Characterization.** Take a fairy tale character and think of at least five emotions that the character feels in the story. Write down each emotion on a separate slip of paper. Think of a way to convey each feeling without using words. Then give one of your papers to a member of a small group. Tell the group who your character is and then try to show the emotion you selected without using words. When the group has guessed correctly, your slip of paper can become a badge of honor you can wear.
8. **Audiences.** Brainstorm opportunities for presenting your fairy tale to a live audience. Work in small groups to think of ideas. Share ideas and list acting opportunities. Select one of the suggestions and prepare a performance of your fairy tale.

The Actor's Logbook

1. ***Learning the Language.*** Organize a section in your logbook for theatre language. Reserve a page for each letter of the alphabet and write that letter in bold print on the outer corner of each page. Begin a chart at the top of each page using the following categories: Word, Page, Definition. Then add each of the words or terms in this chapter that are in dark type to the appropriate page in your logbook. Be sure to make a note of the page on which the word is first used. Copy the definition in your logbook. You could also include any special words or terms your teacher uses and explains in class. Play a game with yourself and think of ways to use one of the words in a phone conversation, at the dinner table, or in a report. Each time you use the word, give yourself a point—or check mark—in your logbook.

2. ***Actor's Etiquette.*** On page 15 you saw a list of guidelines for an audience attending a live performance. There are also certain expectations for an actor's behavior. Make a similar list for actors and write your guidelines in your logbook. You may want to add to your list as you learn more about what is expected.

3. ***Critic's Choice.*** Begin to develop a list of qualities for good acting. Use the advice that Shakespeare gives in *Hamlet.* (See page 13.) Put his advice into your own words and write this in your logbook. Using the qualities you have identified, write a "review" of one of the fairy tale performances done for class. You might include your "review" in your portfolio.

Critical Thinking

4. ***Main Ideas.*** For each of the three sections in this chapter, make a list of at least three important ideas. Try to develop a chapter outline.

5. ***What's Missing.*** The introductory chapter cannot cover everything about theatre and acting all at once. Take a look at your chapter outline and identify at least two things that are missing from this chapter that relate to the main ideas. Then, look at the table of contents or index to see if these topics will be covered in another chapter. Think of one thing you want to learn about the topics in this chapter that was not included in this text. Write this down and figure out how you will get information about this topic.

6. ***Applications.*** Working in a small group, think about how the information about plays, actors, and audiences might apply to your school assemblies. Discuss the best assemblies you have been to. Develop a list for "Assembly Etiquette" based on "Audience Etiquette."

CHAPTER TWO

Characters for the Stage

EXPECTATIONS

After reading this chapter, you will be able to

2.1 define types of stage characters

2.2 use techniques for analysis of characters

2.3 display skill in creating characters

2.4 demonstrate active participation in individual and team characterization activities

The dynamic or energy of acting flows from an actor's analysis and understanding of the character played. Some actors, like Judy Garland as Dorothy in *The Wizard of Oz*, play a character so well they define the role for all others to respect and imitate. An actor's ability to know or create a character helps the audience meet a new personality and see the world through different eyes.

Character Roles

Just as there are types of plays, there are types of characters. The challenge of the actor is to make the **character** become a memorable individual. Most actors dream of playing the leading role in a play, but there are many types of roles. In addition to leading roles, actors play supporting roles, bit parts, and nonspeaking roles.

Character: A role played by an actor on stage.

Leading Roles

In Chapter One, two leading roles were defined. These were the roles of the **protagonist,** the main character of the play, and the **antagonist**, another leading character working against the protagonist in the play. One is the hero of the performance; the other is the villain. Actors playing the role of either the protagonist or the antagonist will probably spend a lot of time on stage and have many lines to learn.

Use the story of *Cinderella* to identify the leading roles for actors. Obviously, Cinderella is the protagonist, the main character of the play. The mean stepmother is the antagonist, the character who makes life very difficult for the heroine.

Supporting Roles

In addition to the leading roles, there are many supporting roles. The challenge for an actor is to make a supporting role come alive despite the number of lines the character says or the length of time the character is on stage.

The protagonist in the story of *Cinderella* is Cinderella herself.

Return to *Cinderella* for a moment. This story has several supporting roles, including the Prince, the stepsisters, and the fairy godmother. The relationship and support they establish for each other on stage enhances each one's performance.

Supporting roles are essential to a play's theme. Think of how dull the story of *Cinderella* would be without the wicked stepsisters!

Most plays also have characters of lesser importance to the overall story but whose presence is necessary for the atmosphere or movement of the play. **Subordinate** roles give actors an opportunity to gain experience on stage and create memorable characters as well.

Bit Roles. A **bit** part is a minor role in which the actor has only a few lines to say during the play. Still, such a role has been used by many actors to get started on stage. In *Cinderella,* the part of someone at the ball might be a bit part. In television programs, some actors have been able to turn a bit part intended for a single performance into an expanded role for future programs. If the audience reacts favorably, or the bit performance is strong, the role is expanded.

Walk-Ons. A **walk-on** gives an actor the opportunity to be seen on stage and to gain the experience of being in a production. Walk-on parts might include the "extras" in a crowd of people or the roles of guests at a party or patients in a hospital waiting room.

Character Roles

Subordinate: A character or position that is of less importance than another character or position on stage.

Bit: A character with very few lines in a play.

Walk-on: A small part for an actor that does not include speaking lines on stage.

Walk-on roles as extras allow actors to gain valuable acting experience.

Casting: The process of choosing actors for the particular roles in a play.

Cast by type: The situation in which actors are selected for parts that are very similar to their own personalities.

Straight role: A role in which the actor and the character are similar. The actor makes only slight changes to portray the character in the play.

Cast by character: The situation in which actors portray traits that are outside their personal experience.

Character role: A role in which the actor and the character do not share many traits. The actor takes on a role that is very different from his or her own personality.

Characterization: The art and skill of putting together all the aspects of a character to make that role believable and realistic on stage.

Casting

The process of choosing actors to play the various roles in a play is not an easy one. This **casting** of characters involves many decisions.

Cast by Type. Sometimes, actors are **cast by type.** In this case, actors are playing characters that are very similar to themselves. For example, if there were a cheerleader character in a play and a cheerleader student were selected to play that part, the actor would be cast by type.

When an actor is cast by type, the personality of the character and the personality of the actor are similar. Other similarities could include age and physical characteristics. For instance, if a young English boy with a limp were chosen to play the character of Tiny Tim in *A Christmas Carol,* the actor would be playing a **straight role** and would be cast by type.

Cast by Character. Sometimes, actors are **cast by character.** In this case, actors take on traits that are different from their own to portray characters very different from their own experiences. If a big, bulky football player were cast to play Tiny Tim, the actor would be challenged to play a character very different from his own age and physical characteristics.

When an actor is selected to play a **character role,** a lot of research will be part of the preparation for the role. It might not be hard for a teenager to portray a young adult on stage because the age differences are not very great. It would be more of a character role if that young adult role involved physical or cultural differences from the actor's background.

Characterization. Every character in a play is unique and individual. The creativity of the actor is a key ingredient in developing a realistic, believable character on stage. This is the fun and challenge of **characterization.**

Actors bring personal experiences and talent to the process of characterization. They are guided by the analysis of the play and the character that is expected of each member of the theatre company. In addition, the director guides the actors in the development of the role.

Many types of roles are part of almost every play. Actors are cast to play the leading roles of antagonist and protagonist as well as other supporting roles. In addition, many lesser roles are usually required in a theatre production. Actors will gain experience and develop skills by being cast by type or by character. In all cases, actors will rely on hard work and creativity to develop the characterization necessary to bring the character to life on the stage.

Understanding a Character

Understanding yourself and your friends and family is hard enough and a continual process. An actor needs to understand stage characters, as well. This is hard work indeed. The actor who truly understands a stage character makes a new friend. All actors consider these guidelines for studying the characters they bring to life on stage.

Learn the Background

A playwright writes a script for a play with a specific story or experience in mind. An actor studies the play to get inside the playwright's head. Learning about what the playwright had in mind will help an actor convey meaning and emotion on stage.

Study the Script. The clues to the intentions of a playwright are found in a careful reading of the script. Read the script out loud several times. At the end of each reading, describe what you see as the playwright's point of view and the theme of the play.

Pay close attention to the director's interpretation of the play. When a director explains a character or a scene, take notes in your logbook. Ask the director questions about the playwright's point of view and the theme of the play.

Company Reading of the Play. An entire company of actors will do a reading of the play together with the director. The basic

Actors want to create a stage role that reflects the intentions of the playwright, or author of the play. Your understanding of the character will grow as you analyze both the play and your part. Your own experiences and imagination will give your character a distinctive personality. Take this opportunity to begin to play a stage character. Here's what to do.

Step One

Introductions. Read and memorize the following short dialogue:

A: You're late.
B: Sorry, I thought you'd understand.
A: Not this time.
B: What's the problem now?
A: I have something for you.
B: Oh my!

Step Two

Experience. The lines may remind you of something or suggest a scene, or context. Share your thoughts with a partner. Together you will become the characters, "A" and "B." Try to identify as many characters and scenes for these lines as possible.

Step Three

Understanding. Now select one of the following pairs of characters. Then, with your partner, select the character you will play. Remember the challenges of straight and character roles. Once you have a character, determine his or her personali-

ty characteristics. You are playing an individual. Describe five important personality traits. Then think about how you will demonstrate those traits in posture, voice, and gestures.

Pairs of Characters:

1. Young man giving sweetheart an engagement ring.
2. Fifty-year-old woman returning wedding ring to former husband.
3. Teacher giving test results to student.
4. Emergency radio dispatcher giving report to ambulance driver.
5. Your choice.

Step Four

Imagination. Bring your experience, understanding, and talent to the creation of your character. With your partner, identify how the scene will be played—as a comedy, tragedy, mystery, or drama. Decide what emotions you want the audience to experience. Rehearse various options, try out different styles. Refine your character and practice your lines "in character" with your partner.

Step Five

Action. From the moment you expect to be called on to give your performance, get in character mentally and physically. The acting of your lines in front of the class will not take long. You want the impression you create with your character to last in the audience's memory.

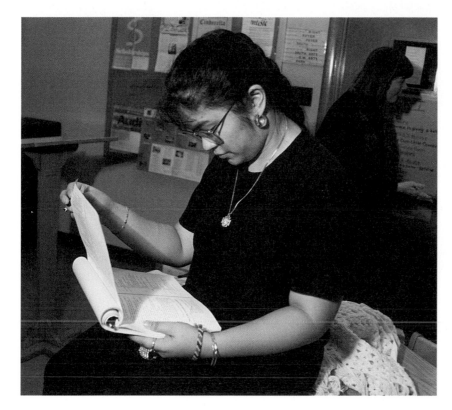

Careful attention to both the script and your director's interpretation will help you to understand a play's tone and theme.

organization of the play should be clarified. The action, mood, and conflicts of each act need to be understood in a similar way by the members of the entire company. The same details will be examined for each scene as well.

Individual actors will pay special attention to their own roles. Still, each actor has to know how his or her particular character contributes to the entire fabric of the play. The playwright would not have included a character unless that character contributed in some important way to the overall theme and experience of the play.

The entire company should reach an agreement about the meaning of the play and the motivations of each character. This common vision and understanding of the play is essential. When everyone has the same approach to the play, the company develops a spirit of creativity and cooperation.

Determine the Theme and Goals of the Play

Most plays deal with themes and emotions that all human beings are capable of experiencing. The specifics of time, place, and characters provide the necessary details to make the story come alive. Use the following process to help determine the theme and goals of a play and the motivations of various characters.

Background Exposition. After reading the script, identify the portions that explain necessary information to the audience. This **exposition** will give information about the time and place of the play, the characters and how they are related, and any background information that explains important events that happened before the play begins.

Exposition: The part of a play that provides important information to the audience.

Include the following exposition information in your logbook:

1. Time and place of the play and each act and scene.
2. Characters and their relationships to each other.
3. Important action that has occurred before the opening of the play.
4. Type of play.

Conflict. Most plays contain conflict to create interest in the action of the play. The conflict is both internal and external. When analyzing the script, transfer to your logbook the following elements of the conflict:

1. General conflict in the historical context of the play.
2. Specific incident that arouses strong audience interest and exposes the basic theme or conflict of the play.
3. Protagonist's internal and external conflicts.
4. Antagonist's internal and external conflicts.

Crisis. In studying the script, pinpoint the scene or lines where the greatest amount of suspense or emotional involvement occurs. This becomes the turning point or crisis of the play. The crisis could be an external event, such as a murder. The crisis could also be an internal change of heart or attitude, such as the decision of Romeo and Juliet to defy family and tradition or the decision of Anne Frank to understand and forgive those who persecuted her. Record this significant event in your logbook.

Climax. In a longer play, the climax is separate from the crisis. In a one-act play, these two are often the same event or change. The climax is the final resolution to the basic conflict presented in the play. The climax claims the greatest emotional response from the audience. It is here that the emotional **catharsis** occurs. This too needs to be recorded. All action will build to this point in the play.

Character Analysis

A character's actions and lines in a play need to be understood in terms of motivation and background. Actors must ask why characters are speaking and acting as they do. Each action and every line has an impact on the entire play. The actor's job is to figure out why the character is speaking and behaving in a certain way.

The Character's Personality. To develop an understanding of why a character speaks and behaves in a certain way, you need to figure out what the play tells you about the background of your character. In the Anton Chekhov play *The Three Sisters*, the schoolteacher, Kulygin, is the only man who has not served in the army. An actor could play the role with a limp, which might suggest why he did not serve in the military. In his character analysis, the actor could develop an explanation for himself as to why Kulygin has a limp even though this is not expressly stated.

It is very important that actors be specific about why their characters are the way they are. When you analyze your character's background, you might make a personal history timeline for your character.

The Character's Activities. Think about what the character does for a living. Imagine activities that your character would enjoy doing in leisure time. Figure out how your character would

Catharsis: The feeling of emotional release during a play when the tensions and conflicts in the characters have been revealed and resolved

spend time during a 24-hour period, or during a week or month. Be as specific as your imagination can be.

Emotional Qualities. Think about what your character likes and dislikes and how he or she shows these preferences. Is your character intelligent, clever, dull, educated, bored, spiritual, confident? Ask yourself what your character believes in. What does the character want in life? Make a list of the words that would apply to your character. Look for real people who you think have the same characteristics. Make mental notes of how they speak and behave. Transfer your notes to your logbook to help you develop realistic gestures for your character.

Relationships. Every character relates to other characters in the play. Ask yourself about the nature of the relationships between your character and other characters in the play. What do other characters in the play say or think about your character? How does your character feel about the other characters in the play?

Begin to think about how relationships change during the course of the play. Think about why relationships change and how the change affects the personality of each character and your character especially.

Summary

Your understanding of a play and the characters in a play involves several things. First, you will learn about the play itself. You will try to figure out the playwright's intention and theme for the play. You will read the script to get a sense of the basic organization for the entire play and each act and scene. It is important that everyone in the theatre company shares a common understanding and vision about the nature of the play and each of the characters in the play. In addition, each actor will analyze all of the characters in the play to determine the motivation of each and to develop a believable character on stage.

The Academy Awards

Great acting performances are a special treat for audiences. They are special because the audience witnesses technical excellence as well as great artistic expression. When that happens, you know it. We begin to judge other acting performances by the best we have seen.

Every year, the movie industry recognizes outstanding actors in the giving of the Academy Awards. The list below reflects the years certain actors received the award. By using the past, you can begin to make judgments about current movie performances.

Year	Best Actors
1991	Jeremy Irons, *Reversal of Fortune* Kathy Bates, *Misery*
1992	Anthony Hopkins, *The Silence of the Lambs* Jodie Foster, *The Silence of the Lambs*
1993	Al Pacino, *Scent of a Woman* Emma Thompson, *Howard's End*
1994	Tom Hanks, *Philadelphia* Holly Hunter, *The Piano*
1995	Tom Hanks, *Forrest Gump* Jessica Lange, *Blue Sky*

1. Select a movie that you have seen and write a brief description of the character the best actor or actress portrayed. Include a description of the emotional traits and personality the character had. In a second paragraph, describe the body language the actor used to emphasize character traits.

2. Select one of the best actors and nominate him or her for your "Critic's Choice" award. You want this award to reflect your own standards of excellence. Prepare a written or oral nomination for the actor of your choice.

3. Take any year and find out who all the nominees were for acting awards. Make your own selection from those nominated and write a "column" identifying your choice and your reasons.

4. Think about the five best acting performances you have seen this past year in the movies. Identify the best actor in each. From this list, nominate your candidate for an Academy Award. Your nomination could be in the form of a speech or a written column. Be sure to include reasons for your choice.

Creating a Character

To create a character for the stage, an actor must come to an internal understanding of the character and practice representing that character visually, emotionally, and vocally. This is a complex process and takes time and effort.

Actors bring talent and experience to the task of creating a believable, natural character on stage. An actor does at least two important things to create a memorable character. He or she develops a character sketch to define the character's personality and then selects and practices voice, posture, and dress to fit the character's personality.

Importance of a Character Sketch

After an actor has studied the character in the manner suggested earlier, it is time to do a character sketch. The character sketch can be a written description or a drawing that defines the character. Armed with a character sketch, the actor will find it easier to stay in character and experience and portray the thoughts and emotions of that character.

Written Description. Write a brief biography of your character. Include personal background, motivation, relationships, strengths, weaknesses, and changes.

After you have written your sketch, identify a real person who closely resembles this character. Make notes about the physical characteristics and mannerisms of that person. Add these impressions to your logbook.

Relationship Diagram. To make a relationship diagram, position the protagonist in the center of the diagram. Cluster all the other characters around the protagonist. You could use relative distance to display the strength or limits of the relationship of each character to the central figure in the play.

To emphasize relationships, develop a symbol to indicate positive, negative, or neutral relationships among the characters. A relationship diagram of *Cinderella* might look like the following:

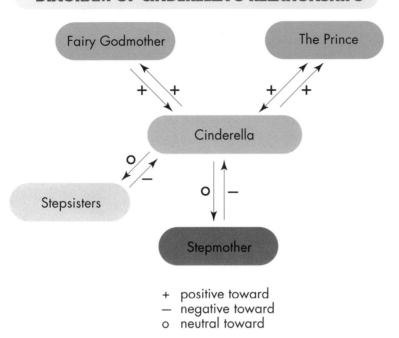

DIAGRAM OF CINDERELLA'S RELATIONSHIPS

+ positive toward
− negative toward
o neutral toward

Body Language

Once you have an understanding of what makes your character tick and how your character relates to the action and other characters in the play, you can begin to create your role. Inner personalities are usually revealed through body language and external appearances. Give much thought to the posture, voice, and gestures your character uses.

Posture. Consider the differences in character roles between Dorothy in *The Wizard of Oz* and Tiny Tim in *A Christmas Carol*. Think of at least five character traits that you associate with either of those characters. For each of those traits, think of a physical way to show that personality trait in terms of posture. Visualize how Dorothy or Tiny Tim would stand.

Practice standing before a mirror in the way you want your character to stand. Get used to seeing that character come alive in the way you stand. Then stand in your own natural way. There should be a visible difference between your own posture and that of your character.

Voice. Your voice is a wonderful and sensitive instrument. It has the power to convey great emotion and differences in tone and volume.

To gain practice in the effective use of your voice to enhance a character's role, practice saying the word "hello" in the characters of Goldilocks, Papa Bear, Mama Bear, and Baby Bear. Your instinct will be to raise and lower the tone of your voice to reflect the differences in male and female voices and the differences in age. Think about what else you could do with your voice to define the differences in those characters.

Finally, practice your voice skills using a tape recorder. Say "hello" as different characters might say it. Play your practice bits back and listen carefully. Think about the changes you can make to your "hello."

Mannerisms: The unique gestures and idiosyncrasies that make each person different. Identifying a character's mannerisms is very helpful in creating a natural and believable character for the stage.

Gestures. Almost everybody has signature gestures or **mannerisms**. These reflect idiosyncrasies of character. Many times a person is not even aware of these gestures or mannerisms, but other people certainly are. Think about someone in your family. Describe a significant gesture that person uses often.

Using appropriate mannerisms is an effective way of making your character seem like a "real" person.

Think about yourself and try to identify some of your own mannerisms. Chances are your friends can identify your mannerisms more quickly than you can.

Imagine playing the cowardly lion in *The Wizard of Oz*. Think of a gesture that will convey the character's lack of courage. Then think of the body language you could use to demonstrate the lion's change of fortune. Show how this character could walk on stage with and without courage.

Summary

Creating a character for the stage is fun and challenging. It requires understanding the personality traits the character has. It means knowing how the character fits into the play as a whole and figuring out the relationship the character has to each of the other characters in the play. Once the personality of the character is firmly in the actor's mind, then the body language that reveals that character can be developed. Actors will pay close attention to developing the skilled use of posture, voice, and gestures.

Active Imagination

1. **Casting.** Make a list of as many characters as you can remember from the movie *Forrest Gump* or another movie of your choice. Next to each character, add the appropriate label from the section "Character Roles" (pages 21–23). Using the people in your class, make a list of students you would cast for each role. Indicate whether you would cast the role as a character role or a straight role.

2. **Auditions.** Imagine that you have just seen an announcement in your local paper about an audition for a Children's Theatre performance of *Goldilocks*. You have given this some thought in your class and want to try out. The director gives you 30 seconds to audition on stage. Think of what you want to do, practice, and then audition for the class.

3. **Dialogue.** Imagine a modern setting for a tale like *Goldilocks*. Write the dialogue for a skit based on this story using modern language. You might work in a small group to develop and polish the dialogue. Then, read the lines out loud.

Body Language

4. **Posture.** Practice sitting on various types of chairs. Get the feel of big, stuffed chairs, hard, straight chairs, or the small chairs in kindergarten. Imagine Papa Bear sitting in his chair; then imagine Baby Bear trying to sit in Papa Bear's chair. Determine which character you are and which chair you will sit in. Practice walking into the Bears' living room in character and selecting one of the chairs to sit in. Then, demonstrate your sitting in a chair for the class silently and in character. If the class can identify your character by your posture, take a bow.

5. **Voice.** Think of a vowel or sound a character might use to express surprise in the story of Goldilocks. This expression of surprise should not be a word, just a sound of surprise. Imagine how a character of your choice would express surprise and practice this sound.

6. **Gesture.** Pretend that the casting director for Goldilocks has asked all the actors at the audition to demonstrate a simple gesture. The director wants you to knock on the cottage door with only your hand or arm showing from the theatre curtain. Your job is to create and display your character using only the gesture of knocking. Give it a try.

Cartoon Characters

7. **Characteristics.** Use one of your favorite comic strips in the newspaper to help you get "in character." Try to exaggerate the characteristics of your cartoon character in terms of posture. Think of a simple prop you could carry or use to help identify your cartoon character. Portray that cartoon character for the class. You might invite them to guess your identity.

The Actor's Logbook

1. ***Learning the Language.*** Add each of the words and terms in bold type in this chapter to the appropriate page in the glossary section of your logbook.

2. ***Voice Cues.*** When you are practicing lines for a role in a play, you want to remind yourself about pauses and tone and volume. Think of symbols you could use to indicate (1) when to pause and for how long; (2) tone of voice that reflects tenderness, anger, and impatience; (3) change in volume for soft, loud, or moderate volume. Use the symbols to prepare your dialogue for an audition. You might copy the lines from page 26 and use your symbols to indicate inflections.

3. ***Critic's Choice.*** Imagine that you will interview an Academy Award-winning actor for this year. Prepare at least five questions you would like to ask and write these in your logbook. If possible, collect some columns written by critics or feature writers about the actor you have selected. You could start a scrapbook of theatre reviews.

Body Language

4. ***Main Ideas.*** Write an outline for each of the three sections in this chapter or make a list of the three most important ideas explained in each section.

5. ***Comparisons.*** Review the list of Academy Award-winning actors on page 31. Think of at least five qualities that all these actors share. Discuss whether the qualities you identified are necessary for every actor. Then think of the specific talents that each individual has. Identify the unique talents of each.

6. ***Judgment.*** As a class, you could listen to a favorite piece of music or song together. Have one student increase and decrease the volume at random. Each student should make a judgment about the volume of music. Use a scale from 1 to 10. If the music is too soft, give it a 1; too loud, give it a 10; and rate variation. Make five adjustments to the volume and rate each change. Compare reactions. Discuss if the class could agree about the level of volume that would make it seem like a 5 to everyone.

Creative Thinking

7. ***In Character.*** Create a character that might use one of the following props in the kitchen: an umbrella, a Halloween mask, a plastic bag, or a postcard. In a short skit, demonstrate the character using the prop.

8. ***New Characters.*** Think of at least three popular characters that did not exist ten years ago. For example, Barney the purple dinosaur did not always have a life. Neither did the Power Rangers. Imagine that you have entered a contest to create the next action "character" for a toy company. The cash prize is enough to pay for your college education. Create a character and describe and demonstrate it as a work of art, a written report, or a scale model. Be prepared to present your new character to the class.

9. ***New Emotions.*** To expand your emotional awareness, begin a list of feelings. Start with ten. Add five each day. Practice describing and acting out those feelings.

CHAPTER THREE

The Stage Environment

EXPECTATIONS

After reading this chapter, you will be able to

3.1 define and use theatre terms about stage positions and stage movements

3.2 develop spatial awareness of different stage arrangements

3.3 practice creative movement in character

3.4 demonstrate active participation in individual and team theatre activities

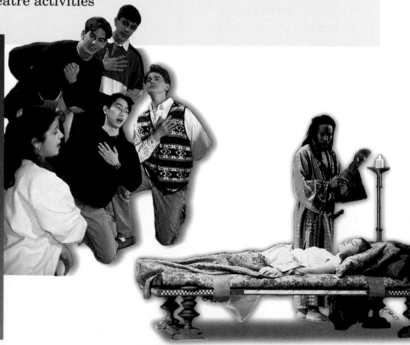

An actor uses the environment of the theatre and the stage to create movement and to stretch the imagination of the audience. Working with simple or elaborate stages and scenery, an actor creates the impression of realities beyond the physical limitations of the space of the theatre. The stage becomes a place of magic and imagination for both the actors and the audience.

The Stage

The relationship between actors and the audience takes place in a special place, the **stage**. The stage is both a physical space as well as a place that lives and grows in the imagination. There are several types of stages.

Stage: The place where actors create performances.

Types of Stages

Most schools have a stage area that is elevated and curtained. This is a conventional stage arrangement, sometimes called a **proscenium stage.** The audience views the theatre action through the "picture frame" of the parted curtains. But there are other types of stages as well. These include the arena and thrust stages.

Proscenium stage: A conventional stage where the audience views the play through a permanent framed opening that is usually curtained.

The Conventional Stage. Look at Figure 3.1, which is a diagram of a conventional theatre. Become familiar with the basic areas identified. The director will use specific terms to refer to specific areas of the stage and to give actors directions about where to be and where to move on stage.

The first thing to remember about the stage area is that all positions and places on stage reflect the actor's point of view when facing the audience. The area closest to the audience is called **downstage.** It makes sense then that the area farthest from the audience is called **upstage.** Important action in the theatre usually takes place downstage.

Downstage: The area of the stage that is closest to the audience.

Upstage: The area of the stage that is farthest from the audience.

Figure 3.1 The Conventional Stage

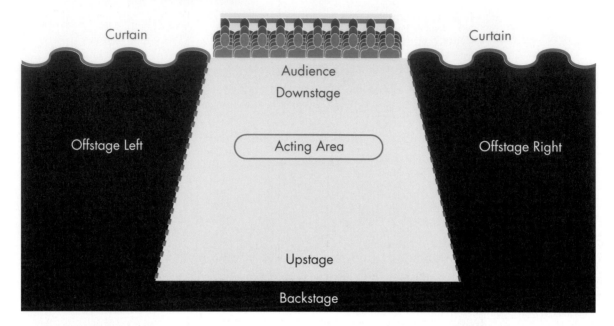

Curtain

Audience

Downstage

Offstage Left

Acting Area

Offstage Right

Upstage

Backstage

Curtain

Arena stage: A stage that is entirely surrounded by members of the audience. This is sometimes called a "theatre in the round."

The Arena Stage. The **arena stage** is sometimes called "theatre in the round" (see Figure 3.2). "In the round" indicates that the stage is surrounded by the audience, either entirely or on three sides. Many theatres and stage areas built in the twentieth century have used this arrangement.

When theatre is performed "in the round," the audience participates more directly in the entire theatrical experience. There are no curtains to shield the actors from the audience. Performing "in the round" presents a variety of challenges for the use of scenery, props, and stage movement. Even entrances and exits on and off stage are affected by the visibility of the arena theatre.

Because actors face the audience in all directions from an arena stage, the areas of the stage are not called upstage and downstage. You can think of the acting area as a giant clock. The director can identify one point as the 12 o'clock position. The hours of 3, 6, and 9 will divide the acting area into four major sections. The acting area could also be organized like a map. Points could be designated as north, south, east, and west. Stage directions and positions could be given in terms of these map locations.

Figure 3.2 The Arena Stage

41

The Stage

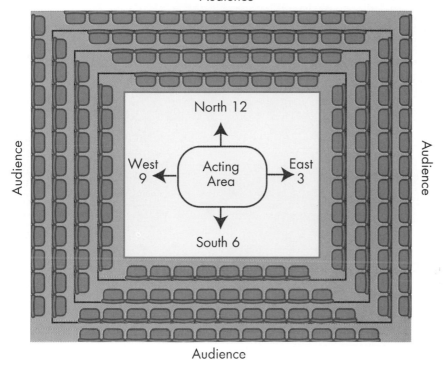

The Thrust Stage. The **thrust stage** combines features of both the conventional and the arena stages (see Figure 3.3). The acting area is surrounded on three sides by the audience. A back section may be attached to the theatre area.

The thrust stage provides flexibility for the actors, who can enter and exit the acting area from the back stage area or from the audience aisles. There is a clear downstage area. Scenery and sets will be designed for the best audience viewing.

Thrust stage: A stage that is surrounded on three sides by the audience.

Stage Areas

To understand the relationship between the actors and the audience, a new world of terms and movement has to become familiar to the beginner. Be prepared to learn new terms and vocabulary. The director will use these terms when **blocking** the positions and movements of the actors.

Blocking: The positions and movements of the actors on stage. Blocking includes entrances, exits, and crosses.

Figure 3.3 The Thrust Stage

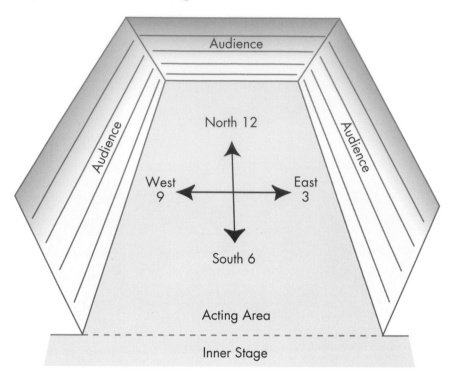

Because most school stages are of the conventional, or proscenium, type, we will focus on the terms used to describe those stage areas. Remember, all stage positions and movement are identified in terms of the actor's right or left when facing the audience.

The conventional stage area is divided into nine places (see Figure 3.4). The sides of the acting area are usually angled so the audience can see the entire area of action more easily. To identify these areas, the abbreviations in the diagram are often used to show actors where they and various props are positioned on stage. Not all of the nine locations in the acting area are created equal.

Strong Stage Areas. Actors consider the locations closest to the audience to be stronger. Audiences commonly respond more readily and strongly to the people closest to them. Thus, downstage locations are considered stronger than upstage positions.

Figure 3.4 Conventional Stage Areas

43

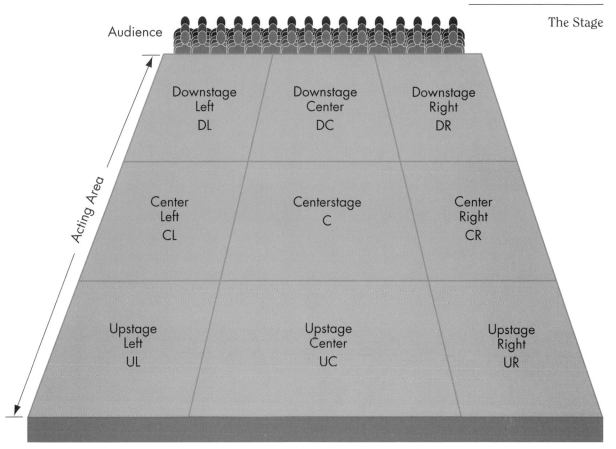

Audience

The Stage

Acting Area

Downstage Left DL

Downstage Center DC

Downstage Right DR

Center Left CL

Centerstage C

Center Right CR

Upstage Left UL

Upstage Center UC

Upstage Right UR

People read from left to right. In the theatre, the audience views the stage from left to right. But the audience's left is stage right. Use Figure 3.4 to locate the strong acting areas on a conventional stage.

When the director begins to block the location of actors, scenery, and props, the important lines and movement will probably occur mostly downstage center and downstage right.

Offstage Areas. In addition to the major onstage areas, an actor should become familiar with other important **offstage** areas. These areas are not visible to the viewing audience, yet provide important support to the entire theatre experience.

Backstage is the area behind the backdrop or stage set or scenery. This area is not visible to the audience and is used to

Offstage: *The parts of the stage not visible to the audience.*

Backstage: *The area behind the set or back-drop that is not seen by the audience.*

Wings: The offstage area to the right and to the left of the acting area. The wings are usually curtained so as not to be visible to the audience.

House: The auditorium or seating area from which the audience views the performance.

prepare for other scenes. Nothing that happens backstage should detract from the action on stage.

Waiting in the **wings** is an activity that actors experience as they await their entrance on stage. Actors wait in the wings to hear the cue that signals their appearance in the acting area. The wings may be a crowded place, but silence is required.

The **house** is an essential part of the theatre experience. This is where the audience sits to view the performance. All actors hope for a full house for every performance. When the house is full, many actors claim to feel more energy, and the performance is more exciting.

Summary

The stage is a special place where actors and audience meet. Actors need to know the different types of stages commonly used for performances. These include the conventional or proscenium stage, arena stages, and thrust stages. All stages have a system for identifying various locations on stage, and actors need to know how stage areas are designated.

Acting Positions of Stage

Just as onstage areas are identified in terms of an actor facing an audience, so basic body positions are also identified in terms of facing the audience. Though there are some common terms for body positions, some directors may have their own way of referring to basic acting positions.

Actors Standing on Stage

Standing is the most common posture of actors on stage. After a walking, running, crawling, or flying entrance, actors will spend most time on stage in a standing position. Where and how to stand becomes an important acting skill. The basic standing positions are full front, full back, one-quarter position, profile position, and three-quarters position (see Figure 3.5 on page 46).

You need to become very familiar with stage areas, body positions, and stage movements. These skills are basic to acting and will be useful in every acting situation. Take this opportunity to practice and perfect basic acting skills.

Step One

Stage Maps. Work in a small group to make a map of a stage. Use your own school stage or imagine creating a stage area in your classroom. To make the stage map, use a large piece of paper or construct a scale model. Include an outline of the stage area with labels to identify the type of stage and the specific areas mentioned in this chapter and a scale to indicate the size of the stage and acting area.

Step Two

Stage Diagrams. Make a diagram of the acting area and use a grid system to identify the major areas on stage. Label each area. Include abbreviations for each area. Put the name of each stage location on an index card and the abbreviation on the back. With a partner, take turns picking an index card and locating the spot on the diagram. Repeat this activity until you and your partner can locate all stage areas in any sequence within one minute.

Step Three

Body Positions. Trace and cut out an outline of your right and left feet. Make posters using your feet outlines to illustrate each of the five positions shown in Figure 3.4. Place these posters on the floor and stand in each of the positions you have drawn. Then practice each body position in each of the major stage areas. Work with a partner and take turns calling for a specific position in a specific location.

Step Four

Partner Locations. Work with a partner to show various body positions in all the stage areas. Start with some of the following and add to these suggestions. Actor A centerstage; B upstage right. Actor A downstage right; B downstage center. Actor A upstage center; B downstage center. Make index cards to identify various locations. Use abbreviations.

Step Five

Partner Positions. Stand centerstage with a partner. Show the following positions. (1) Actor A one-quarter right; B one-quarter left facing toward A; (2) Actor A full front; B three-quarters left; (3) profile for both actors facing each other; (4) profile for both turned away from each other; (5) Actor A three-quarters right; B three-quarters left facing toward each other. Then change locations on stage. Discuss how various body positions and stage locations feel for strength or mystery.

Figure 3.5 Standing Positions

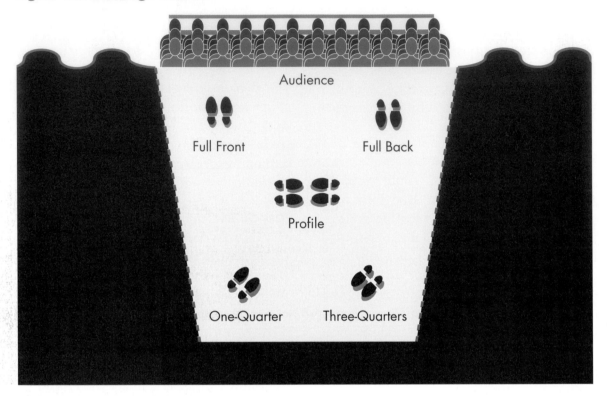

Full front: The position in which an actor faces the audience directly, usually in a standing position.

Standing Full Front. Full front sounds important, and it is. When an actor stands and faces an audience directly, people think something important is going on. They give this actor their full attention. This position is usually used for the delivery of important lines in the play.

The full front position is usually a position of strength. An actor in this position is in a position of dominance or prominence on stage. The actor facing full front will have the audience's full attention. The delivery of lines and use of gestures in this position are especially important. Actors who enjoy a full front position will want to practice and polish their delivery.

Full back: The position in which an actor stands with his or her back to the audience.

Full Back. Full back sounds mysterious, and it is. When actors turn their backs to the audience, it creates a strong impression on the audience. They feel shut off from that character's thoughts or actions. This may cause them to be distracted from other action on stage. This position is usually reserved for special occasions.

The One-Quarter Position. The **one-quarter** position is the most common position when two actors share a scene and talk or respond to each other. In this position, the actor stands with his or her upstage foot parallel to the front of the stage. The downstage foot is turned toward the audience at about a 45-degree angle. In this position, the audience can easily see both actors and gives them equal attention.

One-quarter: The position in which an actor stands a quarter turn from the audience.

Profile Position. The **profile,** or half-turn, position is another common position taken by actors sharing a scene. In this case, the actors stand facing each other so that the audience actually sees the actors' profiles.

The profile position is often used for scenes that involve intense emotions. When actors quarrel on stage, plead, or insult each other, this position is used. It can also be used to mirror actions to obtain a humorous response from the audience.

Profile: The position in which actors face each other directly so the audience sees their profiles.

When sharing a scene with another actor, assume a position that will allow the audience to see both of you, such as the profile position.

Three-quarter: The position in which an actor turns away from the audience so that only a portion of his or her head and shoulder can be seen by the audience.

The Three-Quarter Position. In the **three-quarter** position, the actor turns away from the audience so that only one quarter of the face and shoulder are seen by the audience. This is a transition position and is used when the action or lines shift from one actor to another.

Actors Sitting and Rising on Stage

Sometimes actors need relief from standing on stage, so they are directed to sit and, eventually, to get up. These are simple activities when done at home or school, but on stage, they can be difficult. Actors need to practice the simple skills of sitting and rising naturally on stage.

Sitting on Stage. Just as actors learn to stand as their stage character would stand, so sitting and rising require practice, too. Get in character mentally and review your notes about the gestures and postures of similar real-life people. Then, practice sitting down the way your character would. Do it so often that you do not feel like you have to look behind you for a chair. You will know where the chair is by feeling it with the back of your leg. Then lower your body as your character would.

Rising on Stage. Rising on stage also requires practice. Again, the secret is feeling the activity as your character would feel it. What emotion would the character feel when rising? Practice conveying the specific emotion the character feels when rising. Find your balance when getting up and do not rely on the arms of a chair or sofa for support.

To keep the audience's attention while you are sitting in character on stage requires energy and practice. If you must speak lines from a seated position, use your voice and body posture to give you a more dominant position. Speaking from a seated position or while rising takes more practice than delivering lines while standing.

Summary

On all types of stages, actors commonly stand using five basic body positions: full front, full back, profile, one-quarter, and

Stage Design

Every year, the Antoinette Perry Awards, nicknamed the Tony Awards, are given for the best theatre work on Broadway. The Tony Awards were started in 1947, a year after the death of Ms. Perry. They recognize "distinguished achievement" in the theatre and include an award for best set designer for the stage.

In 1992, John Arnone won the Tony for best scenic design for *Tommy*. Get to know this set designer from the interview excerpts that follow.

Q: Tell us about yourself.

A: I was born in 1949, in Dallas, Texas. I was born of Italian parents and have very joyful memories of going to my grandfather's farm in Irving, Texas, every Sunday. It was this sense of family that enabled me—maybe even conditioned me—to stay, not to seek to leave the family unit.

Q: Why did you want to be an actor?

A: I played Santa Claus when I was five year old? I don't know. I began seeing productions at the Dallas Theatre Center. They did an adaptation of William Faulkner's *As I Lay Dying* that was a total revelation to me. It was a stripped-down production, very elemental—no scenery, simple costumes, and straightforward acting.

Q: When and how did you start to design?

A: The Lion Theatre Company couldn't afford designers. One day Jack [Heifner] wrote a play for three women. Playwrights Horizons offered us $100 for the director, $100 for the playwright, and $100 for the designer. Then Playwrights Horizons wanted to know who the designer was. Well it was Jack's script, and Garland [Wright] was the director, so we told them the designer was John Arnone.

Q: Once you decided to be a scenic designer, what did you do?

A: I did what I had to do: I went to night school.

Q: How do you approach a project?

A: I do a lot of research. This background material becomes the fabric on which I embroider the ideas for the design. But there is another aspect, too, which is I think I'm buying time. The time it takes for the psyche to respond, to create, is very mysterious. And while my active mind is absorbing research, I feel that some deep response from within when my soul is at work.

Q: How do you characterize your work?

A: What characterizes my work is an intellectual/artistic ability to form ideas. Garland says that great designers don't think in terms of sets, they think in terms of ideas. And I would agree.

three-quarter. In addition, actors will sometimes be required to sit and rise from a chair or couch on stage. These actions need to be practiced to appear natural and convincing.

Directions for the Stage

The stage and acting area can be a big place. The actors need to know where to be on stage and how to get there. And getting there needs to seem easy and natural. Actors need to know and practice stage directions and basic movements to make the world of the stage real for the audience.

Guidelines for Stage Movement

Stage movement:
The movement of an actor from one position on stage to another.

All movement on stage has a reason or purpose. Actors need to know why and how **stage movement** occurs. Actors need to understand the motivation for movement. The reasons for stage movement become part of the actor's understanding of his or her character on stage. In general, the guidelines for stage movement are intended to keep the attention of the audience on the speaking character or the main action of the play.

Move in Character. Your understanding of the character you play on stage will help you enter, exit, walk, stand, and sit in a way that is natural to your character. The time you spend understanding your character will have dividends for stage movement.

After writing a character profile, observe how a real person with similar characteristics moves. Notice his or her facial expressions. Pay attention to the position of the person's head, shoulders, arms, legs, and feet. Then try and understand *why* the person moves distinctively.

When you have an idea of how your character moves and why, start practicing. The more you practice standing, sitting, and walking in character, the more your body will feel comfortable with your character.

Move with Reason. All stage movement has a reason, and all stage movement is rehearsed. Nothing happens on stage without motivation and lots of practice. Actors usually have only brief moments to speak and move on stage. The challenge is to make that short time memorable for the audience.

Move with Respect. Movement is not made on stage while another character is speaking. The attention of the audience is focused on the actors who are speaking on stage. They would be distracted by movement or action happening around the speaking characters on stage.

Respect for the performances of all the actors on stage should guide your movement. Respect for your fellow actors should keep you from moving while they are speaking. That same respect should keep you from blocking another actor on stage. The attitude of respect and cooperation will make stage directions and movement easier for everyone on and off the stage.

Movement in a Group. When actors enter the stage as part of a group, the actor who is speaking usually leads. The entrance of actors in a group reflects the relationships of characters to each other. Dominant and subordinate roles are usually reflected in stage movements.

Move in Straight Lines. Movement on stage is usually performed in a straight line. Use a diagram of a stage to place two actors in a variety of positions. For instance, Actor A stands centerstage; Actor B stands upstage right. Move Actor A upstage left and Actor B to centerstage. Block this movement on a stage diagram. Think about how you would direct Actor A and Actor B for this stage movement.

You could work with a partner to try out several stage movements to and from specific stage locations. Practice short, straight movements in an acting area. Then practice longer movement but still keep the movement in a straight line. Discuss with your partner why various positions on stage feel stronger or weaker.

Movement Visible to Audience. The audience needs to be involved with all major action and character development. If some development in the play actually happens offstage, the audience will be informed through dialogue on stage.

Basic Stage Directions

In the course of the play, actors will enter and exit the stage. Actors will change position; they will cross from one location to another. Actors could also exchange positions, or counter-cross, on stage. Even sitting and standing require direction and practice.

Entrances and Exits. An actor's entrance on stage is the debut of the character. This could be the actor's most important opportunity. Remember that first impressions form the basis of the audience's response. As an actor, you will spend much time thinking about your first entrance.

Imagine exactly how you want your character to enter the stage. Then, make that entrance happen. Move and think in character. Anticipate every detail connected with your entrance. Know the target location for your entrance. Check makeup, costumes, and props.

Your exit is as important as your entrance. Lasting impressions are also important to the audience. Actors may experience a sense of relief when their presence on stage is over or they have finished their lines. It is important to stay in character. Keep the character's attitude and posture on stage and through your exit.

Cross: An actor's movement from one area of the stage to another while in character.

Crossing. Stage **crosses** involve a change of position from one area of the stage to another. A stage cross is indicated on a script with an "X." Usually, actors take the shortest route to get from one place to another on stage. This straight cross suggests determination, a sense of purpose, or strength of character. Sometimes a director calls for a curved cross. In this case, the character might be suggesting hesitation, indecision, or a casual attitude.

The actor in the lower right-hand corner of this photograph uses a well-planned entrance to establish his character immediately and to create a favorable first impression.

Actors begin a cross with the foot nearest their destination. The idea is to keep the body turned toward the audience. Practice standing stage right and crossing to the left. Take the first step with your left foot.

The timing of a cross is also important. Actors try to cross between lines. If you must speak and cross the stage, walk in front of other characters. If you must cross while another actor is speaking, move quietly behind the speaker to avoid distracting the audience.

A cross calls attention to the actor. You will want to practice your specific cross movements so they appear natural and emphasize your character's role in the play.

Countercross: An actor's movement in the opposite direction of the cross made by another actor.

The Countercross. Actors need to remember that the acting area on a conventional stage looks like a framed picture to the audience. When one actor crosses the stage, the balance of the picture is destroyed. That is why another actor usually makes a **countercross,** or movement in the opposite direction.

Look at Figure 3.6, which shows two actors moving in a cross and countercross. Practice the movement with a partner. Actor A crosses with the lines, "What shall we do now?" Actor B counters by shifting slightly upstage and then moving to the new position downstage left. Both actors should finish at the same time.

Figure 3.6 Cross and Countercross

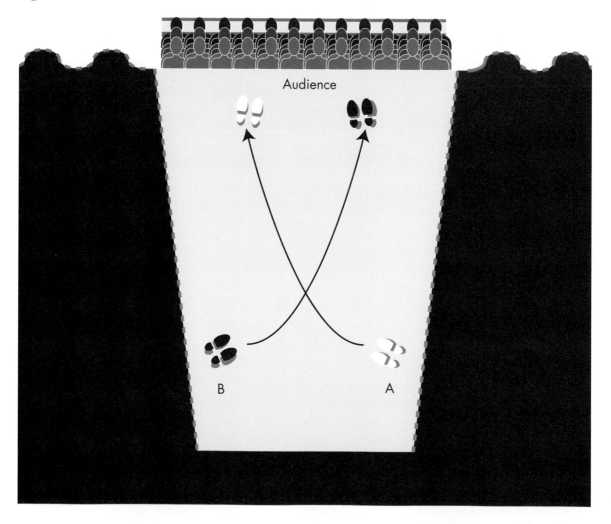

Summary

Actors need to learn the basic stage directions and the basic body positions and movements on stage. The guidelines for stage movement require that actors learn to move as their characters would move and respect the positions and movements of other actors on stage. Actors will have to practice the basic stage directions given for entrances, exits, crosses, and countercrosses so that these movements become easy and natural.

Staging

1. ***Entering the Stage.*** Try to imagine how you would enter a conventional stage if you were playing Goldilocks or Papa Bear coming to the front door of the cottage. Then imagine that same scene done on an arena stage. What would you want to do to use the best features of both stages? Return to the entrance of Goldilocks or Papa Bear as each approaches the cottage door on stage. Think of how you might enter the acting area on a thrust stage.

2. ***Stage Diagrams.*** Make a diagram of each of the three main types of stages. Think about the area on each stage that would enjoy the greatest audience attention. Target that area as the arrival place for your entrance. Practice your entrance.

3. ***Acting Areas.*** The acting area of a stage is usually organized in a grid system as shown in Figure 3.1. Actors have to know how areas on stage are designated. Practice drawing your stage area from memory. Be sure to include labels and abbreviations for each area in the acting grid.

4. ***Stage Scale.*** Take another look at your school stage with fresh eyes. Measure the size of the acting area as well as the offstage areas. Make a drawing of your school stage to scale. Use your scale drawing to locate actors for a curtain call of *Goldilocks* or a play of your choice.

Stage Movement

5. ***Enter in Character.*** You might practice entrance skills in the character of Goldilocks or Papa Bear. Target a specific location in the acting area for your entrance. Imagine that you enter the stage through a forest and take the door knob of the cottage with the words, "Oh, my!" Once you have practiced the entrance to a certain area of the stage, change your entrance location. Display your entrance skills for the class.

6. ***Exit in Character.*** You could practice exit skills, still in the character of Goldilocks or Papa Bear. Imagine that both characters are on stage and have resolved their conflicts. They exit the stage as friends saying, "What a day!"

7. ***Sitting and Rising.*** An important part of the Goldilocks story is the way each of the characters relates to various-sized chairs. To Goldilocks, the small, medium, and large chairs are all strange to her, but one is just right. In the Bear family, each has a chair that is just right. Practice sitting and rising in each of the three chairs in character as Goldilocks or Baby Bear.

The Actor's Logbook

1. ***Learning the Language.*** In addition to the terms in bold type in this chapter, there are many other terms that are used to refer to stage movement and set design. You can impress your family and friends if you add any of the following to your working vocabulary: give a scene; share a scene; take a scene; and dressing the stage.

   These are harder to find, but give it a try: flies, legs, teaser, and tormentors.

2. ***Shorthand, Too!*** The terms for stage areas and stage movement also have a shorthand version. Include all the standard abbreviations for stage areas in your logbook. Learn them by heart. You can develop your own shorthand for words or terms that you use often.

3. ***Stage Directions.*** Plot each of the following stage directions on a diagram of a conventional stage. Practice until you know the nine stage areas and five body positions by heart.

X DR; one-quarter position left	X C; profile face left
X UC; full front	X UL; three-quarters position face right

4. ***Critic's Choice.*** Find out who has received design awards for the Tony or Academy Awards in the 1990s. Prepare a chart or table that identifies the designer and the production. Start a scrapbook with photos, credits, or interviews about scenery and set design. If you have seen any of the productions nominated for best set design, write a description of what you saw and your impressions.

Critical Thinking

5. ***Compare and Contrast.*** Imagine that your school has received a grant to build a new stage. Think about the advantages and disadvantages of the conventional, arena, and thrust stages and prepare a one-minute speech or write an editorial to argue for the stage you want.

6. ***Evaluation.*** Read a review of a movie you have seen. Note the number of "stars" this movie received from the reviewer. Think about how you would rate movies and develop your own rating system. Then rate the movie you selected. Think of the best movie you ever saw and give three reasons why you think it was the best. Then rank other movies in terms of how they compare to the best. You could do the same for the worst.

Creative Thinking

7. ***Three's a Crowd.*** Imagine that your doorbell rings, you open the door and the family baby-sitter arrives just as your five year-old brother comes crashing through the hall. Identify stage locations for this scene and give stage directions to the three actors.

8. ***Time Travel.*** Imagine a reunion of the Star Wars heroes, Princess Leia, Luke Skywalker, and Han Solo fifty years after their victorious battles to save the galaxy. Prepare a short play that uses a flashback or a future dream scene.

CHAPTER FOUR

Actors Using Pantomime and Clowning

EXPECTATIONS

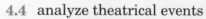

After reading this chapter, you will be able to

4.1 demonstrate body awareness and spatial perception through creative movement

4.2 display skills in pantomime

4.3 define clowning and its relationship to pantomime

4.4 analyze theatrical events

People convey more about themselves through their posture, gestures, and dress than they do through their words. This is an important insight for an actor. The key to strong characterization is the actor's ability to use nonverbal skills to convey character. Just as we learn to crawl and move about before we learn to speak, so beginning actors will focus on body movement before "learning their lines" for a stage character.

Pantomime—Acting without Words

Actors bring a story and its characters to life through their words and actions. In many cases, the story is told without words. The actors rely on their own imagination and gestures to tell the tale. **Pantomime** uses the imagination and physical actions to create vivid, believable characters.

Guidelines for Pantomime

Our bodies mirror the way we feel. When you feel angry, your body tenses, your eyes narrow, your fists might clench, your body goes on a kind of "red alert." When you feel happy, your eyes sparkle, your smiles are easy and quick to come, you walk with a lighter step. Sometimes you may not even be aware of how your body language reflects your emotions. Understanding the link between emotions and the body leads to better acting skills and insights into characterization.

Feel the Emotion. Acting skills are related to the powers of imagination and observation. You can put both of these powers to work to develop acting skills. Observe in your mind's eye an impatient teenager waiting in line to buy tickets to a concert. Describe the teenager's face, the look in his or her eyes, the muscles around his or her eyes and mouth. Think about the body posture and movements that convey impatience.

Pantomime: A sequence of facial expressions, gestures, body positions, and movements that convey a story or character without words.

You could probably impersonate that impatient teenager on stage based on your powers of observation. But go a step further. Bring your imagination to this characterization. Create a character with a family background that gives him or her a reason for impatience. Begin to feel the impatience coming from the emotions inside the character. Your acting will be more convincing when character portrayal comes from within rather than from simple observation.

Relax the Body. The importance of actors having healthy bodies will be emphasized often. In the context of pantomime, a relaxed and disciplined body will convey emotion and help define stage characters. If you want to express positive emotions such as love, courage, or sympathy, hold your head and upper body high, practice free and relaxed movements with your arms and hands, keep your face relaxed yet animated. Stand before a mirror and, by simply standing, practice body posture and facial expressions that convey courage.

Negative emotions are also conveyed through the body and facial expressions. Hate, jealousy, fear, and anger can be communicated through a lowered chest, restricted gestures, and tense facial muscles. Again, gain practice expressing negative emotions without saying a word. Stand in front of the mirror and through facial expression and stance try to express jealousy.

Use Facial Expressions. The face is the best mirror of inner feelings. Some people try to cover up their feelings. Their faces are like masks that hide another self. Actors learn to use facial muscles to express a wide variety of emotions.

What the audience sees is often more important than what is said on stage. And the audience is conditioned to look at an actor's face to "read" a character. On stage, a facial expression usually precedes a gesture or body movement. It takes understanding, observation, and imagination to convey a complex emotion through the face. Loosen up facial muscles with yawns, raised eyebrows, wiggles, and head shaking. Then try to convey a positive emotion such as courage simply through your face. Practice using a hand mirror. Then try to express a negative emotion such as fear.

You can convey an amazing array of emotions through facial expressions.

Human beings are capable of many emotions, and it is important to understand their subtle differences. Consider each of the emotions in the list below:

exhaustion	confusion	guilt
confidence	anger	frustration
disgust	smugness	shame
boredom	embarrassment	suspicion
hurt	shyness	

Pick several emotions you are familiar with and a few that you are not. Describe the emotions. In the course of a week, try to observe someone experiencing those emotions. Describe the person's facial expressions, noting eyes and mouth especially. Imagine the reasons why that person is experiencing those emotions. Then try to express the emotions you select through your own facial expressions.

Use Strong Gestures. In addition to body posture and facial expression, an actor conveys character through the use of gestures. While some gestures will be exaggerated on stage to emphasize meaning, all gestures should appear natural and appropriate to the stage character.

Remember that all gestures should have a reason for being included in the play action. The meaning and intent of a gesture should be clear in the actor's mind. In that way, the audience will have a greater understanding of the character.

You want all gestures to be clearly visible to the audience. When possible, lead with your upstage arm when you make a gesture. This will keep the rest of your body more visible to the audience. Move your arms and hands in lightly curved lines neither above your head or below the waist unless there is a specific reason for doing so. Anticipate what your body will look like and be doing every moment you are on stage. Remember, your body and facial expression convey your stage character more strongly than any words.

As with body posture and facial expressions, choose suitable gestures to convey your character on stage.

Pantomime is a useful technique for the beginner and the experienced actor. At first, pantomime may seem like an exercise to increase body coordination, concentration, and control. But with repeated practice, pantomime will help discipline an actor to create strong characters for the stage. In addition, pantomime can help actors develop specific stories, atmospheres, and locations.

Character Types. The stage presents all sorts of people, and the actor needs practice in observing and imagining different types of characters. Think about the body language, emotional experiences, and facial expressions you might develop to portray any of the following characters on stage:

five-year-old child	sixteen-year-old boy/girl
overworked parent	police officer
store clerk	fast-food cook

Stand in front of a mirror and practice how you would stand, how you would hold your head, and how you would use your hands to create one of these characters for the stage. When you think you can convey the character you have selected, try out your character pantomime for an "audience." If your character is guessed correctly within ten seconds, take a bow and try another character type.

Ready for Action. Pantomime, like all forms of theatre, has a beginning, a middle, and an end to a story. Select one of the following actions to convey through pantomime. Once you have made your selection, use your imagination to create an environment and character for your pantomime. Think of at least five different body movements and facial expressions that are related to the action you select. Then practice to convey each step and create the overall impression you want.

bowling	taking a test
planting a garden	playing a computer game

Pantomimes for Partners and Groups

Actors practice pantomime individually as well as with a partner or with a small group. When working with another person, an actor develops a sensitivity to the character and movement of that other person. A spirit of cooperation and creativity develops that is essential to a theatre company. Consider how the following activities would promote team spirit on stage.

The Mirror. In this activity, pantomime partners work together to mirror each other's body movement. Stand facing another actor. Imagine that a mirror separates you and the other actor. Place your hands against the hands of your partner, then draw them an inch apart. Take turns taking the initiative in changing positions, using gestures, and expressing emotions, but always keep at least one hand "touching." Mirror each other's changes as smoothly as possible.

Discuss how you learn to work with a partner. If a pantomime partner were a matter of your personal choice, figure out what qualities you would most like to have in your partner. Consider how working with a pantomime partner helps focus on the interrelatedness of characters on stage. With the practice of partner pantomime, actors learn to play a character in relation to another rather than simply concentrating on their own characters.

Tug of War. An entire theatre company can practice pantomime with an imaginary game of tug of war. The spirit of give and take reflected in the tug of war can apply to giving and taking in a scene on stage. After developing a feel for the basic tug of war pantomime, you can add variations to the skill. To gain practice in conveying environment, a theatre company can try to create the impression that the game is being played on sand at the beach or another location.

Summary

Actors can use pantomime skills to communicate character, story, and location without using words. Pantomime relies on body posture, gestures, and facial expression to communicate

Pantomime exaggerates movement and gesture so that the actor can apply these physical skills and muscle memory on stage. Take this opportunity to combine pantomime skills with stage movements.

Step One
The Story. Select one of the following story suggestions or create you own. Your job is to make the story and setting clear without the use of words. Think about how to create the environment of the story without words or props.

    a. ***Fast Food.*** An impatient customer orders a diet drink and a baked potato with sour cream in a small cafe. The server takes the strange order to the restaurant and brings the diet drink to the customer, who reads the paper. After finishing the drink, the customer puts a quarter on the table and leaves.

    b. ***Bake Sale.*** A boy sneaks into a kitchen and climbs to a top shelf of a cupboard to cut a piece of a freshly baked cake. His sister enters and is furious. She chases her brother from the kitchen. He sits in a chair and slowly begins to eat the cake.

    c. ***Contagious.*** A student is reading a very funny book in the library and laughs out loud. The librarian reminds the student about silence. Another round of laughter, another reminder, and an apology. Another outbreak of laughter, and this time the student invites the librarian to read the passage. The librarian breaks out laughing.

Step Two
The Characters. Work with your partner to create background and motivation for each character. Develop significant gestures for movement and stay in character.

Step Three
Stage Movement. Include in your pantomime at least three of the following stage movements: enter or exit; sit or rise; cross and countercross; open and close door. Remember to keep all stage movement motivated, simple, and exaggerated for your pantomime. Plan or outline each movement of your pantomime.

Step Four
Rehearsal. Practice your story with your partner. Give each other feedback and make suggestions about character definition and gestures. Modify your outlines based on this feedback. When you have rehearsed at least ten times, you could present your pantomime to the class.

Step Five
The Ratings. After your performance, discuss with your partner the things you think went well in your pantomime. Identify the areas you want to improve. Record your impressions and evaluations in your logbook.

with the audience. Guidelines for using the body, feeling emotion, and developing facial expression can be practiced in a variety of pantomimes for individuals, partners, and teams.

Clowning

Another way to gain experience using exaggerated movements and facial expressions is through the skills of clowning. Many clowns rely on pantomime—acting without words—to relate to their audiences.

Clowns have been making people laugh forever. They are silly, clever, zany, bizarre, and just plain funny. **Clowns** are performers who rely on makeup to exaggerate facial expressions and on gestures to communicate thoughts and actions.

Learning how to create a clown character with an exaggerated personality can help a beginning actor to develop other characters for the stage. Learning basic clown skills, including the use of props and pantomime, will also apply to acting on stage. Finally, learning clown skits and stunts will prepare actors for direct audience contact and teach them to read and respond to their audiences.

Clowns: Actors who entertain an audience through the use of exaggerated facial expressions, gestures, and pantomime.

Clown Characters

Every clown you have ever seen is one of three basic types. Each of these types is associated with a certain "look" and uses a traditional makeup design. Knowing the basic types of clowns will help you find the "clown" inside you and help you develop your own clown character. The basic clown characters are the whiteface clown, the Auguste clown, and the character clown.

The Whiteface Clown. The **whiteface clown** is the classic clown with white facial makeup and features painted on in red and black. The white face is usually topped off with an outrageous wig. Whiteface clowns usually try to play tricks on other clowns and keep their own dignity in the process. The whiteface usually is the straight comedy figure when working with another clown.

Whiteface clown: A traditional clown type that uses white facial makeup with black and red painted features and dresses in a loose jumpsuit to play tricks on others.

A whiteface clown traditionally wears white facial makeup with painted-on features and an outrageous wig.

The costume of a whiteface clown is traditionally a loose-fitting pajama-type jumpsuit. Many of these clown suits have a ruff around the neck and large pompon "buttons" down the front. Many children have been entertained with television performances of Bozo the Clown, a familiar example of the whiteface clown type.

The Auguste Clown. The **Auguste clown** is a less educated, polished, and skilled clown character than the whiteface. This clown will create comedy by misunderstanding directions, mistaking people, and generally messing up. The Auguste clown does not use whiteface makeup. Instead, this clown wears a light color base such as pink, light blue, or yellow. White is usually used around the eyes and mouth, and these features are exaggerated.

Auguste clown: A traditional clown type often paired with the whiteface clown as the silly, bumbling sidekick; these clowns rely on pale facial makeup and exaggerated facial features to create the clown character.

The Auguste clown enjoys a greater variety in costumes than the whiteface clown. Since the Auguste clown is active and always getting into trouble and messes, the costume is usually loose fitting to allow ease of movement. It is also easy to clean after all the spills and falls. A traditional Auguste costume would be a plaid suit or pants and colorful tie. Modern versions of the Auguste costume might include a striped shirt with loud pants and colorful suspenders or vest.

Bozo's sidekick clown, Cookie, is an Auguste clown. If you have seen Bozo or circus clowns who played either the whiteface or Auguste types, try to remember their costumes and makeup.

Character Clowns. In addition to the whiteface and Auguste clown types, some actors have developed delightful clown personalities to entertain their audiences. While there is much variety, several character types are common. These character types include the tramp, or hobo, clown, the police officer, and the rube or country bumpkin.

An Auguste clown traditionally wears pale facial makeup with white around the eyes and mouth and a loud costume.

The great clown Emmett Kelly created the tramp clown, which many actors have tried to imitate. Some tramp characters are happy-go-lucky; others seem down on their luck. Some pretend to enjoy a higher social or economic status than their shabby costume would suggest.

Emmett Kelly was perhaps the best-known character clown as the tramp clown.

The rube character clown is often costumed in baggy over-alls, an old-fashioned straw hat, and a red bandanna or scarf. This type of clown will be amazed by common aspects of modern society.

Develop Your Own Clown Character

To find the best clown character for yourself, look at your own personality and the humor you enjoy. Your clown character is a very personal choice. No one can really tell you what type of clown to play. Your clown character is another part of yourself. Think about the parts of yourself that you routinely mask that could come alive with clown makeup and costume.

You want to choose a distinctive and believable character. Invent a life for your clown character just as you would for a stage character. Your clown character is important because this influences your choice of makeup, costume, props, and stunts.

To help you create your clown character, you might list some of your favorite cartoon characters, funny television programs, and movie comedies. Look at the list and try to find the things that all these funny elements have in common. Then use your imagination to create a clown character that seems to share as many of these qualities that you enjoy as possible.

Remember that the clown character you develop will, like any person, continue to grow and change. Try out your clown character. Pay attention to how the audience responds; then do more of what they respond to and cut out what does not get a positive reaction.

To help you develop your clown character, think about the following skills and how they can help you with your clown, as well as with any stage character you play.

Clown Skills

Any character you play on stage requires your analysis and imagination. The research you do and the description you provide for your character helps to create a distinctive and memorable personality. To play a funny, convincing clown, you will want to give your clown character the same distinctive personality you would give a stage character.

Playing the clown, like playing a stage character, will require costumes, makeup, props, and action. In playing a clown, all these things are magnified. It is this exaggeration that provides useful skill development for beginning actors.

Costumes Make the Clown. In real life, every piece of clothing tells something about the person who wears it. You think you can spot "nerds" by their white socks and the way they dress. Even hair styles tell a lot about a person. The costumes selected for stage characters take much thought and research. The same is true for your clown costume. A good place to start might be the back corners of a closet.

Make a sketch of the type of clown you want to be and the costume you would like to wear. Your clown costume should reflect the kind of clown you will want to play. Think of how gloves, hats, and shoes could be used to create a costume. And don't forget clown hair. The style and color of clown hair is one of the most important parts of playing the clown.

Clown Makeup. All actors use makeup. Clowns use a lot of makeup. Experiment with designing a clown face that fits the clown character you want to create. Remember that the three basic types of clowns require different types of makeup. Make several sketches. Use whatever makeup materials you have on hand. When you are satisfied with the clown face you have designed, consider the following guidelines for applying clown makeup:

1. Makeup is messy. Have a supply of paper towels and/or facial tissues on hand. Aprons or towels also help keep stray powders or paint from getting on your costume. Some clowns use a plastic shower cap or a baseball cap to keep their hair clean while applying makeup. You will not want to pull a shirt or dress over your head after you have applied makeup. Plan ahead.
2. Follow a diagram or plan for your clown makeup. Never copy another clown's makeup. Always add your own

individuality to your design. Keep your lines simple and even. You don't want one eye to be different from the other or one side of a smile to be unequal.

3. Apply the different colors in this order: white, pastels, red, black. Go from light to dark when applying makeup. You can use a few thin art brushes to apply fine detail paint. After applying each color, powder it with baby powder using a sock, brush, or powder puff. Remove excess powder to get an even coat.

4. Practice and experiment before a real performance. Applying makeup takes time and patience. Give yourself plenty of time. You don't want a crooked smile because you hurried and got the outline crooked or smudged.

5. Remove all makeup after your performance. Use baby oil to remove makeup if your skin is normal or dry. Use baby shampoo if your skin is oily. Apply the oil or shampoo to the palm of you hand, rub your hands together, and then rub your hands over your face. You will make a big mess, so use paper towels or tissues to wipe it off immediately. If you have trouble getting all the red off your face, apply another dose of baby oil or shampoo.

Props: Stage properties. Objects used for a performance, including hand props, objects carried on stage by an actor, and set props, which are large items placed on stage, such as furniture.

Clown Props. Almost all actors, including clowns, use **props** in a performance. For a clown, a prop is anything that is used to make an audience laugh. By themselves, props are just objects. A clown uses imagination to give the prop a life of its own. Many clowns use a special hat as a prop. The hat could become a brain, or a conscience, or a troublemaker.

Think about how you could use a hat, or another object of your own choosing, as a clown prop. Describe the personality you would give the hat. Think of the gestures and body posture you could use when wearing or removing the hat. Use your imagination to think of ways to get your audience involved with your prop. What might happen if your clown "passed the hat" around or tried a "hats off" routine?

Clown Skits and Stunts

Many clowns perform in pantomime, using actions without words to communicate with an audience. Other clowns use

Clowns use a variety of props to make audiences laugh.

words. All clowns perform stunts or short skits to entertain an audience. Your class might want to consider entertaining a group of children at a library story hour or a group of senior citizens at a nursing home. Clowns, like all actors, need an audience to make their performance come alive.

A clown needs to make an entrance and an exit on stage and to do something funny on stage. The clown wants to entertain the audience, to be funny. What the clown says or does should be in good taste and interactive with the audience. While most actors must wait for applause until the end of a performance, a clown gets immediate response from the audience.

Say "Hello." Give yourself a clown name. Take time to think of a name that suggests the clown personality you have created. Your choice of a name will condition the audience to respond to you in a certain way. If your clown name is Professor Braino, the audience will expect different gestures and props than if your clown name were Giggles. Now imagine yourself in clown costume and makeup. You want to get ready for your introduction on stage.

There are many ways to say "hello." Your choices will depend on your clown character, what your character wants, and what your character does to get it. Imagine this hello done in pantomime. Then you might practice the routine for your own clown character. Tricky the Magician sneaks on stage to try a quick performance of an unscheduled magic trick. Tricky tiptoes on stage, taking big exaggerated steps and looking around to show fear of being discovered. Tricky moves with her back to the audience from center left, reaches centerstage, and turns to face the audience. Tricky puts an index finger to her mouth and gestures with a large movement, "Shhhhh!" Then Tricky bends her legs and becomes smaller and makes the "Shhhhh!" movement again. This is the character's entrance or hello.

Tricky's exit should also be in character. Tricky pantomimes hearing somebody coming. Tricky freezes and listens carefully, then turns and scampers off stage to center left or right.

Develop a pantomime entrance and exit for your clown character. Think of a reason for your entrance on stage. Your reasons might include (1) a need to escape from your partner; (2) a search for your pet dog or a missing prop; or (3) a scheduled appointment with another clown, doctor, scientist, and so on. Your hello could also include tipping your hat, using your signature prop, taking a bow, or waving.

Your exit could be motivated by the need to continue to look for your dog, to escape from a partner, to run off to join a parade, or whatever you invent for your character.

Practice an entrance and exit for your clown in pantomime. When you are ready, perform for the class. Then you might be ready to take your show on the road for children, adults, or grandparents.

Clown Stunts. Some clowns develop a special set of skills they use in their performances. These could include magic tricks, creating balloon animals, juggling, walking on stilts, or riding unicycles. Any of these special skills can be included in a clown routine. Start with one magic trick or one balloon animal and work it into your performance. If it gets a positive response from the audience, plan to add a similar stunt to your routine.

Props are also used for clown stunts. These could be very large props, such as using a big saw or hammer to perform a very small task. Squirting props are also used commonly. Old catsup bottles or hot water bottles can be dressed up for a variety of purposes for a gag with a partner.

To expand your creativity as you develop a clown stunt, take an ordinary object and make a list of twenty ways that object could be used. Not all the uses need to be funny, but develop as long a list as you can. Let one idea flow into another. Use a balloon or a drinking glass, for example. Think of an unusual way you could change the size, shape, color, or texture of the object. Begin to work this altered object into a clown stunt. Get in the habit of asking yourself, "What else can I do with this prop?"

Clown Skits. Work out a short skit for your clown character. Plan your entrance from any stage location. Say your "hello," incorporating the earlier suggestions. Use your hat or another prop in at least three different ways. Make an exit. Develop the skit as a pantomime.

As you work on your skit, remember to give your character a reason for coming on stage. Brainstorm different ways to think of and use the prop you select. Exaggerate your movements and gestures. Be very clear about what your clown character wants and why.

You may want to work on a skit with a partner or a team. Use your creativity to imagine and develop a clown character and skit that will give you a lot of satisfaction. You could take your show on the road and offer to perform at a child's birthday party. Have fun!

Summary

Clowning develops an actor's skill in character development and the use of movement, gestures, facial expressions, and props. There are three traditional types of clowns, and these types influence the kind of costume, makeup, and routines the clown character develops. Clowns can perform in pantomime or with words. Actors create personalities for their clowns in much the same way that actors develop stage characters. Clowns work to entertain the audience using exaggerated gestures, expressions, and props.

The Clown Hall of Fame

Even clowns cannot escape the critics! Good clowns want to become great clowns. Beginner clowns want to improve their performances. You might be amazed by the "standards" clowns use to evaluate their performances. The Clown Hall of Fame and Research Center (212 East Walworth Avenue, Delavan, WI 53115) is dedicated to maintaining high standards for clowns. The center promotes clowning and operates a museum and national archive for clown information and history.

Imagine that you want to nominate one of your clown classmates to audition for a performance at the Clown Hall of Fame. Based on the clown activity in this chapter, you will use four standards to nominate your choice for Hall of Fame consideration. These standards are: (1) clarity of character, (2) costume, (3) makeup, and (4) pantomime or skit. You could begin a chart using these categories and listing all class clown participants. Begin a simple rating system to evaluate skills in each category.

Clarity of Character. Remember that there are three basic types of clowns. Identify the members of the class who created whiteface, Auguste, and character clowns. Then think about how clearly the personality of the clown character was communicated. Do you think the classmate clown did the homework involved to invent a clown character? Write this category on an index card. On the reverse side of the card, write your nomination and give two reasons for your choice. Put your card in an envelope with the category written on the outside.

Costume. Clown costumes are no accident; they take much planning. Think about the clown sketches or actual costumes your classmates developed. Think about the clever use of accessories like hats, gloves, or shoes. Make your nomination for best clown costume following the same procedure mentioned above.

Makeup. Clown makeup leaves little to chance. Everything is planned. Remember the types of makeup that correspond to the basic clown types. Think about how your classmate clowns personalized their makeup design. After reflection, nominate a classmate for best use of makeup.

Pantomime or Skit. Every classmate had the opportunity to present his or her hello and use of a prop to the class. Based on that performance, identify the most original entrance and exit. Think about the best use of exaggerated movement and gesture. Who used a prop most creatively? Make your nomination as before.

And the Winner Is. . . . The nominations for best clown in each category can be tallied by a small group of judges. Enjoy a presentation of clown awards. Then write the Clown Hall of Fame!

Pantomime Activities

1. ***Charades.*** Most of you are familiar with the party game of charades. Pick a song or music title with at least three words. Practice using body posture, gestures, and facial expressions to convey each word in the title. When you think you can communicate your title, ask a friend to guess the title based on your pantomime.

2. ***Express Yourself.*** Use your whole body to create the letters of your name. Make your body into the shape of each letter of your name. Take your time; try several different body positions. Have fun.

3. ***Dance Your Name.*** Put on some in-strumental music and practice "dancing" your name with the movement of your whole body. Move within the room as you dance your name with feet, legs, body, arms, and head. After printing your name with dance movement, you could also try dancing your name or the name of a friend.

Facial Expressions

4. ***Masking Emotions.*** Either pretend you have a mask or make a simple mask that reflects one of the emotions listed on page 61. With pantomime movement, place the real or imaginary mask in front of your face. Create a facial expression that conveys that single emotion. Then erase the mask emotion with another pantomime motion. Develop a gesture to indicate your taking another mask. Convey a variety of emotions through facial expressions using the mask activity.

5. ***Pantomime Climax.*** Identify the emotion your character feels in the climax of the pantomime story you chose to perform. (See page 63.) Figure out what motivated that emotion in the character you play. Then practice the facial expression you want to convey that emotion.

Pantomime Scenes

6. ***The Machine.*** In a small group, use your imaginations to create or invent a new machine. First think about how you could pantomime being a car or canoe. Then draw a sketch of the machine you create and discuss how it works and who will play each part of the machine. Figure out how one part reacts with another part. Practice your machine pantomime until you feel that it really "works."

7. ***Camp Big Top.*** Imagine that you are the director of a summer camp that will teach young children clown skills. You want to introduce a variety of clown skills, including basic clowning techniques, pantomime skits, costumes, and character development. Put together a brochure that would describe your camp and the activities you provide.

8. ***Cinderella.*** Pantomime the scene in *Cinderella* where two stepsisters and Cinderella try on a glass slipper held by the prince's servant. The scene is watched by the stepmother and the prince. Each character in the pantomime must convey a distinct personality through body language and facial expressions. Create the impression of place and the size of the room.

The Actor's Logbook

1. ***Learning the Language.*** Add each of the words and terms in bold type to the appropriate page in the glossary section of your logbook.

2. ***Critic's Choice.*** Draft a letter to send to the Clown Hall of Fame (see page 77) to obtain information about the organization. Inquire about local organizations for clowning that might be closer to your community. Look in your local paper and identify opportunities for an aspiring clown to perform. These opportunities might be an announcement of a birthday or anniversary, a company picnic, or a county fair. Make a list of these clown opportunities in your logbook.

3. ***Production Schedule.*** Imagine that you have one week to prepare a clown show. In your logbook, identify the things you need to do every day in order to be prepared to present your clown show at a school assembly on Friday. Compare your lists. Add things that you forgot to mention. Discuss how you could best use your time each day in order to have a great performance.

Critical Thinking

4. ***Similarities.*** The main parts of this chapter on pantomime and clowning share some aspects of acting. Make a list of the characteristics that these elements of acting share. Discuss these similarities. Try to make your list of similarities grow.

5. ***Criteria.*** Think of at least two aspects of movement that you want to concentrate on to improve your acting skills. For each aspect, list two things you want to learn to do or improve that will demonstrate your achievement. Over the next week, look at your criteria each day and evaluate your progress. Write a progress report at the end of the week based on your own criteria.

6. ***Compare and Contrast.*** Make a chart to show the characteristics of costume, makeup, and stunts that are typical of whiteface, Auguste, and character clowns.

Creative Thinking

7. ***What's in a Name?*** Brainstorm at least ten zany names for a clown character you might develop. Work with a partner or in a small group to weigh the appeal of each of your possibilities. Based on this feedback, select the best name for your clown character

8. ***Business Cards.*** Design a business card for the clown character you developed. Include the name, your specialty act, and the audiences who enjoy your skills. Display these in class.

9. ***Pantomime.*** Many mimes take to the streets to perform for passersby. Imagine that your class has been asked to develop a pantomime that would welcome students on the first day of school. A mime could also gain experience by volunteering to serve as an usher for school assemblies.

10. ***Design a Face.*** Select either a pantomime character or a clown personality and experiment with creating a face through makeup for the character you select. Work with a face outline and concentrate on eye and eyebrow treatment. Then work on a suitable mouth. Finally, experiment with noses. Have fun. Display the face designs in the classroom and select your personal best for your portfolio.

PART TWO

Use of Body and Voice

CHAPTER FIVE

The Body

EXPECTATIONS

After reading this chapter, you will be able to

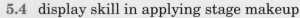

5.1 appreciate the importance of empathy between actor and audience

5.2 use observation skills to create a character

5.3 understand the importance of costume to character portrayal

5.4 display skill in applying stage makeup

good actor makes us care about the character presented on stage. By showing how the character feels and thinks, the actor forges a bond with the audience. We identify with the human aspects of the character. When that character is real to us, we may respond as if to someone we know personally, a member of our family or a good friend.

Empathy

When we watch a play or movie, we are not passive observers. The actor communicates with us as members of the audience through the words, actions, and reactions of the character, and we respond. An actor relies on **nonverbal communication** as well as words to reach the audience.

We identify with the character because he or she is a unique human being with emotions and needs like our own. The relationship that develops between an actor and an audience as a result of identification is known as **empathy.**

Empathy is an emotional connection between the actor and the audience. The audience feels the same emotion as the actor portraying the character feels. You may experience empathy as an everyday response to others. For example, when a friend loses someone dear, you feel some of the friend's pain. Or when one person yawns sleepily, you may start to yawn, too. These are empathic responses. As a member of a theatre or television audience, you have probably experienced empathy. Have you ever cried during a sad movie? Have you cheered when a character won? Because the actor was able to arouse your empathy, you cared what happened to the character he or she was playing.

Nonverbal communication: Any communication that does not involve speech. This could include gestures, body language, and facial expressions.

Empathy: The flowing of emotion from the actor to the audience and its return.

Creating a Bond with the Audience

One reason people enjoy going to the theatre and watching movies is that they find emotional satisfaction in the experience. They feel that what they see on stage or in a film is

Resource: Something that is useful and can be called upon when needed.

about real life. They know that they can identify with the character being portrayed. A good actor makes a character memorable because he or she uses the words of the playwright, facial expressions, gestures, and movement to create a living, breathing character on stage. The actor also calls on certain **resources,** such as experiences, observations, and the senses, to enrich the portrayal of characters.

Experiences. An actor uses resources such as experiences—the actor's own or others'—to enrich a role. To play a believable character, you need not have experienced what the character has experienced. But maybe you know someone who has. A simple way to share experiences is by talking to others and by listening to their stories.

An actor also benefits from recounting experiences in front of a group. It heightens the awareness of empathy and gives

Strive to create an emotional bond with your audience by making your character memorable and unique.

the performer a chance to communicate vividly to others. If the audience empathizes and becomes involved, the actor then experiences an important part of true acting. When you speak of something that happened to you in the past you may communicate on both a verbal and nonverbal level–with words and gestures. Empathy is part of this communication of experiences. When there is active empathy between actor and audience, there is a basis for a good performance.

The actor uses experiences in other ways, too. In studying a script, an actor may find situations in the play that are similar to situations he or she has experienced in the past. By drawing on this resource, the actor can add life and believability to a character portrayal. As a starting point, experiences can aid an actor's character-building. When the character is based on truth and is believable, the audience becomes more involved and empathic.

Observation. Experiences can be even more valuable for the actor who is a keen observer of life. Observing is being aware of what is going on in life. People, places, objects, and situations all add to an actor's depth of awareness. Watch people and take mental notes on their physical habits and body movements. Notice how they walk and move their hands. Observe their facial expressions when they are happy, sad, or lost in thought. These mental notes may become the basis for a character in the future and can be triggered when needed to create a character's physical movements within the structure of a play. Eventually these mental notes will become so natural that they become part of you and part of the character.

An actor can use the powers of observation for the following purposes:

1. to learn human characteristics in walking, gesturing, talking, and sitting that may be reproduced on stage

2. to stimulate creative imagination

3. to incorporate qualities learned from watching animals, such as the gracefulness of a cat

Stimulus: Anything that starts the thinking process or that awakens one of the senses.

Using Your Senses. An actor must develop a sensitivity to the senses—sight, touch, smell, hearing, and taste. Be aware of your senses during daily activities. Think about what it is that you are perceiving. When you are walking to school, notice the wind on your face, hear the noises of cars and the sounds of voices and birds, feel the cold or warmth of the air, smell and taste the raindrops. The character you are playing should be attuned to the sights, sounds, smells, tastes, and textures in the context of the play.

An actor can use the five senses in everyday life to sharpen awareness of the world around him or her. To create a real character that responds to the **stimuli** in the context of a play, the actor should become more observant of those sights, sounds, smells, and tastes in daily life.

The actor can create a more believable character by paying attention to details such as how different people respond to a stimulus. Imagine how you might react to the following:

Sight: a red, juicy apple; your image in a mirror; a large, hairy spider; a smooth, calm lake

Touch: a steaming, hot cup of tea; steel wool; the fur of a rabbit; a steel pole on a sub-zero day

Smell: a pepperoni pizza; ammonia; a garbage dump; roses; a new car

Sound: a fire alarm; rain on a roof; fingernails on a chalkboard; robins in the morning; a train in the night

Taste: a lemon; a juicy peach; garlic; hot chili peppers; vanilla ice cream

You know how you would respond to these stimuli in real life. It is also important as an actor to know how a character you are playing might respond. For example, how might a homeless person react differently to that red, juicy apple or that steaming, hot cup of tea? Would a character who just lost a front tooth respond differently to the image of her face in the mirror? How would a vegetarian react to the smell of pepperoni pizza? Would a teacher react differently than the students to the sound of a fire alarm?

Summary

Empathy is the flowing of emotion from the actor to the audience and back again. It is a critical element of an actor's performance. Empathy helps the audience care about what happens to a character in a play. In order for the actor to create this emotional bond with the audience, he or she needs to rely on experiences and observations about the way people behave. The actor must also develop an awareness of the world of the senses: sight, smell, taste, sound, and touch.

Costume

Theatre is in many ways a visual experience. What the audience sees on a stage enriches its understanding of a play. The actors' facial expressions, movements, gestures, and costumes all affect the audience. The clothing, or **costume,** an actor wears is particularly important in giving the audience clues about the character being portrayed.

Costume: Clothing that is used to further the portrayal of a particular character on stage.

What Costumes Tell the Audience

The costume designer works with the director and actors to come up with costumes that enhance the meaning and mood of the play and help to define the characters. Costuming must be carefully planned in order to add to the total experience of the play. It can also provide important clues to the audience. Costume can suggest a historical time, show a character's social status, and give insight into character.

Setting of a Play. Costumes help the audience know the **setting** of a play. The costumes worn by actors in Shakespeare's *Romeo and Juliet* let the audience know immediately that the play is set in the past because women no longer wear long, full skirts and men do not wear tights and short tunics. The modern costumes for Leonard Bernstein's *West Side Story,* an update of Shakespeare's play, show the audience that this play is set in recent times. Costumes for a modern play will be different from the costumes for a **period play.**

Setting: The time and place of a play.

Period play: A play set in a particular historical period with the speech patterns, manners, and costumes of that time.

Makeup can transform your appearance from that of a teenager to an old person. There are certain basic steps you need to take when applying stage makeup to achieve the effect of old age. Study the drawing below and note the lines, shadows, and highlights that help create the appearance of old age. Use the drawing as a guide, but follow the natural contours of your face when applying the makeup.

Step One

Use a Light Foundation. The skin tones of older people tend to look faded. Use a pale color that is lighter than your natural skin tone. If you are dark skinned, use a foundation with a yellow tint. Apply the foundation to your face and neck.

Step Two

Create Deep Shadows. The face of an older person has more contrasts between light and shadow than a younger person's. The bones are also more prominent. Shade the following areas using a small brush and brown makeup:

1. hollows of the cheeks
2. sides of the nose
3. recessed area between the eyelids and the brows
4. area under the eyes
5. jaw line and neck

Step Three

Draw Lines and Wrinkles. Facial lines and wrinkles are crucial to playing an older part. Along with the proper highlights and shadows, a few well-placed lines can create a look of old age. Use brown liner to make the lines. Draw two or three thin lines across your forehead. Make the lines parallel if possible. Lines under the eyes also give the impression of age. Find the bone under each eye and draw a curved line along each.

Step Four

Along Each Shadow and Line, Apply a Highlight. Use a light-colored makeup and highlight only one side of the line or shadow.

Step Five

Powder Your Face and Neck. Take care not to smear your makeup.

Step Six

Wear a Gray Wig or Use White or Gray Hair Spray. Glasses and conservative clothing will complete the look.

Costumes such as the ones worn by the actors in this production of *Romeo and Juliet* can convey much information about a play's setting, as well as a character's personality and social status.

When the curtain rises at the beginning of a play, the audience may know immediately in what historical period the action of the play takes place because of the **costume silhouettes** (see Figures 5.1 through 5.4). The costume silhouette of a man and a woman in a Civil War play, for example, can be identified by the man's stovepipe hat, suit coat, and straight-legged pants and by the woman's bonnet and long, full skirt.

Costume silhouette: *The outline of a costume worn by an actor on stage.*

Social Rank of Character. Besides showing the time and place of a play, costuming can reveal the social rank or economic status of a character in the play. In *Cinderella,* for example, the stepsisters wear rich dresses, but Cinderella's clothes are dirty and ragged, showing that she is poor and of lower rank, at least in the eyes of her stepfamily.

Color and Costume. Color on the stage set helps to establish the mood of the play. The colors of costumes worn by the characters on stage add to this dominant tone. Dark or dull colors often lend a feeling of seriousness, sadness, even depression. Lighter, brighter colors lift the spirits and show a less serious mood. Imagine going to a party and finding everyone in attendance dressed in gray or red or purple. Think of the effect each color would have.

Figure 5.1 Costume Silhouettes: Ancient Greece

Characterization:
*Putting the particular
facets of a character
together to make a
believable person on
stage.*

Color in costuming also affects the way the audience perceives the action on stage. An important character will often be set apart from the others on stage by a bright or contrasting color. Members of a family or a social group may wear the same or similar colors to show that they belong together.

The color of a costume is also important in increasing the depth of a character. Dynamic, expressive characters may wear red or other vivid colors. Meek or weak characters may wear pale colors, such as light blue or beige. Colors can help distinguish **characterizations** for both the actor and the audience.

Figure 5.2 Costume Silhouettes: The Elizabethan Era **91**

Costume Gives Insight into Character. An important function of costuming is to give insight into a character. People often dress to impress others in a particular way. In Shakespeare's play *Hamlet,* Polonius tells his son, "The apparel oft proclaim the man," or, in modern English, "Clothes make the man." Think of how much time is spent in selecting the right clothes because people are often judged, rightly or wrongly, by the clothes they wear.

Notice what characters in a play or movie wear. Is there anyone whose clothing is conspicuous for some reason? Ask yourself why that character may choose to dress that way. A

Figure 5.3 Costume Silhouettes: The Restoration Era

character in extremely elaborate clothing may be trying to impress others with his or her wealth and importance. Along with the words and actions of the character, the costume may show that this is a shallow character who is more interested in appearances than substance. A carelessly dressed individual may not care at all what others think. He or she may be rebelling against the norms of society or may just be too busy to worry about what others think. A scientist working in a laboratory trying to discover the cure for a disease will probably look disheveled.

Think of how someone may be pigeonholed, or put into a certain category, because of the clothing he or she wears. Ask

Figure 5.4 Costume Silhouettes: The Victorian Era   **93**

Costume

yourself how the following clothing choices might give you clues about the personality of the person wearing them:

a T-shirt celebrating a band that is no longer popular

blue jeans that are faded and full of holes

blue jeans that are stiff and new and never washed

a brand of blue jeans with a label no one has heard of

a hot pink coat

black shirt, black pants, black hat

a big hat

Costume Design

Costumes are a major element in our visual enjoyment of plays and movies. Excellent costume design is recognized in the theatre and in the movies. Each year a Tony Award is given for the best costume design for a play. The movie industry also presents an Academy Award for costume design.

You may have seen some of the movies listed below. They were all winners of an Academy Award for costume design. Notice that because many of these movies were set in the past, they presented a special challenge. The designer had to research the clothing styles of the time of the movie to create an authentic feel for the movie. Other movies, such as *Dick Tracy* and *The Addams Family,* required that the costumer be true to the spirit of the comic strip or cartoon characters.

1984	*Amadeus*
1985	*Ran*
1986	*A Room with a View*
1987	*The Last Emperor*
1988	*Dangerous Liaisons*
1989	*Henry V*
1990	*Cyrano De Bergerac*
1991	*Bugsy*
1992	*Bram Stoker's Dracula*
1993	*The Age of Innocence*

1. Select one of the movies listed above or another in which you thought the costumes were outstanding. Describe the costumes the main character(s) wore. Why do you think you can still remember the costumes?

2. Watch one of the movies listed above on video. Study the costumes the main characters wear. How do they suit the personalities of the wearers? Notice the costumes of the minor characters. In what ways, if any, are they different from those of the main characters?

3. Pause the action of the video in a scene where there are at least five people. Describe the mood of the scene. Is it happy, sad, lively, dull? Make a rough diagram showing where the characters in the scene are standing. Write the dominant color of each character's costume over each figure. Do certain colors predominate? Do the colors help create the mood of the scene? Are the colors of the costumes similar or in contrast to other colors in the scene?

Costumes Help an Actor Portray a Character

A costume can be a psychological boost for an actor in portraying a character. It can help the actor feel like the character he or she is playing. Would you feel more like a villain if you could wear a cape and mask than if you were dressed in your everyday clothes? Would Batman be Batman without the costume and mask?

An actor playing Queen Elizabeth I may wear a stiff costume, forcing her to stand erect, feeling like a queen. To walk gracefully in the long skirt, she may have to take short, even steps and avoid her normal bouncing walk. The costume may make her feel psychologically like the character she's playing, and physically it may make her walk in a queen-like manner. By contrast, a young man dressed in loose-fitting rags to play a poor beggar may walk in a slouched, dejected manner because the clothing is ugly and ill-fitting.

Wearing a Costume Comfortably on Stage

Because a costume should add to the meaning of a play, it is important that the actor be comfortable wearing a costume. Movement is key to acting, so the actor must not let wearing a costume interfere with movement on stage. Sometimes even small details become distracting if the actor has not adjusted to them before the performance. Costumes that are different from the type of clothing one normally wears can make stage movement difficult. The following are tips for wearing costumes on stage:

1. Wear your costume as much as possible before opening night.
2. Learn to walk, stand, sit, and bend naturally and comfortably in your costumes.
3. Do not forget to practice wearing all the details of your costume, such as boots, gloves, wig, glasses, and mustache.
4. Be familiar with all of your character's costumes.

5. Familiarize yourself with all accessories, such as a fan, glasses, or a cane, that your character will use in the play.

Summary

Costumes serve several functions in a play. They tell the audience when and where the play takes place. The costume of a particular character can suggest social standing and personality. Color used in costuming affects the mood of the play and can add to characterization. Wearing a costume can help an actor "feel" a part. In order for costuming to enhance a character portrayal, however, the actor must practice wearing the costume naturally and comfortably.

Makeup

Makeup: Color or lines applied to the face and features of an actor to aid in creating a character.

Makeup is essential to an actor. It not only completes a costume but also enriches the characterization. It also gives the actor a psychological boost in portraying the character. The actor who looks the part can more naturally play the part.

Why a Modern Actor Needs Makeup

The invention of electric lights made stage makeup necessary because stage lighting washes out the faces of actors on stage. Makeup defines their features. Actors work hard to create realistic characters, and the audience needs to see the actors' facial expressions to get a true understanding of the play.

Makeup also gives the audience information about a character. Properly applied, makeup can show age, health, even character. An actor can add years to his or her age by the use of shadows and lines. Color can make a character can seem young and healthy or old and sick. Personality and character can be emphasized by makeup that enhances certain facial features.

Character makeup: Makeup that changes the appearance of an actor into that of the character being portrayed.

Character Makeup. Sometimes an actor uses makeup in order to play a character who looks nothing like the actor himself or herself. This type of makeup is called **character makeup.**

Character makeup includes items such as nose putty and false hair that drastically change an actor's appearance. Through the skillful use of character makeup, Robin Williams was able to change his face into that of an older woman in the movie *Mrs. Doubtfire*.

Straight Makeup. Sometimes an actor plays a part that does not require a change in appearance. At such a time **straight makeup** is needed.

Some Guidelines for Applying Makeup

Actors usually apply their own makeup for a part in a play. Following are some general guidelines for applying stage makeup:

1. Strive to look natural by not using too much makeup.
2. Have a good reason for whatever makeup choices you make.
3. Work with your facial features; do not expect to totally change your looks with stage makeup.
4. Focus on shadows and highlights rather than lines.
5. Follow the bone structure of your face.
6. Practice applying your makeup for a part before opening night.

How to Apply Makeup

Learning to apply stage makeup is an art that requires practice. There are certain steps in putting on stage makeup. The following discussion shows the order in which you should apply makeup.

Foundation. First, be sure that your face is clean and that your hair is covered. Then use your fingers or a sponge to apply the foundation, or base. This is a makeup close to your natural skin tone that you will use to cover your face, neck, and other

Using makeup to emphasize or even change your facial features, you can transform yourself into an entirely different person.

Straight makeup: *Makeup that enhances the features of the actor without changing his or her appearance.*

Greasepaint: Oil-based stage makeup.

Pancake makeup: Water-based makeup.

exposed areas. Dark-skinned actors may not need a foundation because their features show up better under stage lights. There are two basic types of makeup that you can use. One is **greasepaint.** The other is **pancake makeup.**

The color of the foundation that you choose will be determined by your natural skin tone or by the character you play. If your character is young and healthy, use a pink-toned foundation. Sallow, gray colors indicate advanced age or poor health.

Shadows and Highlights. Skillful use of shadows and highlights can mold your face to help create the character you are playing or to enhance your natural contours. Your bone structure is important. Notice how your face is made up of various planes. Some parts come forward; others recede.

Remember that dark colors recede and light colors advance. Add a touch of white to the foundation to highlight the features you want to call attention to. Add brown to the foundation to darken those you want to downplay. To make your nose look larger, use lighter makeup on it. You can also narrow it by applying darker makeup on the sides. If you want your chin to recede visually, you would use a darker color on it.

Keep in mind that for every shadow there is a highlight. If you highlight your cheekbones, add a darker shade in the area beneath the cheekbones.

Eye Makeup. An actor's eyes show emotion and character, so they should be visible to the audience. Use eye makeup to call attention to your eyes and visually enlarge them. To accent your eyes, use a fine brush or eyebrow pencil to draw a thin line along the upper and lower eyelids. Have these lines meet slightly beyond the outer corners of your eyes, and your eyes will appear larger. Some makeup artists suggest making a small red dot at the inner corner of each eye to add sparkle.

Eye shadow should be close to the color of your eyes unless there is a good reason to do otherwise. Brown-skinned actors should use lighter colors of eye shadow, such as pale yellow or beige, to accent their eyes. The eye shadow of a colorful, showy character could be bright to match her personality. Mascara and false eyelashes can also be used to call attention to the eyes of female characters.

Figure 5.5 Eyebrow Shapes That Convey Character

99

Makeup

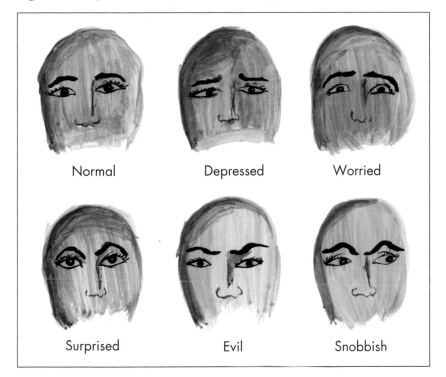

| Normal | Depressed | Worried |
| Surprised | Evil | Snobbish |

The shape of the eyebrows can suggest character (see Figure 5.5). Think of how your eyebrows lift when you are surprised. To create a look of perpetual surprise, conceal your natural eyebrows with makeup and draw high, rounded eyebrows. Of course, you would only do this if a look of surprise were the main characteristic of the part you were playing. If you were playing a villain, you could draw twisted brows to suggest your character's deviousness. Think of Captain Hook's eyebrows in the Disney cartoon *Peter Pan*.

Rouge. Rouge adds color and contours to the actor's face. It can impart a healthy glow. Fair-skinned actors should use light pink or peach tones. Darker, orange-tinted rouge is more effective for brown-skinned actors. When using rouge, blend the color along the cheekbones and up toward the hairline.

Powder. Powder helps set makeup and remove the shine caused by greasepaint. Choose a color of powder that is either essentially colorless or lighter than your foundation color. Use a powder puff to apply the powder. Be gentle so that you do not smear your makeup. Brush off any excess.

Lipstick. Since the shape and expression of the mouth help to show character, lipstick can be a useful tool to help you create a believable character (see Figure 5.6). With upturned lips, you can show a happy character. Thin, pursed lips may show a stingy character. Down-turned lips can show a bitter, unhappy person. Experiment and see what other characteristics you can create with lipstick.

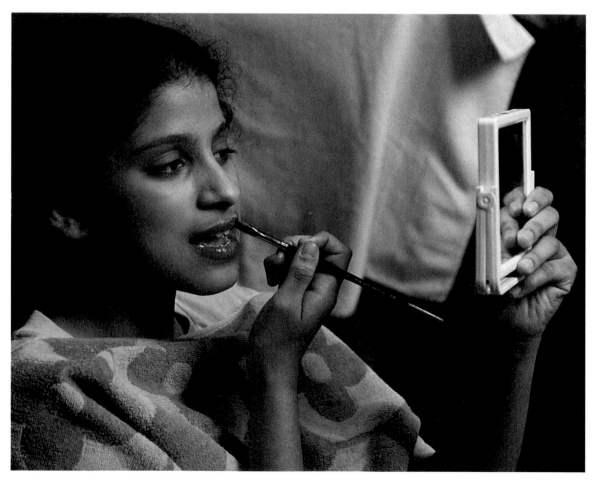

Carefully applied lipstick can help you to achieve the look you want to further develop your character.

Figure 5.6 Lip Shapes That Convey Character   **101**

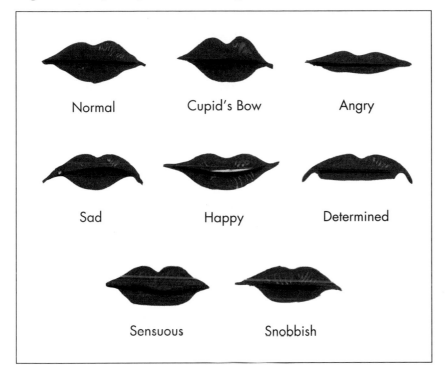

Normal   Cupid's Bow   Angry

Sad   Happy   Determined

Sensuous   Snobbish

Summary

Modern actors need stage makeup. Makeup helps the audience see the actors' expressions in a large theatre. It also aids the actor to more accurately portray a character. Actors need to know how to apply their own makeup and should practice applying their makeup for a part before opening night.

Empathy

1. **Telling Stories.** Break up into groups of three or four. Each person will tell the rest of the group "My Most Embarrassing Moment." As you tell your story, pay attention to the feedback from your listeners. Are they eager to hear what you will say next? Do they appear to be bored? Adjust the way you are telling your story to their reactions.

2. **Listening.** As others in the group recount their embarrassing moments, listen carefully to what they say and notice their expressions and gestures. If you have not yet told your story, do not be planning what you are going to say when it is your turn. Just listen.

3. **Observing.** Find a place to sit in public where you can observe people walking by. This can be in a park, at a bus stop, in a mall. Notice the different ways people walk and the expressions on their faces. Find one person and remember the way he or she walked and looked. Give that person a made-up name. Imagine where that person is going and why. When you get home, try to recall the characteristics of the person you saw. Practice his or her walk, gestures, and expressions in front of a mirror.

4. **Sensing.** At lunch time, notice the sights, sounds, and smells of the world around you. Eat your lunch slowly and note the way it feels, smells, and tastes. Then take notice of the noises you hear–the noises in general and the sounds of the people right around you. Make a habit of sensory awareness that will carry over into your acting.

In Character

5. **Acting Out.** Be your favorite character for a day. Everyone in the class should choose a character from TV or the movies. Select one whose characteristic ways of moving and speaking you think you know well. Do not tell anyone who you are. Just plan to be that character throughout the class period. Walk into the room at the beginning of the period as that character. Sit at your desk as that character would sit. Ask or answer questions as that character would. Try not to use expressions that will give away the identity of your character. Rely instead on the way that character would behave based on your observations of him or her. Near the end of class, try to guess the character each student is playing.

6. **Props.** To emphasize the character you play in the activity above, add a piece of clothing or a personal prop that will accentuate the character traits of the role you are playing. Select the article of clothing or the personal prop carefully. Keep it simple. When students guess who your character is, explain why you selected the prop you did.

The Actor's Logbook

1. ***Learning the Language.*** Review the vocabulary words in boldface print in this chapter.
2. ***Supplies.*** Make a list of the basic makeup supplies that you would need in playing a role on stage. Divide the list into those supplies that you already have and any supplies that you would need to obtain. Try to determine the color of your skin and the shade of foundation and rouge that would suit your skin tone.
3. ***Critic's Choice.*** Make a list of at least seven guidelines to follow in planning costumes for a play. List them in order of importance.

Critical Thinking

4. ***Basics.*** Imagine you are in an acting troupe with a small amount of money to spend on costumes. You can afford to provide only one item for each character in the play. All the characters will wear black pants and shirts and the one item you provide to indicate who they are. Decide what one piece of clothing or item would best serve to identify each of the following characters: king, farmer, teacher, dancer, police officer, child. Explain your choice.
5. ***Evaluation.*** Sometimes a play set in the past is produced with the actors in modern dress rather than period costumes. What do you think would be the effect of actors in modern dress acting plays by Shakespeare, for instance?
6. ***Analysis.*** Think of a favorite character from television or the theatre. Why do you like the character? What are the traits that appeal to you? Is the character at all like you or like someone you know? In what ways?

Creative Thinking

7. ***Costume Design.*** Imagine you are a costume designer for a production of *Hansel and Gretel*. You want to present personality and character through the costumes you create. Describe the costumes you would design for these characters: the father, the stepmother, Hansel, Gretel, the witch.
8. ***Creating a Mood.*** You also want the costumes to show the overall mood of the play. How will you accomplish this?
9. ***Getting the Most Out of Makeup.*** You have been also been asked to suggest makeup for the above characters. Decide the effects you would like the makeup to produce on each of the characters. Select either straight or character makeup for each role.

CHAPTER SIX

The Voice

EXPECTATIONS

After reading this chapter, you will be able to

6.1 understand the basic terms used to refer to the voice

6.2 breathe properly in order to produce the best vocal quality

6.3 project your voice more effectively on stage

6.4 read aloud with greater expression

**A**n actor's voice is a wonderful instrument. It infuses life into the words of the playwright. It helps create memorable characters. Actors depend on their voices. An actor with a strong, flexible voice can play many roles. It is especially important for a stage actor to develop a voice that will carry to all the members of an audience seated in a large theatre.

Talking about the Voice

Because of the importance of this tool to an actor, it is helpful to know how the voice is produced. You should also know the terms used to describe the voice and ways you can improve your own voice.

How the Voice Is Produced

When we breathe, air is forced from the lungs and passes over the vocal cords, which are the thin folds of muscle that stretch on either side of the windpipe. The vocal cords vibrate, creating sound. At the same time, the bones and spaces in the head and chest act as a soundboard to reinforce and amplify the sound. See Figure 6.1. The tongue, lips, and jaw help to create the consonant and vowel sounds, producing words.

Qualities of the Voice

You are born with a voice that is uniquely your own. People may recognize your voice when you call them on the telephone. Your voice may be low or high, smooth or gravelly, dull or expressive. There are some aspects of your voice that you can change, and there are others that you cannot change. In this chapter, we will learn what can be changed and some ways to make these changes.

Pitch, Range, and Timbre. All voices have certain qualities that together produce a distinctive sound. We are born with these

Figure 6.1 How the Voice Is Produced

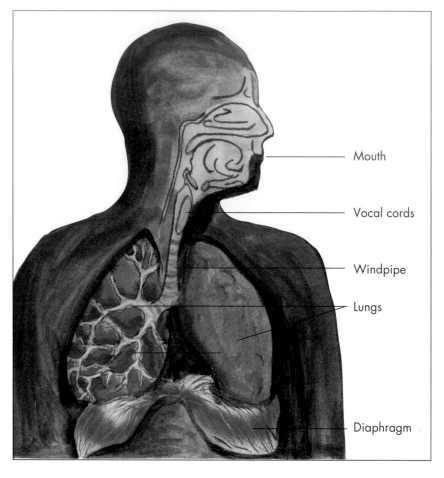

- Mouth
- Vocal cords
- Windpipe
- Lungs
- Diaphragm

When we exhale to speak, air passes over the vocal cords, causing them to vibrate, which creates sound.

Pitch: The relative highness or lowness of a person's natural speaking voice.

characteristics and cannot change them significantly. These include pitch, range, and timbre.

Some people have very high or very low voices. Most of us are somewhere in between. Women tend to have higher voices than men because women's vocal cords are shorter. Longer vocal cords produce a deeper pitch. When the vocal cords tighten, the pitch of the voice becomes higher. At certain times, a person's mood may affect the pitch of the voice. Anger or excitement can cause the pitch to become higher. People can speak with a variety of pitches. When we refer to the **pitch** of someone's voice, we usually mean the pitch at which a person speaks most of the time.

Range is the distance between the lowest and highest pitch of a comfortable, effective speaking voice. Some people have a broad range. They can speak comfortably at more pitches than someone who has a narrow range.

The **timbre** is the characteristic sound a voice has. Some people may have naturally pleasing voices; others may have harsh, raspy voices. Timbre is the unique quality that helps you to recognize a voice such as Dustin Hoffman's or Jack Nicholson's. Musical instruments are also described as having a certain timbre. It is what makes a violin sound different from a guitar or any other instrument.

Resonance. **Resonance** is another vocal quality that we are born with. It affects the timbre of the voice. Resonance depends primarily on the openness and flexibility of the cavities of the mouth and throat. We can, however, greatly improve the resonance of our voice with proper practice and training.

The variation in size and shape of a person's **resonators** accounts in part for the differences in voices. We have control over some of the resonators, such as the mouth, which we use in forming consonant sounds.

When you have a head cold and cannot breathe through your nose, your voice sounds different. Resonance is affected. Good resonance produces a voice that has warmth, richness, and beauty. A resonant voice is not just an asset for an actor. It is a necessity.

You can improve the resonance of your voice in the following ways:

1. Practice good breathing and breath control.

2. Keep your jaw relaxed and flexible.

3. Relax your throat by yawning.

4. Emphasize the vowel sounds in words by holding them longer.

5. Practice reading along with tapes of actors with resonant voices.

6. Learn to sing.

Range: The distance in pitch between the highest and lowest tones a person can make without straining the voice.

Timbre: The natural tone of the voice that makes it sound different from other voices.

Resonance: The vibrating quality of the voice that amplifies and enriches the tone.

Resonators: The spaces in the head and chest, along with the nose, throat, and mouth, that play a part in voice production.

Diaphragmatic breathing: The special kind of deep breathing, using the muscle between the abdomen and rib cage, that is necessary to produce a strong voice.

Breathing from the Diaphragm

Developing the voice takes time and energy. The first step in voice development involves learning to breathe correctly. Everyone breathes to support life in his or her own body. The actor must learn to breathe correctly to support a strong voice on stage. This takes a certain type of breathing. It is called **diaphragmatic breathing.**

Diaphragmatic breathing means that when a person inhales, the diaphragm contracts and flattens. The diaphragm is a muscle located between the abdomen and the bottom of the rib cage. At the same time, the abdominal muscles expand, forcing the ribs up and out. This enlarges the size of the chest cavity, creating a partial vacuum. Air rushes in to fill the vacuum. The air enters through the mouth and nose, goes down the windpipe into the lungs, and expands them.

When a person exhales, the abdominal muscles contract, pushing the diaphragm upward and pulling the ribs in. This reduces the size of the chest cavity and compresses the lungs. The air is driven out through the windpipe, past the vocal cords, where sounds are produced, and out of the body through the nose and mouth. See Figure 6.2.

Breath Control

Besides the deep breathing described above, an actor must modify his or her normal breathing when speaking. Learning to breathe properly for speaking is essential for an actor. The following are the basics of proper breathing for speech:

1. Stand up straight to give your lungs room to fill with air.
2. Inhale briefly through your mouth, because you can take in more air quickly through your mouth than through your nose.
3. Exhale slowly and with control as you speak.

In regular speech, our breathing in matches our breathing out. But to breathe properly for speech, we need to exhale longer. This is because when we speak, we automatically breathe out. We need to try to have enough air to speak comfortably as long as possible on one breath. So we let the air out slowly as we

Figure 6.2 Diaphragmatic Breathing

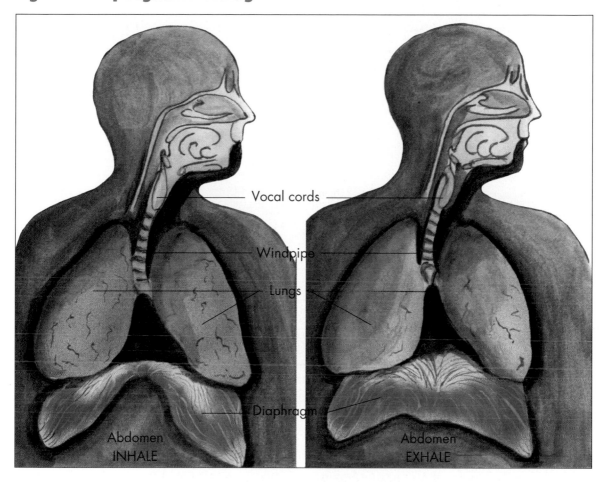

Vocal cords

Windpipe

Lungs

Diaphragm

Abdomen
INHALE

Abdomen
EXHALE

When we inhale, our diaphragm contracts and flattens as air rushes down our windpipe into our lungs, causing them to expand. When we exhale, our diaphragm expands upward, pulling our ribs in and forcing air out of our lungs.

speak. Proper breathing and breath control need to be practiced every day in order to become a habit. See "Take One" on page 110 for exercises for proper breathing and breath control.

Summary

The voice is produced by air passing over the vocal cords, causing them to vibrate and produce sound. The sound is amplified and changed by structures in the chest and head. Characteristics of the voice include pitch, range, timbre, and

Everybody loves to hear a good story. Children love bedtime stories. Families share stories around holiday dinner tables. You can improve and practice your own storytelling skills and contribute to the fun. Enhancing your storytelling skills will improve your acting skills, as well.

Step One

Choose Your Story. Well-told stories help us develop a better understanding of ourselves and others. A good story needs to have an intriguing beginning, interesting characters, conflict, and a believable ending. Shorter stories work better for telling than longer ones. Select a story that you like, that moves you. Consider these suggestions:

1. Fairy tales and folktales have widespread appeal.
2. Return to a favorite childhood story like *Stone Soup* or *Peter Rabbit*.
3. Read the classic myths, such as the adventures of Ulysses or King Arthur.
4. Think about selections in your literature book that you enjoyed.
5. Find a human interest story in a magazine such as *The Reader's Digest*.

Step Two

Visualize Your Story. As you read or remember your story, enlist the help of your imagination. See the characters in the story. Imagine details about clothes, appearance, posture, and motivation. Visualize the setting of the story. Consider how the senses of sight, hearing, smell, touch, and taste enhance the impact of the story.

Step Three

Identify the Story Line. Every story has a beginning, a complication, and an ending. Identify each part of the story you have selected. For your introduction, think about a "hook" to create interest in the story within the first ten seconds. Help listeners identify the episodes or complications in the story by emphasizing transition words and specific words and phrases for each character. Plan how to end your story so that its message is clear and memorable.

Step Four

Use Your Voice Effectively. Practice telling the story in your own words. Use strong, simple words that help listeners visualize the characters and events. Articulate your words, use pauses, and vary the volume and pitch of your voice. Be aware of the tempo and timing of the story.

Step Five

Rehearse. Practice telling your story to a friend. Use a tape recorder for feedback. Spend time thinking about the meaning of the story and the characters. Try to articulate why you like the story or a particular character and try to convey that quality as you practice. Now, get ready for a live audience and tell your story!

resonance. Good resonance produces a strong, pleasing voice. In order to have a strong, resonant voice, an actor must learn and practice diaphragmatic breathing. In addition, breath control enhances an actor's speaking ability. An actor must practice diaphragmatic breathing and breath control every day so that they can be done easily and naturally.

Using Your Voice Effectively on Stage

One of the first responsibilities of the actor is to be heard at the back of the theatre. The actor must be able to speak loudly without shouting or straining the voice. At the same time, the actor's voice must sound conversational and natural. He or she must speak clearly, so that the audience can understand the words being spoken. To be heard and understood, the actor must cultivate a flexible, expressive voice.

Projecting the Voice

In everyday life, you are not expected to speak as loudly as you would if you were performing on stage. In fact, your teachers and parents may tell you to tone down your voice and speak more softly—at least in the school halls or at the dinner table. On the stage, however, you must **project** your voice.

To project properly, you must practice correct breathing. The sound of your voice must carry throughout the theatre. You must also clearly enunciate your words so that the audience can hear exactly what you are saying.

You may fail to appreciate the distance factor between the stage and audience, so you must always focus on the need to project your voice. Always remember that even the people in the last row of the theatre have to be able to hear your words clearly. It may help you to imagine that you are speaking personally to someone sitting in the back of the theatre.

No Need to Shout. A good actor can be heard in a large auditorium without straining his or her voice. Relaxation is key. The throat and jaws should be relaxed in order to produce full

Projection: Controlling the volume and clearness of the voice so that it can be heard by the audience.

resonance. To relax your throat, try yawning, humming, or exhaling quickly and then letting the air rush back in. You do not have to strain your voice in order to increase **volume.**

Volume has nothing to do with shouting. It has everything to do with a relaxed throat and correct breathing. Remember that breathing from the diaphragm lets an actor control the quantity of air taken in and helps to sustain and regulate the speed of the air going out. Faulty projection may arise from faulty breathing. Excellent projection comes with time and hard work.

As an actor, you must project your voice so that everyone in the audience, even those people in the back row, can hear what your character is saying.

Volume: *The force of air that determines how loudly or softly a person speaks.*

Open Your Mouth Wide. Speaking on stage differs from other types of speaking. You cannot expect to be heard if you speak on stage the same way you speak to your friends. You have to exaggerate. One of the ways you exaggerate is by opening your mouth wider than you would in normal conversation. You have to let your voice out so that the audience can hear it.

As mentioned before, proper breathing provides you with the force of air to increase volume. To make the most of this force of air, you need to open your mouth wide to let your voice out. Opening your mouth wide may feel strange at first, but this is a necessary way of projecting your voice. The practice and experience of speaking on stage will make this type of speaking seem natural after a while.

Speaking Clearly

Clear pronunciation is also an absolute necessity for an actor. If the audience cannot understand the actor, the character in the play is lost. Even the actor who can project his or her voice still needs to make the words clear through proper **articulation.**

Articulation: *The clear and concise pronunciation of words and sounds.*

You may be in the habit of not speaking clearly because you speak the way everyone else speaks. If you watch situation comedies, you may hear speech that reflects the way you and your friends talk. That is fine for TV. But the kind of speech you hear on television may not be appropriate for the stage.

There are few role models of good pronunciation. We live in a relaxed culture, and our speech tends to be informal. But you can improve your articulation. The following may help:

1. Listen to the speech of actors with excellent articulation, such as Meryl Streep and James Earl Jones (see "Critic's Choice" on page 115).

2. Relax your jaw and open your mouth wide to articulate properly.

3. Close your mouth firmly on consonant sounds.

4. Look up words in a dictionary if you are unsure of their pronunciation.

Regional Accents

A good actor must be able to speak without an accent in order to be understood by people from all parts of the nation. A heavy accent can prevent the audience from understanding an actor's words. No matter where you live in the United States, there is a dominant accent. If you speak like most of the people in your part of the country, you probably pronounce some words differently from the way that they are pronounced in other parts of the country. Or you may stress different syllables in some words. You may even drop or add certain sounds from words. The word *accent* refers to the pronunciation used by people speaking in a common region.

Midwesterners and Westerners often pride themselves on speaking without an accent, but they too have their own accents, especially in large cities. For instance, some people mimic the Chicago accent when they refer to that city's basketball team as *da Bulls*. You hear a nasal quality in Midwestern speech and certain characteristic inflections. Some people in Los Angeles speak with an accent sometimes referred to as *valley talk*.

Southerners are known for their drawl and their tendency to drop the R's from the ends of words. Northeastern cities such as New York and Boston have distinctive speech pat-

Clear articulation will help you ensure that the audience understands every word you say.

terns. New Yorkers may say *oo-off* for *off* or *thoidy-thoid* for *thirty-third*. On the television show *Cheers,* some of the characters spoke with a Boston accent. The postal worker, Cliff, for example, pronounced *park* as *pack* and *Norm* as *Nahm.*

Speaking without an Accent

Actors need to speak with a voice free of any regional accent so that they can be clearly understood by audiences from all parts of the nation. Of course, at times an actor may need to speak with an accent for a role, as Tom Hanks did in *Forrest Gump.* Otherwise, serious actors work hard to acquire what is known as **Standard American English.**

Standard American English: *American English spoken without a regional accent.*

Most newscasters and radio announcers have been trained to speak Standard American English. It is important that national newscasters speak without an accent so that viewers from all regions of the country can easily understand them. You can learn to recognize Standard American English by listening to national newscasters. Dan Rather of *CBS Evening News*, for example, grew up in Texas, but you would not know where he came from by listening to his speech.

You can work at erasing your regional accent by listening to Standard American English. Watch the national nightly news. Notice the pronunciation of words. Does the newscaster pronounce any words differently from the way you pronounce them? Make note of these differences and practice the standard pronunciation.

Some aspiring actors may have a heavy regional or foreign accent. The most effective way to eliminate such accents is to train with a voice coach. Obviously this is expensive and time-consuming, but it will pay off for the actor in the long run. He or she will be able to play a greater variety of roles without the limitation of an accent.

Summary

An actor must be able to project his or her voice in order to be heard by every member of the audience. Correct breathing plays an important role in projecting the voice. Proper articulation is also important, so that the audience can understand

Great Voices

Meryl Streep and James Earl Jones are actors with rich, resonant, and versatile voices. Both have won critical acclaim for their vocal and acting skills.

Meryl Streep won the 1982 Academy Award for Best Actress for her portrayal of a Polish woman in *Sophie's Choice*. Critics praised her authentic accent, which she learned for the role. She has worked with dialect coaches to develop convincing accents for many roles. In *Out of Africa,* she spoke with a Danish accent, and she portrayed an Australian in *A Cry in the Dark*. More recently, her role as an Italian-born woman in *Bridges of Madison County* has been praised by critics.

Streep's skill in creating characters with convincing accents is recognized throughout the acting world. She has won two Academy Awards as well as many nominations for her work in films.

James Earl Jones has appeared on stage, screen, and television, in roles ranging from Othello to the voice of Darth Vader in *Star Wars*. In 1969, he won his first Tony Award for Best Performance by an Actor in *The Great White Hope*. He was nominated for an Academy Award for the same role in the movie version of the play. He has won countless other awards, including Emmys for television work and Obies for off-Broadway theatre.

Like many actors, Jones was not born with the gift of great speaking ability. He has had to work hard to acquire it. Eight years of his childhood were spent in silence as he struggled with stuttering—a struggle that continues even today.

In Jones's autobiography *Voices and Silences,* he talks about an actor's voice: "You hope you have worked so hard for so long that you don't have to become self-conscious and think about it. You use it organically as the instrument of your art."

If you want to develop your voice, listen to and learn from Meryl Streep and James Earl Jones.

1. Think of an actor who you think has a good, expressive acting voice. Watch a movie that actor has appeared in. Close your eyes and listen to the voice of that actor. Notice the pitch, the resonance, the unique quality by which you recognize it as that actor's voice.

2. Watch a movie in which Meryl Streep or James Earl Jones appears. Focus on the way she or he uses the voice. How does Streep or Jones use voice to create the personality of the character? In each scene, how does the actor change her or his voice to show the emotional state of the character?

the individual words the actor speaks. An actor's speech should be free of any accent. If there is any trace of accent, the actor should attempt to learn Standard American English.

How to Use the Voice to Stress Meaning

An actor must strive to make the meaning of the playwright's words clear to the audience. He or she can use certain devices to create shades of meaning in the words the character speaks.

Pause

Pause: A brief suspension or hesitation of the voice.

The silences between words can be an effective tool for the actor. The actor may use these **pauses** for a variety of purposes. Pauses can be used to do the following:

1. separate thoughts and ideas
2. give listeners time to grasp a point
3. increase curiosity
4. call attention to an important word or idea
5. give the speaker time to establish breath control for better speech

With practice you will be able to judge the proper length of a pause by the way the audience is responding. Is the audience eagerly waiting to hear what you are about to say next? Or are they losing interest? Pause just long enough to be effective and to make your listeners want to know what you are going to say next. If your pause is too long, the audience may think you have finished speaking, when in fact you have not. Confusion will result when you resume speaking.

Add Emphasis

Emphasis: The stress placed upon a syllable, word, group of words, or portion of a speech.

Each word and idea should not be given the same weight. Some words or ideas are more important and should be stressed. The actor may use **emphasis** to underscore meaning.

Emphasize the words or ideas that are most important. Notice how in reading the famous words of Patrick Henry, you naturally stress the two most important words: "Give me liberty or give me death."

Speed Up or Slow Down

An actor adjusts his or her **rate** of speaking to convey the tone of what is being spoken. A sad or serious speech is spoken at a slower rate. Think of how sad music is often slow and formal sounding. To convey a feeling of excitement, an actor should speak faster. A character who rushes onto the stage with an urgent message or exciting news is going to speak faster than an actor who must reluctantly tell another character bad news.

Rate: The speed of speaking.

Feel the Rhythm

The words of a play are like the notes in a musical composition. Certain parts are stressed and others downplayed in a regular pattern. An actor must be attuned to the musicality of the play. He or she must sense the **rhythm** when speaking the words of the play.

Rhythm does not necessarily imply time. It is more a matter of accenting syllables. Rhythm is usually a succession of pauses and phrases, along with an alternation of strong and weak syllables within the phrases. The rhythm of a comedy is often staccato, or abrupt.

Rhythm: The alternation of silence, sound, strength, and weakness in speech.

Change the Volume

An actor with a flexible voice can control its loudness or softness to stress the meaning behind the words his or her character speaks. A character who is ranting and raving may suddenly whisper a word. This change in volume highlights the word. Speaking louder or softer can set the words apart by contrast. By speaking in a weak voice with little change in volume, an actor can show a character who is insecure, weary, or sad.

__Intensity:__ The use of vocal variation to produce a feeling of power and control in the voice.

Speaking expressively enables you to convey your character's feelings at any given moment.

__Inflection:__ The voice's rise and fall in pitch.

Sheer volume may not be enough to show depth of emotion. The actor may need to speak with added **intensity.** Intensity arises from strong feeling. It is not just loudness of tone. It is a controlled vocal energy that reflects emotional tension. A skilled actor can show depth of feeling by the intensity with which the words are spoken.

Change the Pitch

You can change pitch to make your voice more interesting, to provide a clue about how a character is feeling, and to add emphasis. Using a higher pitch to say a word or phrase calls attention to it.

The overall range in pitch of a character's voice can show his or her inner state. Changes in pitch can be slight or they can be dramatic. When a character is sad or depressed, there is little variation in pitch. Wide variation in pitch can convey anger or excitement.

Speak Expressively

The actor should strive to have an expressive, flexible, pleasing voice. As with other aspects of voice, this too requires constant practice. You can add expressiveness to your voice by using **inflections.**

Inflection enables a voice to show shades of meaning or feeling by underscoring the important words that the audience should pay attention to. Note how the meaning of the following sentences changes with the different inflections:

> *Karen* told me not to tell you.
> Karen told me not to tell *you.*

Practice Oral Reading

An excellent way to train your voice is to do oral reading. When doing oral reading, practice adding pauses, emphasis, varied reading rates, rhythm, changes in volume, intensity, changes in pitch, and inflection.

Make Eye Contact. Look at the audience as much as possible, around 75 to 80 percent of the time. Practice scanning the words ahead, concentrating on the meanings expressed, and then looking up and speaking. At the end of the thought, look down and find the beginning of the next thought and then look up and speak again.

Be Familiar with the Material. You should be comfortable looking away from the script. Drawing slanted lines between thoughts in the script helps to avoid losing your place. By separating the ideas in the script, it is easier to speak more clearly. This is because the ideas are divided and can be expressed in concise phrases.

Find the Right Rate. Generally, a good rate of delivery is about 125 to 150 words per minute. When you practice, count out 150 words to read while you time yourself. If you finish before a minute is up, slow your rate. If you find yourself reading too slowly, speed up your rate of reading.

Do not read too slowly or rush key ideas. A good reader pauses to give the audience time to think and respond but not too much time to get distracted. It is generally good to use pauses and let the important ideas take hold of the audience.

Summary

An actor uses various methods to underscore words and ideas. Pauses and emphasis can signal key points. An actor should adjust the rate of delivery to suit the words being spoken. Volume and pitch can be adjusted for emphasis. In order to practice using these methods, an actor should become skilled at oral reading.

On Stage

1. *Speaking Up.* Stand at the back of the classroom. Relax your throat by yawning several times. Project your voice to the front of the classroom without straining. Say your name. Repeat it. Say it louder each time, as if the person you were talking to were walking away. Stop when you can no longer say it comfortably.
2. *Stage Whisper.* Practice saying the words "He did it" in a stage whisper. Repeat the sentence with greater volume each time but retain the element of a stage whisper.

Stress Is Meaningful

3. *Changing Inflections.* See how many different meanings you can create for the following sentences by changing the inflections:

   * Ann wants me to help her with math homework.
   * Where did you learn to dance like that?
   * Did you spend all afternoon at the beach?
   * That was a really smart remark.

4. *Oral Reading.* Read the following passage several times until you are sure that you understand its meaning. Underline the key words that you think should be stressed. Decide where the pauses will be most effective. Check the dictionary to learn how to pronounce any words you are unfamiliar with. Working in groups of three to four, read the passage to each other. Make sure you use eye contact as you read.

   Drought is, throughout each summer, the master scourge of the Plains. No rain—or next to none—falls on them from May till October. By day, hot suns bake them; by night, fierce winds sweep them; parching the earth to cavernous depths; withering the scanty vegetation, and causing fires to run wherever a thin vesture of dead her-bage may have escaped the ravages of the previous autumn.

   —Horace Greeley, from "The Plains as I Crossed Them Ten Years Ago"

5. *Acting Out.* Sentence by sentence, put the above reading into your own words. Write it down. Be prepared to read it before the class. This time, imagine that the year is 1850. You are describing to listeners the conditions of life on the Plains, where you have lived for several years. Speak the words you have written using pauses, emphasis, changes in pitch, and inflection to underscore the meaning of your words.

The Actor's Logbook

1. *Learning the Language.* Make sure that you understand all the terms that relate to the voice. Write these words in the glossary section of your logbook.

2. *Applying What You Have Learned.* Of the vocal characteristics discussed in this chapter, choose one to work on to improve your voice. Consider pitch, resonance, projection, volume, accent, or inflection. If you are unsure, ask for your teacher's advice.

3. *Critic's Choice.* Start paying attention to actors' voices. After watching a movie, jot down in your logbook anything positive or negative you noted about an actor's voice. Did the actor have an accent? Was the actor supposed to have an accent? Was the actor's voice rich and resonant? What did you notice about the actor's articulation? Did the actor change his or her voice for the role? How did it affect the role? Does this actor's voice sound the same for every role?

Critical Thinking

4. *Analyzing Speech.* Write down the following terms on a sheet of paper: *pitch, resonance, projection, volume, inflection.* Form groups of four or five students. Each student will read the same paragraph from the textbook to the rest of the group. The other students will rate each category with a 1 (low), 2 (medium), or 3 (high). See if there is general agreement within the group. If some members of the group assigned a category a 3 while others gave it a 1, try to determine how each person came to his or her decision.

5. *Compare and Contrast.* Watch a video of a national news broadcast. How does the broadcaster's speech differ from your own? What are the peculiar accents that people from your area use that are not found in the broadcaster's speech? Does he or she pronounce any words differently from the way you pronounce them?

Creative Thinking

6. *Delivering the News.* Write a two-minute news broadcast for events that have taken place in your classroom. Each student will come to the front of the classroom to read his or her news. Try to read the news loudly and clearly so that all the class can understand. Be aware of your articulation, and try to speak without any trace of regional accent.

7. *Reading with Expression.* Stand before the class and read the first three paragraphs of a front-page story from a local newspaper. Do not read it as a newscaster would read a news story. Use inflection and changes in pitch to make the news sound dramatic and exciting. Choose a story that lends itself to this type of presentation, such as a feature about a rescue or a fire.

CHAPTER SEVEN

Stage Characters

EXPECTATIONS

After reading this chapter, you will be able to

7.1 find clues about minor characters from the text of the play

7.2 enrich a character portrayal by creating a subtext for your character

7.3 analyze the structure of a play in order to better understand a character

7.4 describe the different ways an actor can relate to a role

**A**ctors are responsible for bringing life to the characters they portray. To do this, an actor may need to look beyond the words the character speaks in the play in order to create a complete character. Often the key to understanding the character is only hinted at in the words of the play.

Using Subtext to Enrich Character Portrayal

Actors must flesh out the meaning beneath the words and actions of the characters in a play. The playwright provides the **text** of the play but relies on the creativity of the actors to bring the words and the characters to life.

Text: The words of a play.

The text is the bare bones of the play. It contains all the words the characters will speak, but the actors must decide how to say those words to show a deeper meaning. In this chapter, we will look at some ways you can enrich character portrayal by using subtext. To create a well-rounded, believable character, the actor should try to discover or create a **subtext**.

The prefix *sub* means below. Subtext refers to the meaning beneath the words of the text. We have to go deeper than the surface meaning of the words to find the subtext.

Subtext: The foundation of character traits, and perhaps actions, not specifically outlined in the action of a play.

Where to Find Clues about a Character

The first place to look for clues to your character is in the script. Useful information may be hidden in places where you may not think to look, such as stage directions. After you have discovered the subtext of the play, you can use these clues to emphasize this other level of meaning.

If your character speaks few words in the play, you may have to do some detective work to get more information about your character. Read the entire play not only to find out what your character says but also to discover the relationships among characters. The text of the play may be filled with hints that you could easily miss.

Stage Directions. Stage directions instruct the actors and director about where and how the actors should move, what objects are on stage, and other information not contained in the words of the characters. A stage direction that mentions a cluttered drawer may tell you that the character's house is messy and that maybe the character also has a sloppy appearance. This carelessness could affect the character's relationships.

If the stage directions suggest that a person has been standing all day, then you can create a subtext of the character working in a state driver's license facility or as a bank teller or a department store clerk. When the character walks onto the stage, he or she may trudge wearily over to a chair and plop down.

What Other Characters Say. You may find that another character can be a clue to subtext information. For example, a character may say to another, "You look mad enough to kill somebody." The actor can then create a meaningful subtext to motivate an angry look. The actor may imagine, for instance, that the character is angry because his brother just hung up on him during a quarrel on the phone.

The Character's Own Words. Read all the words your character speaks in the play. Shut your eyes and imagine what kind of person might utter such words. Do you get an image of a certain type of person? Is that person strong or weak, emotional or cool, loud or quiet, simple or complex, a thinker or a doer? Then notice if the character repeats certain words or phrases. Analyze why the character might choose those particular words.

In Chekhov's play *The Three Sisters*, the minor character Solony often repeats the phrase "Quick as a flash, the bear made a dash." An actor may become aware of how the viciousness of Solony's nature relates to that of a bear. A meaningful subtext can result from the actor's awareness.

You may find that your character is not truthful. The character may lie outright or may fail to tell the whole truth. Ask yourself why the character would lie. How does the character benefit by lying? The fact that the character lies is helpful in uncovering a subtext.

Creating a Subtext

Creating subtexts for all characters enriches them. Frequently, actors who play minor characters feel that they have insufficient time on stage to establish a believable characterization. They fail to consider, however, that every character who appears on stage, no matter how briefly, can contribute to a scene or an entire play. By bringing out certain characteristics, the actor creates a fuller character.

A Character's Mannerisms. You can begin to create a subtext by looking for small clues about special mannerisms. For example, Roday, a minor character in *The Three Sisters*, is a member of a military brigade stationed somewhere in the Russian countryside at the turn of the nineteenth century. His first lines reveal that he is the leader of the gymnastics team for the local boys. An actor who plays Roday may infer that the character might do the following:

1. walk fast and be muscular, since he follows a physical fitness routine

2. speak with a loud voice and have forceful gestures

3. stand and sit very erect

4. wear clothes that fit him well but are not restrictive

A Character's Pet Phrases. An actor can call attention to the pet phrase the character speaks. In *The Three Sisters*, the tone with which an actor speaks Solony's line, "Quick as a flash, the bear made a dash," may provide a key to the character. Because the line is unusual and provocative, it lends itself to creating a vivid speech pattern. If you find a certain expression your character is fond of saying, decide how you should speak it. Will

Create a subtext for any character you play to emphasize certain characteristics of that character and to contribute to every scene in which you appear.

Coloring: *Creating shades of meaning by inflecting or changing the pitch of the voice.*

you speak it in a matter-of-fact way? Or will you try to enrich the meaning by **coloring** it?

Think of the words "Mirror, mirror on the wall, who's the fairest of them all?" from *Snow White*. Or "Life is like a box of chocolates. You never know what you're going to get," from *Forrest Gump*. What do these expressions tell you about the characters who speak them?

Other Sources for a Subtext

The actor who studies a script may need more information about the character and the play as a whole. Sometimes the actor has to go to sources outside the play to find information that may help in the creation of a subtext.

Books and Magazines. Turn to other sources, such as newspapers, magazines, and books, to help you to think about the locale, setting, and dress of the play. You can create a more believable character if you understand the current social events and major issues of the time in which the play is set.

An actor with a role in *The Three Sisters* may want to know what Russian society was like at the time of the play. Where in society did the characters fit? Were they among the weak or the powerful? Was it a time of war or peace? Turmoil or stability?

Other Works by the Playwright. You may find that it helps to study any short stories, novels, or other plays by the same playwright. An actor studying the part of Tchebutykin, an army doctor in *The Three Sisters*, can gain additional insight into the character through other works by this author. The actor would see more of the types of people Chekhov created, especially doctors.

Summary

Actors often rely on subtext to create believable characters. To find clues for a subtext, an actor should study the stage directions of the play and the words of the other characters as well as the words of the character being portrayed. The actor can emphasize a subtext by creating mannerisms and habits of speech for the character. Other sources for a subtext include books and magazines that provide information on the time and place of the play and other works by the playwright.

The Actor and the Role

An actor can relate to a role in different ways. One way is to become totally immersed in the portrayal of a character. Another is to keep a great distance between the character and oneself. Often the relationship between actor and role falls somewhere between these two extremes. Over the centuries, different aspects of this relationship have been stressed. Modern actors often put more of their own emotion into acting than actors did in the past.

Changes in the Relationship of Actor to Role

Actors sometimes question their relationship to the character they portray. They wonder to what extent they should "feel" or "become" the part. How much of their true selves should they expose to the audience? How objective should they be? Should they emphasize the external aspects of the character? Or should they try to get inside the character and feel the same emotions?

An External Approach. Actors of the eighteenth and nineteenth centuries generally tried to keep a clear separation between themselves and the characters they portrayed. An actor did not "become" the character. The actor tried to keep a distance between the self and the role. Objectivity and lack of emotional involvement characterized acting of this period.

Actors concentrated on the external appearance and actions of their characters. They were always conscious of themselves as actors while on stage. They tried to look the part and act the part without necessarily feeling the part. There were exceptions to this objective approach, however, such as the great actress Sarah Bernhardt, who was more emotionally involved with her acting. See the Critic's Choice on page 133.

Imagine that you have been given the chance to play one of the following roles:

Grandmother in *Little Red Riding Hood*
Mother in *Jack and the Beanstalk*
Woodsman in *Little Red Riding Hood*
Farmer in *Jack and the Beanstalk*

You want to make your character real, but he or she has only a few lines to say in the play. You want this character to be well-rounded. The best way to develop a believable character is to create your own subtext.

Step One
Use the Facts of the Play's Text to Help in Creating a Subtext. You already know a few things about the characters, such as that Grandmother is old, the woodsman is strong, Jack's mother is frustrated by his behavior, and the farmer is trying to get a good deal. You also know something about their relationships to the other characters. How the mother deals with Jack may tell you something about her.

Step Two
Create a Life for Your Character. Give the character a past. Make the character real. Imagine as many details about his or her life as you can. Make sure that the life you create for your character fits in with the facts that you already know about the character from the play.

Step Three
Decide What Your Character Has Been Doing Just before the Scene Opens. Was Jack's mother counting out coins and wondering how they were going to have enough money to survive? Was she daydreaming about better times?

Step Four
Use Your Voice to Accentuate the Subtext. Make sure you understand the meaning of the words your character speaks. Then speak those words to emphasize their meaning beneath the surface. If the character repeats any expressions, determine how best to reveal the subtext in those words.

Step Five
Let Your Movements Reveal the Subtext. The character will have a certain way of walking, gesturing, and sitting, depending on the subtext. Use your intuition and logic to create a way for the character to move that fits the subtext.

Step Six
Be Aware of the Subtext as You Are Acting. There will be times on stage when you will not be playing an active role. You may just be standing around. It is important at such times that you keep in character. Being aware of the subtext can help you to stay focused on the character you are playing.

An Internal Approach. Reacting to this earlier approach to acting, the famous Russian stage director Constantin Stanislavski (1863–1938) taught his actors to be natural to the point of almost totally uniting their personalities with those of their stage characters. Stanislavski's technique is called **method acting**.

Although the actor was to feel the same emotions as the character being played, Stanislavski did not advocate losing artistic control and objectivity. An actor following Stanislavski's approach had to do intensive internal work. This internal work included using emotional memory and experiences to enrich acting. Stanislavski's approach has had a huge impact on modern acting.

Method acting: An acting technique in which an actor tries to identify with the character emotionally in order to create a realistic performance.

Illusion Versus Reality

No matter how emotionally involved the actor is in playing a role, the actor's task is not to "become" a part. The paradox must be that the actor appears to be the character but in fact is not. The actor must create the **illusion** of being the stage character.

You can see why some of the activities on stage have to be an illusion. Actors in a production of *The Three Musketeers,* for example, cannot engage in real sword fights on stage and risk injury or even death.

At times, actors have overstepped the boundaries between illusion and reality. The nineteenth-century English actor Edmund Kean became too personally involved in the parts he played, despite the fact that actors of his day kept a distance between themselves and their roles. His style of acting was radically different from that of the typical actor of his day. Kean's acting reflected a volatile, romantic temperament. Eventually, he became psychologically unbalanced and was unable to tell the difference between his stage roles and his own personality.

Illusion: Making the audience believe the actions on stage within the framework of the play.

Creative Forces

An actor must rely on more than acting skills, techniques, and actions. He or she must also rely on creative forces. Because these creative forces are intuitive, they cannot be taught. They are within the actor, who must be aware of them and call on them in playing a role. These creative forces include empathy, sympathy, imitation, and identification.

Empathy. When you have empathy for someone, you experience the same emotion that the other person is feeling. In the theatrical sense, empathy means that when you act you feel the feelings of the character. The word empathy literally means "in-feeling. When you act, the emotions of the character become part of you. You can read more about empathy in Chapter Five.

Sympathy. When you have sympathy for another person, you are not necessarily feeling the same emotion that the other person is feeling. Instead, **sympathy** allows you to understand your character's emotional response to a situation. Your sympathy for the situation of a character helps to enrich your portrayal. An actor playing the role of Anne Frank would understand her hopes and fears and sympathize with the character because of her plight.

Sympathy: An emotional understanding between two people.

Imitation. Empathy also involves imitating the physical actions of a character. **Imitation** lets the actor get closer to the character in terms of external portrayal. If you use costume or makeup to look like the character you are playing, you may find it easier to act like that character. Think of the actors in the musical *Cats*. Looking like a scruffy alley cat helps an actor act and sing like one. Actors who take an external approach to acting often rely on imitation in order to create a believable character.

Imitation: Reproducing the appearance and actions of a character in order to create a believable portrayal.

Identification. Finally, there is the creative inner force known as **identification**, which enables actors to alter their personalities and become strongly influenced by the characters they play. As an actor you must relate to the character in terms of similarities and differences. You need to ask yourself how you are like the character and how you are different. Try to imagine how the character feels.

Identification: Taking experiences from an actor's life and, for motivation, relating them to a character.

You should be able to find some aspect of a character's personality or experiences to identify with. An actor playing

Cinderella, for example, may be able to relate to the role by remembering times when others treated her unfairly. What if you have to play the role of the Big Bad Wolf in *Little Red Riding Hood*? How can you identify with that role? Think of aspects of the wolf. He can be charming, smooth-talking, sly, tricky, determined. Pick a trait that you and the wolf have in common, and then work from that point to identify with him.

Summary

An actor has a special relationship to the character he or she plays and can put much or little of herself or himself into the role. In the last two centuries, there was a clear separation between actor and role. Stanislavski brought change with his belief that the actor should feel the same emotion as the character in the play and have a close relationship to the role. Apart from acting techniques, the actor should call on creative forces such as empathy, sympathy, imitation, and identification to get closer to his or her character emotionally.

Find some aspect of the experiences or personality of any character you play to identify with. For instance, an actor playing Cinderella could remember times when others treated her unfairly, as Cinderella's stepsisters treat her.

Character within the Structure of the Play

It is important that an actor understand the structure of a play. Knowing where his or her character fits into the larger scheme of the play gives the actor a better grasp of the role. The actor should know how the playwright uses the elements of the play to build suspense, create conflict between characters, and reveal information about characters.

Plot

The terms we use today in describing the structure of a play go back to a work entitled *Poetics*, which was written by the ancient Greek scholar Aristotle. Understanding these terms will help you to analyze plays and aid you with character development.

Stage Characters

Plot: *The events of a story organized by a playwright to achieve a dramatic effect.*

When somebody wants to know what happened in a play or movie, he or she may ask you to tell them the **plot**. But plot is more than a summary of happenings or incidents in a play. Plot is the overall organizing part of drama; it is the shaping part. Plot in a play is like architecture in a building. It gives structure and form to the events that take place in the play. There can be no drama without a plot.

The playwright arranges the events of the play for maximum impact. When the play opens, we are introduced to characters in a certain time and place. In a traditional plot, there are usually several events that are part of the rising action of the play. These events may have to do with a conflict within or between characters in the play. In *Cinderella*, for instance, the protagonist wants to go to the ball. Conflict arises because her stepsisters and stepmother do not want her to go. The conflict is resolved by the character achieving or not achieving a goal.

Suffering: *Undergoing or experiencing any emotion or feeling within a character.*

Suffering. A plot must include **suffering**. You may think of suffering as enduring or submitting to pain, loss, or grief, but it can include even positive emotions. Suffering includes joy as well as misery, remorse, and physical pain. It includes the emotional effect of one personality upon another. Suffering is the basic, primary material out of which plot and drama are made. The unfairness of the protagonist's situation provides the suffering in *Cinderella*. The joy Cinderella feels when she attends the ball and dances with the prince is also an example of suffering.

Discovery: *The finding out of important information within a play that was previously unknown.*

Discovery. When **discovery** occurs in a play, new information is revealed. This revelation changes the course of the play. Discovery may range from learning somebody's name to its most important form, which is self-discovery—a character's coming to know herself or himself. In *Beauty and the Beast*, the discovery centers around the Beast's true identity being revealed.

Reversal: *A change of flow of the action within a play.*

Reversal. **Reversal** refers to a turning around. Every complex plot has a major reversal, but simple plots may only have minor reversals. One of the best known examples of reversal in comedy is the "tables turned" situation. An example of reversal occurs in *Cinderella,* when the girl in rags is transformed into the beauty at the ball.

A classic example of a reversal is Cinderella's transformation from a
poor girl in rags into a beauty at the ball.

Character

A play needs a character to play an active role in the plot. This
character must want to achieve a certain goal in the play. The
character should be emotionally involved in working toward
this goal. Think of how badly Cinderella wants to go to the
ball. Her strong desire to attend the ball conflicts with her
stepsisters' not wanting her to go. When conflict arises, the
character must come to a decision and exercise will. When this
happens, dramatic action occurs, even though the exercise of
will may be merely an outpouring of grief, anger, or hate.

In a play, someone or something may be opposed to the protagonist achieving his or her goal. Characters can often be
divided into those who are sympathetic and those who are
antipathetic.

The **sympathetic forces** include the protagonist and other
characters who want the protagonist to reach the goal. The
protagonist usually starts the action.

The **antipathetic forces** include the antagonist. At times,
you may find it hard to decide if a character is sympathetic or
antipathetic. To determine the nature of a character and his or
her function, state what the character desires. You can then
decide whether what the character wants is the same the
same thing the protagonist wants.

Sympathetic forces:
Those forces working
for the good of the
protagonist.

Antipathetic forces:
Those forces working
in opposition to the
protagonist.

Theme

Theme relates to the central idea or message of the play. The
theme is conveyed by all that the characters say that relates to

Great Actors of the Past

You may have heard the names of the following actors because of the impact they made on the theatre. They were the stars of yesterday. The names of these actors live on because of their great acting.

Sarah Bernhardt (1844–1923) was born in France. She became known as "the divine Sarah." Her theatrical style was passionate and emotional, and her voice was clear and beautiful. Sarah Bernhardt was an international star. Crowds flocked to her performances when she visited the United States, where she played the leading role in *Hamlet*.

Edwin Booth (1833–1893) is still considered one of the greatest American actors. Booth's style of acting was not emotional but restrained and low key. His portrayal of Hamlet won him critical acclaim. Unfortunately, his brother, John Wilkes Booth, assassinated President Lincoln. Because of that scandal, he left acting for a few years.

Laurence Olivier (1907–1989) was an English actor known for his portrayal of Shakespearean characters, especially Hamlet and Othello. He won the Academy Award for the film version of *Hamlet* in 1948. Olivier took an external approach to acting. He first concentrated on looking like the character. In his book *On Acting*, Olivier claims that he never actually cried or felt the emotions of grief that he was portraying on stage. Instead he worked toward creating illusion. Audiences and critics found his acting real and convincing.

1. A hundred years from now, which of today's actors do you think will be remembered for their great acting? Choose one man and one woman. Tell why you think they will be remembered.

2. If you have a chance to see Laurence Olivier's film version of *Hamlet* on television or video, watch it to find out why he was acclaimed for his performance in the role. Then watch the Mel Gibson film version of *Hamlet*. Note differences in their acting styles. Olivier claimed not to get emotionally involved in acting a role. Do you feel that Mel Gibson put more of himself into the role? Which version do you prefer?

3. Bernhardt, Booth, and Olivier are only three of the great actors of the past. Other great names are associated with the theatre, such as the Barrymores (Lionel, Ethel, and John), David Garrick, Ellen Terry, and Eleanor Duse. Choose one and find out when and where the actor lived and what his or her acting style was.

this central idea. In *The Wizard of Oz,* the characters begin their journey hoping to find the magical Wizard of Oz, who will solve all their problems. The dramatic argument of the play is that the heart, wisdom, and courage the characters are seeking are within them. The dramatic argument of a play is highly emotional, particularly if the matter is of great importance to the characters. It must move people to action.

The major dramatic question in *King Lear* is whether Lear will discover the error he has made in rejecting Cordelia and will reconcile with her. This stems from the dramatic argument that parents should be selfless enough to recognize true, unselfish love in their children.

Discourse

The characters in a play use language to communicate. **Discourse** is, therefore, an essential part of a play. Discourse includes the art of writing stage directions and descriptions, as well as dialogue. In drama, however, dialogue is the most important part of the discourse.

Discourse: The formal combination of words into meaningful patterns.

Spectacle

The word *spectacle* may bring to mind a kind of garish display. That is not what spectacle means in regard to the theater. Technically, spectacle is an integral part of drama. Spectacle is what the audience sees and hears. Costume, scenery, lighting, off-stage noise, the stage business of a fight, and the movement and gestures of the actors all are spectacles.

Summary

An actor should understand the structure of a play in order to understand the character's role in the scheme of the play's action. Plot, or the structure of the play, includes suffering, discovery, and reversal. The character in a play moves the action of the play. Overlying the action of a play is its theme, or central idea. In order for the play to be communicated to an audience, it needs discourse. What happens on stage is part of the spectacle of a play.

Reading for Clues

1. This exercise will help you to see exactly where you need to look for clues about a character when reading a play. Photocopy the first scene from a play. After reading the scene, look at the following:

   a. *Stage Directions.* Use a yellow marker to highlight the stage directions (they are usually printed in italics).

   b. *Character's Words.* Use a green marker to highlight all the words spoken by one of the characters in the scene, whom we will call Character X.

   c. *Other Characters' Words.* Use a pink marker to highlight any places where another character refers to Character X.

   d. *Putting It All Together.* Go back to see what information you have found about Character X in all the highlighted areas.

   e. *A Picture Emerges.* Ask yourself what kind of picture of Character X takes shape when you put together these clues from the stage directions and dialogue.

Subtext

2. *Searching for Subtext.* Imagine that you have been given a part to play in the musical *Grease.* You want to know more about what life was like for teenagers at the time of the play so that you can create an accurate subtext for your character. Ask your local librarian to help you find books or magazines about the 1950s. Find out who was president, what was front-page news, what kids did for fun, what they watched on television, what music they listened to.

3. *Changing the Subtext.* How would another character say Forrest Gump's famous line, "Life is like a box of chocolates. You never know which one you're going to get"? Choose a character from a play or movie and speak Gump's line the way the other character would speak it. Does the way your character speaks the line change the meaning?

Acting Out

4. Pretend that you have a short walk-on role playing one of the characters below. You want to create an impact on the audience by creating a well-rounded character. Make up one or two sentences for the character to speak. Imagine a subtext for your character, and then use gestures and mannerisms as well as speech characteristics to emphasize the subtext.

   a. letter carrier
   b. waiter
   c. scientist
   d. librarian

The Actor's Logbook

1. *Learning the Language.* Add the vocabulary words from this chapter to your logbook.

2. *Common Traits.* Make a list of play or movie characters whom you identify with. Note the personality traits or experiences that you have in common.

3. *Discover the Subtext.* The next time you see a film or play, try to get beneath the words of a character to uncover the subtext. Choose one character to concentrate on. Note any expressions that he or she repeats. Are certain words emphasized? Discovering the subtext will enrich your understanding of character.

4. *Critic's Choice.* Watch a movie that was made before 1940. Notice the acting styles. Do you think the main actors tried to present their characters from the inside or the outside? How do their acting styles differ from those of the major film actors today?

Critical Thinking

5. *Analysis.* In each of the plays below, where would you find discovery? What emotion would constitute the suffering? Decide which of the main characters in each of the plays would be sympathetic and which would be antipathetic.

   The Wizard of Oz
   Goldilocks
   Hansel and Gretel
   Snow White and the Seven Dwarfs

6. *Discovery.* Imagine that you have been chosen for a part in the school play. Think of experiences from your own life that you would use to identify with a character from each of the following plays:

   Beauty and the Beast
   Cinderella
   Hansel and Gretel
   Snow White and the Seven Dwarfs

Creative Thinking

7. *Creating Subtext.* Imagine a subtext for each of these characters. Then think of an expression that you would have them repeat as a clue to the subtext:

   Hansel and Gretel's father
   Cinderella's stepmother
   Prince in *Cinderella*
   Dorothy's aunt in *The Wizard of Oz*

8. *Changing Subtext.* Take the same characters and create a very different subtext. Imagine how their behavior would change. Find a different expression to fit the new subtext.

CHAPTER EIGHT

Imagination

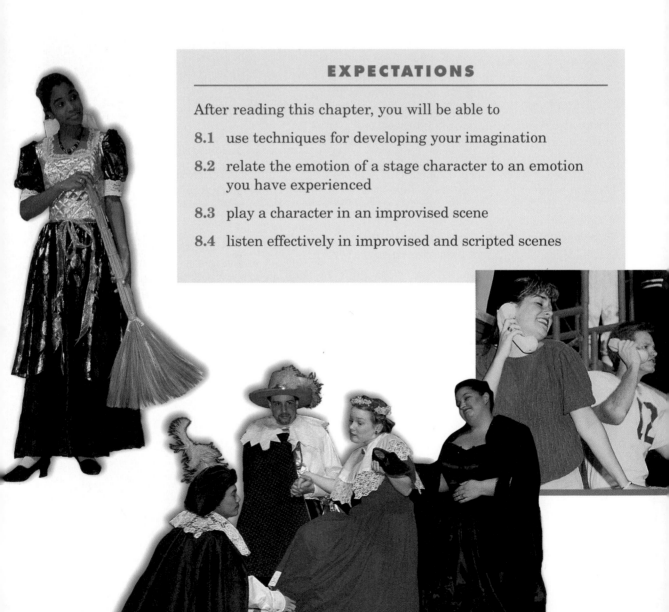

EXPECTATIONS

After reading this chapter, you will be able to

8.1 use techniques for developing your imagination

8.2 relate the emotion of a stage character to an emotion you have experienced

8.3 play a character in an improvised scene

8.4 listen effectively in improvised and scripted scenes

n actor needs a strong, vivid imagination to be able to step out of his or her personality and into that of the character on stage. Imagination enables an actor to play a variety of characters, some vastly different from the self. Imagination is the lifeblood of good acting.

Imagination

Acting on stage is like the games of pretend that children love to play. As children, we have very strong imaginations. By adulthood, we may have lost our ability to imagine and pretend because we no longer use it. If you want to become an actor, you can and must develop your imagination.

Developing Your Imagination

You can have fun developing your imagination. You do not have to read or study or take classes to do it. It is not like learning algebra, which you have to work at to acquire. You already have imagination. You just have to exercise it and let it free.

Trust Your Intuition. As we grow up, we often think before we say or do something. This is good—in most situations. When it comes to acting, however, we often have to trust our **intuition** more than our logical abilities.

We all experience intuition. Intuition is a feeling that we know something instantaneously without having to think about it. When we have an intuition, an answer to a problem may come to us out of the blue. Intuition bypasses logic. Sometimes a person has to make a decision, and he or she knows intuitively which is the right course to take. It can be a gut feeling or a hunch. You do not have to work at becoming intuitive.

Intuition: Immediate knowing or insight without going through a logical process.

The following are ways you can be open to intuition in acting:

1. Go with your feelings about how a character should speak or move.

2. Trust your approach to creating a character instead of looking for the one "right" way to act a part.

3. Spend time picturing the character in your mind.

4. Follow your instincts rather than logic when creating a character.

Experience Life. Human beings are creatures of habit, but habit can inhibit imagination. Life is easier if we form habits so that we do not have to make decisions about all the things we have to do each day. We get up at a certain time each day; we eat certain foods for breakfast; we take the same route to school or to work each day. Sometimes we become so accustomed to the routine of our lives and the people and places that we see every day that we are not awake to the world around us.

An actor cannot afford to live that way. An actor must be alert and use his or her imagination every day. Since acting is about people and life and the world, an actor must always pay attention to the life around him or her.

Start living your life as if each day were a new and different experience. Notice how a toddler is bright-eyed, alert, and inquisitive. He or she is seeing much of the world for the first time. An actor needs this kind of awareness because acting a role is experiencing a part of life for the first time.

The following are some suggestions for how you can work at seeing life with freshness and curiosity:

1. Start noticing the details of life, like the color of a friend's eyes or the slant of light on a winter morning.

2. Change your habits every so often, such as your morning routine.

3. Trade television time for more engaging activities like getting together with friends or going for a walk.

4. Spend time outside and experience nature, even when the weather is cold or wet.

Experiencing life and broadening your outlook will help you to become a more imaginative actor. Keep your eyes open to the world around you.

Broaden Your Outlook. An actor must be interested in the world in all its variety. Your imagination will grow if you stretch the boundaries of what you know and experience. Many of us grow up and spend our lives in one place. Or we may live in different places, but we keep mental blinders on. We may begin to think that the rest of the world acts and thinks and lives just like we do. We develop a narrow view of life.

Chances are that no character you play will be just like you. Learn about people and places outside your immediate experience. The more you see and know, the more resources you will have to draw on in acting. Your knowledge and experience can become a springboard for the imagination.

The following are some ways you can broaden your outlook:

1. Talk to people outside your immediate circle of friends—students at school from different backgrounds or with different interests than yours.

2. Get to know people outside your age group, both older and younger.

3. See a different kind of movie from what you are used to seeing, such as a film about cultures different from your own or a film in another language with subtitles.

4. Read many different types of books and magazines.

Using the Imagination in Creating a Character

An actor relies on imagination when creating a character. An actor's responsibility is to create a character with feelings, expressions, mannerisms, and attitudes. To round out a character in this way, an actor must use imagination.

A playwright does not supply everything needed to create a role. He or she gives an actor dialogue and some stage directions, but an actor must analyze and interpret the thoughts of the character. The final character must be living, vital, and truthful. Imagination helps when we seem to reach a dead end in creating a character. We may know only the facts about a character, but we cannot bring the character to life. Or there may be gaps we need to fill. Imagination can help us bridge those gaps.

Imagine the Character in Detail. Be specific in imagining a character you are playing. The more details you can imagine, the more concrete the character becomes—and the more real. Know your character right down to what he or she had for breakfast and which part of the newspaper he or she turned to first—the comics or the editorial page or the sports page. Along with these mundane details, imagine an interior life for your character, one of hopes, secrets, and dreams for the future. Ask yourself what your character hopes to accomplish in life. Use your imagination to uncover a secret from the past that affects his or her behavior. If your character could have one wish, what would it be?

Imagine the Character's Feelings. Knowing yourself and your own feelings helps you to understand the feelings of a character you play. Human beings experience the same basic emotions—joy, sorrow, hope, fear, anger, depression, and contentment. Remember your own experiences of these emotions when you act. Use your imagination in relating these feelings to the character you are playing.

If you have trouble understanding your character's emotion, imagine a way to make the experience real to you. A helpful technique in portraying emotion is **substitution**.

For example, you may find it hard to relate to your character's fear of flying because you love to fly. But you do have fears. You dread snakes. Think of a time when you came into contact with a snake. Imagine how you felt. Close your eyes and remember the snake. Think of how you reacted physically. What was your facial expression? What happened to your posture? How did fear affect your breathing and your voice? Use that memory of fear to show your character's fear.

Stanislavski used a technique similar to substitution, which he called **emotion memory**. He taught that the feelings of an actor should be the same as those of the character being portrayed. He wanted actors to delve into their experiences and recall emotions in order to portray their character's feelings accurately. He had actors use this technique when they were preparing a role. By using emotion memory, you try to get closer to the character and feel the same emotion that the character is feeling. You use your memory of that emotion to help.

__Substitution:__ The use of one of an actor's experiences to relate to the experiences of a character within the play.

__Emotion memory:__ The replacement of an actor's feelings for a character's feelings.

Summary

Imagination is essential to an actor. Some ways to develop the imagination include trusting intuition, becoming more awake to everyday life, and getting to know people outside your immediate circle of friends. Imagination can help an actor in creating characters by helping the actor to expand character and to understand the character's feelings.

Improvisation

Improvising scenes exercises the imagination and creativity and gives an actor practice in creating characters. **Improvisation** also helps actors become more comfortable being on stage and responding to the words and actions of the other actors. Because an actor does not have a script to rely on, he or she has to communicate with the other actors on stage in a spontaneous, unrehearsed way.

__Improvisation:__ Creating a brief acting scene on the spur of the moment with little preparation.

To improvise a scene, you need only actors, a bare space, an imaginary situation, characters, and their motivations. Using these essentials, you can come up with endless possibilities for improvised scenes. Below is an example of one way that you can go about setting up an improvisation.

Step One
Form Groups. Divide the class into groups of three or four students.

Step Two
Decide on a Situation. Below are some examples of situations that can be used for an improvised scene.

1. Two people waiting in line to use a pay phone while a third chatters away.
2. Three people surveying the damage from a three-way car accident.
3. Three students waiting to be called in to the principal's office.

Step Three
Assign the Characters. The descriptions of the characters do not have to be detailed. A character in scene number one, for example, may be a teenager with strict parents who will ground her if she comes home late without calling. Or a character in number two could be a sixteen-year-old boy who just got his driver's license. A character in the third could be an honor student who finds himself sitting between two problem students.

Step Four
Decide on Objectives. Each student should be given an objective for the character. If the objectives are to be kept from all the other characters in the scene, a description of each character's objective can be written on a slip of paper or told to the performer in private.

Step Five
Prepare. Get together for about fifteen to twenty minutes to plan the basic outline of the improvisation. Decide on the details of the situation. Plan how to begin and end the scene. Do not rehearse the dialogue. It should be spontaneous.

Step Six
Perform the Improvisation. The performance area should be bare except for chairs, if needed. Use pantomime for any props. Performers should keep in mind the guidelines for improvisation found on page 146. The details of the situation can be given in the dialogue.

Step Seven
Critique Each Improvisation. The rest of the class should discuss whether the actors stayed in character, whether they listened to each other and responded accordingly, and whether the characters were believable. They should tell what was best about the improvisation and what needed improvement.

Basics of Improvisation

An improvisation contains one or more characters involved in a specific situation. For example, the characters may be a fourteen-year-old boy who has skipped school for the day, a pizza delivery person who must return to work, and a woman who is on her way to deliver a speech at a meeting. The scene may be an elevator in which the characters are trapped. The form of the improvisation grows out of the basic conflict in the scene.

This conflict arises because the characters each have a certain goal or objective in the scene. These objectives may conflict. Maybe two of the characters want to climb out the top of the elevator, but the other character is afraid to and wants to wait for help. Out of this conflict comes the drama of the scene. Improvisation allows you to be creative because you are not tied to a script. Improvisation is spontaneous and fresh and unpredictable, just like real life. The sky's the limit when it comes to creating characters and dialogue in improvised scenes.

Types of Improvisation

Improvisation can be performed by one actor alone on stage or by two or more actors. There are special advantages and challenges with each type of improvisation. But the basics are the same: character, scene, and objective.

Solo Improvisation. In solo improvisation, an actor improvises alone on stage. He or she is given or chooses a character, scene, and an objective. The actor must ask these questions: "Who am I? Where am I? What am I doing here? What do I want?" Being alone on stage may seem difficult for you. The secret of solo improvisation, however, is to decide who you are and to keep focused on what you are doing in the scene. To prevent the improvisation from turning into pantomime, the actor should speak as well as use movement and gestures. After all, people, sometimes do talk to themselves when they are alone.

When doing a solo improvisation, stay focused on who you are and what you are doing in the scene.

You can turn the elevator scene described above into a solo improvisation. You can be one of the above characters or a different character. You are alone in the elevator. All you have is the emergency button and the telephone—but no one answers it. Your task in the scene is to try to get out of the elevator. Using your imagination and creativity while keeping in character, you do what your character would do in the situation.

Group Improvisation. Improvising in a group may seem easier than solo improvisation because you are not alone on stage. You do not have to do all the work in the scene. But improvising with others can be more complicated because each character has his or her own goals or objectives, which may be in conflict with those of the other characters. Group improvisation can be even more challenging if you decide to perform it so that some of the characters do not know the intentions of the other characters.

When you improvise with other actors, you have less control over the scene and must adapt your actions according to the words and actions of the other characters. Total commitment to the scene, intense listening, and rapid **adaptation** are required for good group improvisation.

Adaptation: A change on the spur of the moment due to unforeseen circumstances, usually used in relation to improvisation.

Despite its challenges, group improvisation can be fun and exciting, and it is excellent training for stage acting. Anyone who is serious about acting should try to gain experience in group improvisation.

Guidelines for Improvisation

When improvising, there are certain guidelines to keep in mind. The following are general suggestions to follow for successful improvisation. For step-by-step information on group improvisation, see the Take One feature on page 144.

Know the Character. Improvisation may be spontaneous and unrehearsed, but there are a few essential things that an actor needs to do before the scene begins. An actor must know who the character is, where the scene is taking place, how the character is involved, and what the character is trying to achieve in the scene.

It is important to keep in character throughout the improvisation. By always keeping the character's motivation in the scene in mind, you will know the words and actions that are right for your character in the scene.

Forget the Audience. An actor in an improvisation must keep focused on what his or her character is trying to accomplish in the scene. An actor also must listen and react so that there is a give and take among the characters. When actors are only concerned with what their characters are saying and do not pay attention to the words of the other characters, the characters tend to talk at each other. There is no real interaction.

Speak with a Purpose. You should only speak when you have something to add to the scene. Do not chatter aimlessly. If the actors listen carefully to each other and respond in a natural manner, the dialogue will flow naturally. Never say, "Well, what do we do now?" or indicate that the scene is not working. Hang in there and bring the scene back to life or end it quickly.

Do not be afraid of silence. You do not need to fill in every pause with words. Instead, use the silence creatively. Use it as a time to reflect before speaking, as you might in real life. Or use it for a purpose, such as suspense.

Be Spontaneous. Improvisation stretches your imagination and creativity. Do not think too much before speaking or performing an action in improvisation. If it feels like the right thing to say or do, try it out. If the other actors do not like the direction the scene is taking, they can always steer it in another direction. Do not be afraid to experiment, but do not try too hard to be original. Just work on creating a believable scene.

Convey honest emotion. You do not have to strive to be dramatic. Use your voice and gestures naturally to underscore the emotion of the scene. On the other hand, be wary of hiding your emotion under a mask of boredom while improvising. If you appear bored, the scene will be boring. Improvisation requires interaction between characters, something boredom inhibits.

Keep It Moving. Begin the scene with high energy and keep it moving. If the action droops, take it in another direction. Be careful, though, that all actions are natural and not contrived. Keep your character's objective always in mind. The words and actions of your character in the scene should flow from that objective.

Summary

Improvisation provides practice in using the imagination to create character. One actor alone or two or more actors together can perform improvisation. Guidelines for improvisation include knowing the character, forgetting the audience, speaking with purpose, focusing on the other actors, being spontaneous, and keeping the scene moving.

Listening

Listening well to the other actors on stage is a critical skill for an actor. In a play, the performers must work together to create real characters who respond to each other in a believable way. For these characters to seem real, the actors must listen to each other and react as if they truly were the characters.

Listening in a Play

The challenge for an actor in a play is to act as though he or she is hearing the words of the other actors for the first time. In the context of the play, the character really is hearing them for the first time, and the audience is, too. Experience in improvising helps an actor to listen convincingly in a scripted play despite knowing the words the characters will speak.

Cue: A signal for an actor to speak or move on stage, often the last word or action of another character.

Hear the Words. When actors prepare for a play, they know the lines they will speak and the times when they will speak them. They know that certain cues will tell them it is their turn to speak their lines. Memorizing lines and then waiting for the **cue** to speak them may make the dialogue seem artificial and stilted.

The Second City

You may have never heard of The Second City, but you have probably seen many actors who started there. "Saturday Night Live" cast members John Belushi, Dan Aykroyd, Gilda Radner, Martin Short, and Bill Murray and many other entertainers began their careers on the stages of The Second City.

The Second City has been the mecca for improvisation since it opened in 1959. It evolved from The Compass Players, the first professional improvisational theatre group in the country, which was founded by Paul Sills. His mother, Viola Spolin, the author of *Improvisation for the Theater,* pioneered the use of improvisational games to teach acting. Sills used many of these techniques to train the actors of The Second City, which he founded with David Shepherd and others.

Today The Second City is still housed in an intimate theatre on the north side of Chicago. On its bare stage, a small group of actors performs the improvised material for which it is known. The Second City has grown over the years to include other troupes, including ones in Toronto and Detroit, and several traveling troupes.

Improvisation takes place after the scripted show. The actors ask the audience to call out ideas for improvisation. These can range from topics in the news to off-the-wall suggestions. The actors never know what to expect from one night to the next.

Then the actors take the ideas backstage to plan the improvisation. Later they return and perform for the audience. The most successful improvisations are saved and reworked and rehearsed to become main-stage shows. The humor that The Second City is known for derives from the characters they create and their relationships. The actors try not to go for the easy laugh.

1. Find out if there are any improvisational theatre groups in your area. If there are, call and ask them to send any information about programs and workshops for young people.

2. Take turns improvising scenes based on ideas from the class. Take one idea and plan an improvised scene. You do not have to attempt to be funny. But see how well you can work on the spur of the moment.

Forget about your cue for the time being when you are on stage. Instead, listen as the other characters speak. Pretend you have never heard those words spoken before. After all, the character you are playing has never heard those words, so you must not anticipate what you know that character is going to say. Respond to the way the character speaks the words. Listen for inflections and pauses that change the meaning from performance to performance. Then when your cue comes, your words will seem natural and spontaneous.

Stay in Character. When you attend a play, notice the actors who are not actively involved in the action on stage. Are they gazing around the room? Or are they focused on what is taking place on stage? Even when you are not playing an active part in the scene, you must stay in character, acting as the character instead of yourself.

Actors need to be as good at listening as they are at speaking. If you anticipate what another character is going to say, your own lines may not seem natural. Instead, focus on what other characters say, as if you had never heard their words before. In that way, your responses will seem more spontaneous.

When another character is speaking, keep in character. Listen to what is being said and react to it naturally. Do not spend this time thinking of anything except what is taking place on stage. Think the thoughts your character might think.

For example, if you were playing a part in the funeral speech scene of *Julius Caesar*, you might be listening to Mark Antony giving his oration. You might be wondering whether Mark Antony was sincere in his praise of Julius Caesar. You would not have to make deliberate facial expressions to show your doubts but just think and act in character. Your attention to the speaker's words would come through to the audience.

Avoid Distraction. While listening to another actor on stage, do not call attention away from the character speaking. The audience and actors should be listening to the speaker. Listen attentively without any distracting gestures or facial expressions. Do not try to **steal the scene**.

Listening during Improvisation

Improvisation provides practice in listening. Since the dialogue is unrehearsed and spontaneous, each character must listen attentively to what the other characters are saying in order to know how to respond. An actor cannot reply appropriately if he or she does not understand what the other characters have said. Effective listening involves hearing the words and also the shades of meaning, such as those created by pauses and changes of inflection.

Focusing on the Speaker. During improvisation, while you are listening to the other characters speaking, focus on the meaning of their words. Do not plan what you are going to say next because you have to be totally involved in listening. Really concentrate on hearing the words and understanding their meaning. When the character is finished speaking, your reply will be more natural and spontaneous.

An actor must concentrate while performing improvisation or other kinds of acting. To give full attention to the words and actions of the characters, an actor must ignore distractions,

Steal the scene: To divert attention away from the actor on stage who should be the center of attention.

such as noises in the audience or a fly buzzing around the stage.

Intuitive Listening. An actor in an improvisation must be alert to the words of the other actors and to the changes in voice and body language that help convey meaning. All of an actor's inner energies must be rallied to project truthfulness of character. The actor needs to be alert to all signals given by others. Vocal variations and body action offer meaning and feelings about what is being said. The actor must also keep emotional responses appropriate so that they are in keeping with the mood established by the actors.

Teamwork. Acting is teamwork. When actors improvise, they depend on each other for the success of the improvisation. Help yourself and the other actors by listening to what all the actors say. Respond to their words with appropriate facial expressions and gestures. Then your words will be a natural response to the words of the other characters and will help to create a good improvised scene. Effective **communication** is at the heart of good improvisation.

Communication:
The exchange of ideas through speech or other forms of interchange.

When actors begin an improvised scene, they may have little clue as to where the scene will lead. As in life, each character has his or her own agenda. Each wants something in the scene. The actors have to focus on communicating what their characters want and on listening to find out how the other characters are responding to them. By focusing on good communication within the scene, the actors can work as a team to create a good improvisation.

Developing Listening Skills

An actor needs to be a good listener. If you are serious about acting, you should develop good listening skills. There are many opportunities for such practice.

Practice Better Listening. Much of your day is spent listening to others—your friends, your family, your teachers at school. Think of these times as opportunities to practice better listening so that you will be a better listener on stage. The most important ingredient in becoming a better listener is to want to develop your listening skills. If you set that as your goal, you will find countless opportunities for practice.

Tips for Better Listening. It is helpful to focus on certain aspects of listening. The following guidelines will help you to listen more effectively:

1. Pay full attention to the speaker's words and body language.
2. Focus on the meaning of what is being spoken rather than on individual words.
3. Listen actively by questioning or agreeing or disagreeing with the speaker's words.
4. When you are done listening, tell yourself in your own words what the speaker said.

Summary

An actor must be able to listen well. In improvised roles, listening is necessary so that the actors can communicate. In a play, actors must listen and appear to be hearing the words spoken in the play for the first time. Good listening habits are crucial for aspiring actors. Listening well in daily life prepares actors for the listening they do on stage.

Imagination

1. ***Find a Treasure.*** Look for an object at home that could belong to a colorful character in a play. Examples are an old lace fan, a tarnished harmonica, or a faded baseball cap. Sit for five minutes holding the object and observing it carefully. Imagine who might use such an object. Make up a story about an imaginary character who owns the article.

2. ***Create a Character.*** Notice a house or apartment building that you pass frequently. Imagine a character who might live there. Write a detailed description of that character. Give him or her a name, describe the living room, and tell about one item in the home that the character treasures.

Stage Skills

3. ***Listening.*** Choose a television show, such as a courtroom drama, to watch and participate in as a listener. Pretend that you are part of a scene where you have to listen. Choose a character to play who will be in the background. Concentrate on what the characters are saying. Try to put yourself into the part. Try not to let anything distract you for ten minutes.

4. ***Concentration.*** Divide the class into groups of four or five. Two in each group will perform an exercise in which the first student will tell the second student a string of eight numbers. The second student will have to repeat the numbers correctly to the first student. The other two or three students will try to distract the students performing the exercise. Students will change places so that each will have a chance to do the concentration exercise.

Acting Out

5. ***Solo Improvisation.*** You are a teen-ager practicing a speech in front of a mirror. You have to explain to your parents the D on your report card. Next imagine the same teenager two weeks later rehearsing a speech asking the boss for a raise. Finally, the same teenager is trying to get up courage to ask someone on a date to the prom.

6. ***Group Improvisation.*** Find two or three other students to perform an improvisation. Follow the steps in the Take One on page 144. Plan a short improvised scene. Create your own characters.

The Actor's Logbook

1. ***Learning the Language.*** Add the vocabulary terms from this chapter to your logbook. Because some of the vocabulary words in this chapter are difficult, explain each definition in your own words to make sure that you understand it.

2. ***Imagination.*** Write down three things you can do in the coming week to exercise your imagination. Focus on things that you do out of habit. For example, you can try to see your neighborhood in a new way by taking a different route to school. Or you can make a point of talking to one person at school each day whom you would ordinarily not talk to. Or you can start reading a different cartoon on the comics page of the newspaper.

3. ***Listening Better.*** For each day this week, note how you plan to practice effective listening. You may decide to listen well in English class on Monday, to your best friend on Tuesday, or while watching a movie on Wednesday. It is easier to achieve a goal if you can think of concrete ways to work toward it.

Critical Thinking

4. ***Analysis.*** Listen to a discussion on the radio for fifteen minutes. Listen carefully to try to understand what the speaker is saying. As you follow the points the speaker is making, ask yourself what main idea the speaker is trying to get across. Is the speaker convincing? Do you agree with the speaker?

5. ***Compare and Contrast.*** When you are at a friend's house, notice ways your friend's home life resembles yours and ways in which it differs. What is the most striking difference? Then notice the objects in the house. If you could imagine a character living in this house, what would the character be like?

Creative Thinking

6. ***Emotional Recall.*** Pick a vivid memory you have of your childhood. Try to remember the details. Recall what emotion you felt. Take that same emotion and imagine a situation in a play when a character might feel that same emotion. Make the situation different from the one in which you experienced the emotion.

7. ***Creating Characters.*** Imagine three characters for improvisation. State three of the most important facts about each character. Come up with a favorite saying that each character uses. Say each expression the way that the character would say it.

8. ***Coming up with a Situation.*** Describe a situation in which those same three characters find themselves. Ask yourself how the situation affects each character.

9. ***Attributing Motives.*** Provide each character with a motive or objective in the scene. Note how these motives may conflict with each other.

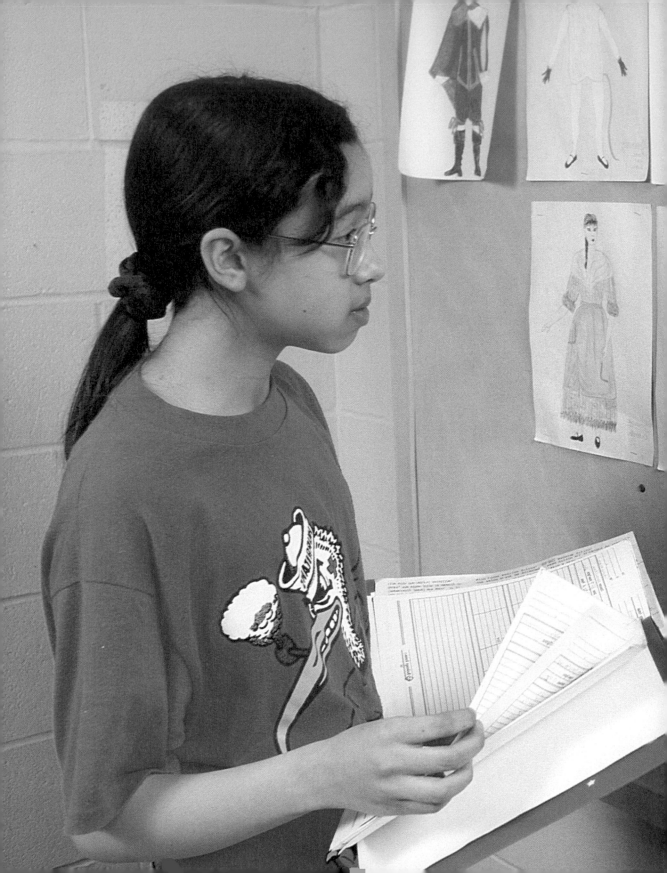

PART THREE

Theatre Production

CHAPTER NINE

Auditions

EXPECTATIONS

After reading this chapter, you will be able to

9.1 apply expressive movement to the interpretation of a script for an audition

9.2 demonstrate basic acting skills in an audition

9.3 use dramatic reading skills for an audition

9.4 prepare a script for a dramatic reading

ne of the first steps in theatre production is the selection of a play. The director makes the choice based on the available resources, the talents of students, and the support and interest of the local community. Once the play has been selected, the director wants widespread involvement and calls for auditions and volunteers to start the production process. This chapter introduces the audition process and the early stages of theatre production.

The Call to Audition

The news is out. The theatre director has selected a play and is calling for **auditions.** The audition, or invitation to try out for acting parts in a play, is one of the most important experiences for an actor. Preparing for an audition requires work, timing, and basic acting skills.

Audition: An opportunity to try out for a part in a play.

Types of Readings

Sometimes directors make copies of the play's script available and invite interested students to read them and prepare a scene for the audition. In other cases, the director prefers to have actors do a cold reading of a script. There are also auditions in which actors prepare a monologue of their own choosing for delivery on stage.

Script Audition. Before the audition, you will want to find out as much as possible about the play that has been selected for performance. If the audition is a **script audition,** you will have some idea of the character for which you want to audition. Do a preliminary character analysis and read the scene selected for the audition out loud several times.

    When doing a script audition, applicants still need to be very flexible and sensitive to the director's approach to the play. They need to show they can take direction. Directors

Script audition: An audition in which an actor reads an actual scene that involves the character the actor would like to play.

often have ideas about the type of actor they want for particular parts before the audition process takes place. One applicant may resemble the image the director has, and another may not.

With a script audition, applicants can use the opportunity to dress in such a way as to suggest the parts they are trying out for. In general, when auditioning for a part, you will want to dress appropriately and avoid being overdressed or dressed too casually.

Cold Reading. In this situation, applicants come to an audition without knowing what they will be asked to read. The director will have scripts distributed, and you will be asked to read a

In a script audition, you will be given the opportunity to read a particular scene that involves the character you would like to play. Try to dress as you think the character might dress and be sensitive to the director's approach to the play.

part. You will have a few minutes to prepare, so make the most of your time. First, skim the script to get a sense of the play or the scene you will read. Then go back and read for an understanding of character and scene.

To practice for a cold reading audition, you need to read out loud with clarity and expression. Read out loud every day. Learn to recognize the subject and verbs in sentences before you speak and practice emphasizing them vocally. Learn to recognize the emotion of the speaker or writer when you read out loud.

Monologues. In some cases, the director will ask applicants to prepare a short monologue for the audition. If you participate in this type of audition, you will want to prepare a couple of types of monologues—one classic and serious, another that is more modern and perhaps humorous.

The monologue you select should reflect an understanding of the character you are representing. Learn the monologue in the context of the entire play. Do a character analysis. Prepare simple but effective gestures to accompany your monologue.

Audition Procedures. You might be amazed at the number of people who show up to audition for a part in a play. The director has probably used a lot of publicity to inform interested students about the audition opportunity. The director usually wants a lot of people to try out because casting decisions can make or break a play. The director wants to make good choices to insure the play's success.

After all the applicants for the audition are assembled, the director will briefly describe the play and the characters in it. Applicants will probably be asked to fill out an audition form to help the director learn about the applicants' skills and experiences (see the sample in Figure 9.1). If you are asked to complete such a form, be as truthful as possible. Do not give false information about age, weight, or experience.

Callbacks

After the audition, many actors wait nervously for a call inviting them to return for further consideration by the director.

Figure 9.1 Audition Information Sheet

Name ——————————————— Class ——— Age ——————— Sex ———

Address ——————————————— Phone ——— Height ——— Weight ———

Class Schedule

1 ————————————— 4 ————————————— 7 —————————————

2 ————————————— 5 ————————————— 8 —————————————

3 ————————————— 6 ————————————— 9 —————————————

Previous Acting Experience

——

——

——

Special Acting Skills (Sing, Dance, Dialect, Musical Instrument, etc.)

——

——

Rehearsal Availability (When can you rehearse? Do you have conflicts or complications?)

——

——

Please check areas you would be interested in working on.

Costumes ————————   Makeup ————————   Props ————————

Sets/scenery ————————   Lighting ————————   Publicity ————————

Sound ————————   Prompter ————————   Manager/crew ————————

Director's Comment:

——

——

A **callback** is another opportunity to demonstrate acting skills.

Director's Choice. The director will make preliminary decisions about the candidates for specific roles in the play. Callbacks help the director make final decisions about casting. Actors invited to a callback should be encouraged; their first audition obviously went well. Being in a select group of invited actors is a challenging experience. If you are among those selected for a callback, practice courtesy and cooperation with everyone involved. A spirit of competition will not be considered an asset by the director hoping to build a theatre company's team spirit.

Callback: Asking selected actors to audition for a second or third time for a part in a play.

What to Expect. During callbacks, actors may be asked to demonstrate acting ability by presenting a monologue, reading a scene from the play as a specific character, or participating in an improvisational activity. If you are asked to do an improv, you will be assigned a character and a situation and given a set amount of time to create a memorable story and character. Repeated practice with improvisation is a real benefit to actors invited to callbacks.

After a callback, the director may ask a candidate if he or she would consider taking a part other than the particular one auditioned for. For beginners, gaining any experience on stage is a benefit. Not getting a particular part often leads to unexpected opportunities in other roles.

Guidelines for Auditions and Callbacks. Attitude, skill, and availability are all factors the director considers in making casting decisions. When you audition, make sure you follow these guidelines:

1. Be prepared. Read the play and learn about the characters before the audition or callback.

2. Be courteous. Develop a friendly and flexible approach to all those who audition. Reject a spirit of competition and foster a spirit of cooperation.

3. Listen carefully. Pay attention to the directions given to all the candidates. Listen to the auditions of the other candidates to become sensitive to other interpretations.

4. Be flexible. After casting, be understanding and supportive of those who were chosen for parts as well as those who were not chosen. If a lesser part is offered, be cheerful and accept it. If no acting part is offered, volunteer to work backstage or in some other capacity. Get involved.

Summary

The audition is the start of an actor's involvement in the production of a play. There are several types of auditions, and the director will decide to ask candidates to do a prepared reading of the script, a cold reading, or a monologue. In some cases, actors will be invited to a callback. Whether a candidate is selected for a major or minor role, an attitude of cooperation and flexibility will be an asset to the theatre company.

Blocking the Play

After the director has made the casting decisions for the play, the theatre company will spend time together going over the play to refine meaning and build characterizations. The end result will be a common vision and interpretation shared by all members of the cast. The director will then begin **blocking** the movement and positions of actors on stage. Blocking the play requires both imagination and technical skills. In addition, strong doses of patience and cooperation make the blocking process go more smoothly.

Blocking: Planning the actors' movements and the positions of sets for a play production.

The General Plan

Once an actor has a successful audition, much time will be spent learning about the general plan for the play. Even though an actor will be eager to begin learning and practicing lines, the preliminary steps are equally important. Learning about the physical, psychological, and emotional aspects of the scenes and characters will enhance the overall interpretation of the play.

How to Prepare a Monologue

Sooner or later, actors will have the opportunity to demonstrate skills in character analysis by presenting a monologue. Prepare either of the following monologues for presentation to the class:

Female Monologue

From *The Diary of Anne Frank* by Frances Goodrich and Albert Hackett

Background: The Frank and Van Daan families are hiding from the Nazis during World War II. They have been living in a small attic over a store for two years.

Character: Despite the horrors of war, Anne is convinced that "people are really good at heart."

ANNE (Looking up through the skylight): Look, Peter, the sky. What a lovely day. Aren't the clouds beautiful? You know what I do when it seems as if I couldn't stand being cooped up for one more minute? I *think* myself out. I think myself on a walk in the park where I used to go with Pim. Where the daffodils and the crocus and the violets grow down the slopes. You know the most wonderful thing about *thinking* yourself out? You can have it any way you like. You can have roses and violets and chrysanthemums all blooming at the same time. . . . It's funny. . . . I used to take it all for granted . . . and now I've gone crazy about everything to do with nature. Haven't you?

Male Monologue

From *You're a Good Man, Charlie Brown* by Clark Gesner

Background: Charlie Brown is the born loser from the comic strip *Peanuts*.

Character: Charlie Brown suffers from a lack of self-confidence but has a great sense of humor.

CHARLIE BROWN: I think lunchtime is about the worst time of the day for me. Always having to sit here alone. Of course, sometimes mornings aren't so pleasant, either—waking up and wondering if anyone would really miss me if I never got out of bed. Then there's the night, too—lying there and thinking about all the stupid things I've done during the day. And all those hours in between—when I do all those stupid things. Well, lunchtime is *among* the worst times of the day for me.

Step One
Research for Background. Research the play, playwright, and characters in the monologue you select.

Step Two
Develop the Character. Imagine the activities and emotions the character experiences. Represent those emotions with appropriate posture and gestures.

Step Three
Practice. Read out loud and then memorize the lines. Read in character.

During the blocking process, the director will plan the movements and positions of the actors on stage. Because this can be a long and rather tedious process, patience and cooperation are essential.

Physical Arrangements. Even though the sets and scenery are not ready for use, the director will help the cast anticipate what the physical appearance of the sets will look like. This is especially important if the acting area is broken into different levels or has a revolving set. The physical dimensions of the stage will influence the blocking in very important ways.

The physical set will determine entrances and exits and all stage movement. Actors will need to know how the acting area will be referred to if there are variations in the traditional stage grid area.

The physical set will also become the environment in which actors convey characterization and movement with conviction. The more an actor is able to envision the physical arrangements of the stage, the better his or her actual portrayal will be.

Psychological Arrangements. While the director is blocking the action on stage, actors must be noting all the details of a scene and relating them to the character being played. Each actor will have to figure out the psychological motivation for all movement on stage. A character does not speak or move or perform any physical action without a reason for doing so. Getting to know the psychology of a character can take weeks.

Emotional Arrangements. The early preparation time for a play production can seem tedious to beginning actors who think the important business is just learning lines. Because of the long hours required for the early planning, patience and cooperation between the cast and the director are important. Actors need to remember that the time spent blocking will save time later during actual rehearsals.

Prepare for the waiting time during blocking by bringing your actor's logbook and making notations of the director's instructions. Begin taking notes about the interpretation of the play and the character you will play, as well as the relationship of your character to the others in the play. Keep yourself involved with all phases of a play production.

Blocking Details

During the course of the audition and the early blocking, you may hear many new expressions. You will want to learn the language of the blocking procedures so that you can begin to mark your script using the terms the director uses.

Blocking Terminology. The following terms are commonly used in the audition and blocking process. You should add these terms (and any others the director uses) to your logbook:

Ad lib: When an actor is asked to add lines that might be lacking in the script to enhance a particular production. This gives an actor a chance to show real creativity and understanding of his or her character and the entire play.

Aside: A line spoken on stage but directed solely to the audience, as if the other characters in the play cannot hear it.

Build: An increase in the speed or volume of voice to reach a climactic theatrical moment.

Cue: The last word or the end of an action that indicates the time for another actor to speak or act.

Drop: Dropping the volume of the last word or words of a speech.

Pick-up cue: A direction given to actors to avoid undesirable time lapses between lines or action.

Top: Delivering a line with more volume or intensity than the preceding lines.

Stage business: The actions performed by an actor on stage that involve the use of props.

Planning Stage Business. Not all time spent on stage in character involves speaking lines. To pass the time on stage in character, the actor will develop **stage business** to strengthen the personality of the character. Stage business is essential to the development of a realistic character.

The actor uses a variety of props to convey messages in character. Stage business usually involves the use of props such as:

1. Hand props—small objects that the actor can carry on stage; these might include papers or glasses on a tray.

2. Personal props—items worn or carried by the actor; these include watches, purses, briefcases, bow ties, rings, and so on.

3. Costume props—accessories that relate to the historical costume worn by the actor; these include fans, gloves, handkerchiefs, and swords.

4. Stage props——objects that relate to the physical set or scenery; these include stools, pillows, and lamps.

All of these items can enhance an actor's portrayal of a character. An actor should use props to his or her full advantage but still keep all stage business motivated, concise, and simple. Think, for example, of how you would conduct the stage business of writing a letter or drinking a cup of coffee. Use as many senses as you can to create realistic stage business.

You need to have an understanding of the purpose for any props in order to use them to your full advantage.

Summary

Immediately after a successful audition, members of the cast will spend time with the director in the early blocking of the play. The general interpretation of the play as well as the character development of each role becomes more defined through the blocking instructions. It is important to learn how the acting areas of the stage will be designated and what terminology will be used for stage direction and marking the script. In addition, actors will begin to develop stage business to enhance the role of their characters.

Auditioning for *The Wizard of Oz*

Auditioning is a skill that every actor needs to develop. An actor has only several short minutes to demonstrate his or her skills and personality. A director needs to see a special something in an actor to invite the aspiring actor for a callback and assign a role.

Think about the classic story written by L. Frank Baum, *The Wizard of Oz*. In 1903, a musical based on the book was produced at the Majestic Theatre in New York City. In this version, Dorothy and her cow, Imogene, are blown out of Kansas by a cyclone and land in the faraway land of Oz. They meet a Scarecrow, Tin Man, and Cowardly Lion as they travel to visit the Wizard who will help them get back to Kansas.

The 1903 version had 293 performances and starred Fred Stone (Scarecrow) and Dave Montgomery (Tin Man), who were a very popular musical-comedy team at the time. The roles of Dorothy, her cow, and the Cowardly Lion were minimized to spotlight the two stars.

The movie version of *The Wizard of Oz* debuted in 1939. Judy Garland starred with Ray Bolger, Bert Lahr, Jack Haley, Frank Morgan, Billie Burke, and Margaret Hamilton. The movie has become an American classic.

In 1975, an original, African-American musical, *The Wiz*, used the same story. This two-act musical ran for 1,672 performances. Stephanie Mills played Dorothy; Hinton Battle, the Scarecrow; Tiger Haynes, the Tin Man; and Ted Ross, the Lion.

1. To learn how *The Wizard of* Oz has been done in the past, find out more about one of the actors mentioned above. If possible, learn about his or her audition process and share this information with the class.

2. Watch *The Wizard of Oz* or *The Wiz* and write a "Critic's Choice" review of it. Award the production and each of the actors an appropriate number of stars.

3. Imagine that you are going to audition for the school production of *The Wizard of Oz*. Select the part you are most interested in. Prepare a one-minute monologue or reading for that part.

4. Imagine that the director of the school production of *The Wizard Of Oz* has invited all who audition to think of an alternate pet for Dorothy. This is an opportunity to be creative. Create a new role to replace Toto, Dorothy's dog.

5. Try your hand at writing a song that could be used with your school production of *The Wizard of Oz* or *The Wiz*.

6. Make a list of all the characters in *The Wizard of Oz* and indicate who you think could play each role in a new movie version.

Marking a Script

Whether an actor is preparing a script for an audition reading or to portray a character in a play, the skill of marking a script is essential. In the case of an audition, candidates will want to indicate voice emphasis, pauses, and voice volume in their scripts. In an actual play production, each actor will mark his or her script to be aware of the action of the entire play, as well as the cues and stage movement for his or her character.

Theatre Shorthand

In general, movement and location on stage are indicated through abbreviations. The stage locations and the positions and movement of actors are marked on the script. Review the abbreviations for stage location and stage movement on pages 41–54. In addition, actors can use the following symbols to prepare the script for reading:

+	slight pause	<	increase pitch
/	one second pause	>	decrease pitch
//	two second pause	→	speed up reading
///	three second pause	←	slow down reading
___	simple stress	↑	rising inflection
====	greater stress	↓	falling inflection

Use these script symbols on one of the monologues on page 165. Mark the monologue as you would want to practice it for an audition. You should copy these symbols into your logbook so you can use them often. Develop additional symbols to help you use voice and gestures effectively.

Stage Movement Symbols. Actors record all stage movements and locations in the margins of their scripts. Some of the more common notations are:

X	Cross stage	XDL	Cross downstage left
XC	Cross center stage	XDR	Cross downstage right
XR from C	Cross from right to center		
Enter UL, exit DR	Enter from upper left, exit downstage right		

Making and Using a Promptbook

Soon after the auditioning and casting, the director will begin making a promptbook that will be used and copied by the cast. This book helps everybody stay focused and keeps the production running smoothly. The promptbook will use a lot of theatre shorthand, and individual actors will add their own instructions to their own scripts.

How to Make Your Own Promptbook. When you receive a copy of the script, place the pages in a large loose-leaf notebook. Try to leave large margins around the text area for marking your cues, positions, movement, and stage business.

In addition, leave blank pages between acts and scenes so you can sketch diagrams of the acting areas, sets, and location of props. Stage groupings can also be indicated with the initials of each character.

How to Use a Promptbook. You will continue to add to your promptbook as the play production goes on. Since there are always changes in direction and interpretation, it is best to use a pencil when making marks in your promptbook. You might want to use a color code to indicate your cues, entrances, and exits.

Others, besides the director and cast, will be using a promptbook. The backstage people will also rely on the promptbook to develop lighting, costumes, props, and sound effects. The stage manager and prompter will also need copies. Keeping the promptbook up-to-date and complete will be a challenge for the entire theatre company.

Sample Prompt Page. Study the sample prompt page in Figure 9.2. Make sure you understand all the symbols and directions used. Add new symbols to your logbook. Then, take a sample script page and begin to mark your script as if you were playing one of the characters.

Summary

Actors rely on a common system for marking their scripts to read at an audition or to act in a play. When preparing a script

Figure 9.2 Example of a Promptbook from *The Three Sisters* by Anton Chekhov

X to W.S.

MASHA: ▼I am not talking about my husband. I'm used to him, but among the civilians generally there are so many people who are crude and *unfriendly*

X to desk chair — and haven't ▼any *manners.* ▲*Rudeness* upsets me and *Sit on desk chair* offends me. I suffer when I see that a man is not fine enough, gentle enough, polite. When I happen to be among the teachers, my husband's colleagues, I'm simply miserable.

Standing by sofa

VERSHININ: Yes . . . But it seems to me it's all the same whether they are civilian or military, they are equally uninteresting, at any rate in this town they are. It's all the same! If you listen to one of the local intelligentsia—civilian or military—what you hear is that he's worn out with his wife, worn out with his home, worn out with his estate, worn out with his horses . . . A Russian is quite supremely given to lofty ways in thought, but will you tell me why it is that in life he strikes so low? Why?

Taking off gloves, while Xing to window, drops gloves on chair

MASHA: ▼Why?

VERSHININ: Why is he worn out with his children, worn out with his wife? And why are the wife and the children worn out with him?

MASHA: You are not in a very good humor today.

VERSHININ: Perhaps. I haven't had any dinner today, nothing to eat since morning. ▼One of my *Pacing twice* daughters is not very well, and when my girls are ailing, I am seized with anxiety, and my conscience torments me for their having such a mother. Oh, if you'd seen her today! What a miserable wretch!

Figure 9.2 (Continued)

X to Masha ——→ We began to quarrel at seven o'clock in the morning, and at nine I slammed the door and went out. (A pause.) I never speak of it, and strangely enough I complain just to you. (Kissing her hand.) Don't be angry with me. But for you alone, I'd not have anybody—nobody . . . (A pause.)

In front of Vershinin, off UC   *X up to level, look at UR*
MASHA: ▼What a noise in the stove! ▼At home, just before Father died, it was howling in the chimney. There, just like that!

Turn to Vershinin

VERSHININ: Are you superstitious?

Stepping off level
MASHA: ▼Yes.

X to her
VERSHININ: That's strange. ▼(Kissing her hand.) You are a magnificent, wonderful woman. Magnificent, wonderful! It is dark here, but I see the sparkle of your eyes.

X to loveseat
MASHA: ▼(Moving to another chair.) It's lighter here.

Xing down with her   *By left ear*
VERSHININ: ▼I love, love, love . . .▼Love your eyes, your gestures, I see them in my dreams . . . Magnificent, wonderful woman!

Look at candle on desk ——— MASHA: (*Laughing quietly.*) When you talk to me like that, for some reason or other, I laugh, though I'm frightened.▼Don't do it again, I beg you . . . (In a low voice.) But talk, though, it's all the same to me. ——— *Lean on arm of loveseat with hand on head*

Rise, X DL ——— (Covering her face with her hands.)▼It's all the same to me.▼They're coming here—talk about something else . . .

Pick up gloves on chair

for an audition, actors will use certain symbols to indicate pauses and differences in volume and pitch of voice.

In addition to marking a script for an audition, actors will need to follow the promptbook that the director starts for the play production. This promptbook will be individualized according to the skills and interpretations of each actor.

Auditioning

1. ***Overcome Stage Fright.*** Prepare at least ten index cards, each containing a positive comment you have received about your voice, your posture, your appearance, your gestures, your acting skills, and so on. On the reverse side of each card, add the name of the person who complimented you and the occasion. When you need a boost of self-confidence, such as before an audition, review the cards and keep them with you for moral support. Remember to add to your collection of cards whenever something encouraging is said to you.

2. ***Develop a Positive Attitude.*** Make a point to say one positive thing to each person who auditions. In finding something good about each candidate's audition, you will be more aware of your own strengths. Smile often to relax your facial muscles.

3. ***Create a Portfolio.*** Imagine that you will audition for a local summer theatre group. Prepare a résumé that will represent your acting skills and experience in a professional manner. In addition to a résumé, think of other material that could represent your work. Perhaps you could make an audiocassette or videotape of your performance.

Blocking a Play

4. ***One-Act Fairy Tale or* Cinderella.** Use a diagram or scale drawing of your school stage. Make a grid to refer to the acting area of the stage. Prepare a blocking diagram for a scene in a one-act play of your choice or use the *Cinderella* scene in which the stepmother and stepsisters receive the invitation to the ball.

5. ***Stage Business for* Anne Frank *or* Charlie Brown.** Develop a hand prop and a personal prop that would be suitable for the character you choose. Work both props into stage business for the monologue you prepare.

Marking a Script

6. ***Actor and Prompter.*** Work with a partner on the monologue you prepare. One student should mark the script for pauses, pitch, and emphasis using the symbols in the text. The other should mark the script as a prompter, indicating when to use props.

7. ***On Stage/Backstage.*** Work in small groups, with each group representing an aspect of a production such as lighting, sound, props, sets and scenery, and actors. Each group should prepare a list of cues that would be helpful in making a scene go smoothly. Compile a master list of all the cues each special team wants.

8. ***Dialogue.*** Select a dialogue suitable for male and female partners. Prepare a character sketch for each role in the dialogue. Practice with your partner to develop gestures and stage business. Mark your scripts for emphasis, pause, and pitch. When you have practiced and memorized your lines, present your dialogue to the class.

The Actor's Logbook

1. ***Learning the Language.*** Add the blocking terminology to your logbook. You might want to add a section for the symbols commonly used to mark a script or to indicate stage positions and movement.

2. ***Monologues.*** Prepare a script so that you can practice a monologue with the voice pitch, emphasis, and pauses that you think best convey the emotion of your character. Make a list of ten short monologues that you could add to your portfolio. Select the monologues on the basis of variety in character development and skills required for a sensitive portrayal.

3. ***Audition Forms.*** Practice filling out a form such as the one on page 162. Add the names, addresses, and phone numbers of any teachers or other adults you would give as references in a callback. Be sure to request permission to use their names as references. Carry this information in your logbook so that you have it handy when it is requested.

4. ***Critic's Choice.*** Add your review of the movie version of *The Wizard of Oz* or *The Wiz* to your logbook. Include both positive and negative comments. Decide how you would rate the movie and identify the criteria you would use.

Critical Thinking

5. ***Main Ideas.*** Make a list of your "ten commandments" for the auditioning process. These should include the most important things to remember and do during an audition.

6. ***Comparisons.*** Compare your blocking diagram for a scene with a partner's or those in a small group. Identify the stage locations of the main characters you suggested and the stage movements required in the scene. Discuss how each of you sees the scene played and identify similarities and differences.

7. ***Choices.*** Imagine that you are the director calling for an audition for a production of *The Wizard of Oz* or *The Wiz*. Make a list of the important qualities you would want in each of your leading characters. Then prioritize your list. Identify the single most important quality you would want in the actor you select to play Dorothy, for example.

Creative Thinking

8. ***Monologues.*** Imagine that you are going to present a series of ten short monologues on stage for the children's hour at your local library. Keep your monologue selections short—no more than one or two minutes each. You can develop a simple mask as a personal prop to represent each character. Make a list of your monologues. Draw a mask for each character.

CHAPTER TEN

Production Preparation

EXPECTATIONS

After reading this chapter, you will be able to

10.1 use expressive movement to portray a stage character

10.2 demonstrate creative problem-solving strategies for stage performance

10.3 understand the interdependence of production elements

10.4 manage preparation time for a theatrical performance

10.5 practice basic safety guidelines for theatre activities

Theatre production involves a lot of people and takes organization, coordination, and team spirit. Students with a wide variety of interests and skills will find a welcome place in the theatre company and have fun learning new skills "on the job." See if one of the following theatre jobs seems most appropriate for you.

Job Descriptions for One and All

Putting on a play requires great team effort. For each actor on stage there are many people backstage whose work is essential to the performance. The director serves as the great organizer, trainer, and motivator. The production crew works with lights, sets, sounds, and props to create the environment and mood for the performance. Actors bring characters to life on stage. Without a spirit of cooperation, the theatre company cannot stretch and grow and feel the exhilaration of the stage. Everyone contributes something essential.

The Director

Even before the play production starts, the **director** has been busy. The director, who is the drama teacher in most schools, has the task of selecting the play or musical and coordinating performance dates with the school administration and other departments. Once these basic decisions have been made, the director tackles the tasks of organizing people, time, and money.

Director: The person in charge of bringing a theatrical production together by coordinating the acting, technical requirements, and business functions.

Organizing People. One of the keys to a smooth production is to prepare students to handle many of the production tasks associated with a play performance. Older, more experienced students can be encouraged to help mentor younger students in the areas of set and scenery design, lighting, costume and makeup, and prop management. Younger students can apply for the job of interns to help older student production managers with their designated responsibilities.

In addition to coordinating the work of the cast and crew, a director must keep a production on schedule and under budget.

Students might enjoy the process of applying for various production jobs just as acting candidates apply for roles on stage through the audition process. Job descriptions should be posted with clear definitions of duties. Some of these positions include the jobs of stage manager, technical director, business manager, set director, costume head, prop master, lighting director, and publicity manager. These will be described in the following section.

Organizing Time. Producing a play requires more time than is usually anticipated. Some students overextend themselves with the time commitment of play practices, homework, and part-time job responsibilities. A preliminary production schedule needs to be available to all interested students so that the investment of time can be assessed. Usually, you will have six to eight weeks for the production process. Everyone needs to make the most of available production time.

A Policy for Cuts and Tardiness. Unexpected complications affect everyone. The director should make the cut policy very clear for all students. Usually, students are allowed a specified number of excused cuts from practice and a specified number of unexcused cuts. Once the quota of cuts is used, the student will be dropped from the cast.

A simple statement of the cut and tardiness policy should be given to all in the cast and crew at the beginning of the production. Sign-in sheets can be maintained by the stage manager. If a potential problem develops, communication between director and students is essential. Cuts and tardiness can be reduced if students understand their responsibilities from the beginning and are busy and productive during practices.

Production Budgets. The director will work closely with a business manager to keep play expenses and revenues reasonable. The play selection will be influenced, in part, by its appeal to the students, parents, and local community members who will buy tickets to the performances. Large casts appeal to a wide audience.

Play expenses will include the **royalty,** if required, as well as playbooks for each of the cast. Scenery, props, costumes, makeup, and the printing of tickets and programs will also require money.

Revenues will come from the sale of tickets and advertising in the play program. Some schools have budgets for school performances, while others want productions to be self-supporting. In all cases, students can learn to participate in budgetary responsibility.

The Cast

The actors and extras who will be on stage at one time or another need a clear sense of their duties and time commitment during the production of a play. In some cases, the director will ask members of the cast to sign an agreement that specifies their responsibilities to the theatre company and the play production.

Responsibilities of Cast Members. Individual actors have a responsibility to themselves, the director, and the entire theatre

Royalty: The payment made to a playwright for permission to perform his or her play.

company to be and do their best. Students need to manage their own time well. A calendar and assignment book can help students to keep track of practices and homework assignments. A watch can help punctuality.

Students need to have a positive attitude at practices. Patience, cheerfulness, and flexibility will be appreciated and contagious. Students should not let others in the company down by being tardy or neglecting assignments.

In addition, students have a responsibility to communicate with many people. Parents must be familiar with rehearsal schedules. The director and stage manager must be kept informed about study, job, or medical complications, and the cast and crew need to know specific requests for props, cues, costumes, and prompts.

Learning Lines. Once an actor has been cast, the job of creating a character and learning lines begins. While studying the character and discovering the meaning of the lines in relationship to the theme and action of the play, the actor starts to memorize lines.

There is no set way to memorize lines. Some actors like to read their lines over and over by themselves. Others like to go over them with someone else listening and reading the lines of other characters. You will have to find the method that works best for you. Try copying your lines by hand to increase your memory. If you do this, start a promptbook for yourself. You could double-space your lines and leave wide margins for cues, marks, and prompts. You might try reading your lines into a tape recorder and playing the lines back for additional reinforcement.

The process of memorizing lines is gradual. The actors and director will talk about the various interpretations of the lines. The blocking process will also reinforce the meaning of the spoken words. Play an active role in taking notes and marking your script so that the words and meaning are emphasized appropriately.

Most directors prefer that actors learn their lines as quickly as possible. This involves intense study and concentration but has great results during rehearsals. You should aim to have your lines memorized by the third week of rehearsals. After that time, your hands will be free to work with props, and you will be able to concentrate on movement, stage business, timing, and interpretation.

While actors are busy learning their lines and blocking scenes, many other minds and hands are also at work creating the sets, costumes, props, and lighting that the play requires.

Actors use a variety of methods to learn their lines. Find the method that works best for you.

Summary

The early stages of the play production process involve many people, many tasks, and a shared sense of responsibility and enthusiasm. The director will select the play, plan the schedule, and organize teams of people to work on the production, business, and staging of the play. The cast will be busy learning the director's expectations for their time and performance. In addition, actors will begin to learn their lines so they can devote more time to the skills of movement, the use of props and stage business, and interpretation.

Production Backstage

A well-organized and motivated crew is the backbone of every theatre company. This group supports all the people on stage and helps them to look and do their best. The crew's work is essential to the theatre experience. Consider each of the following job descriptions and you may find one that suits your own talents and interests.

Major Managers

The following briefly describes the tasks expected of the technical director and the stage manager. These people provide

Developing a group sense of responsibility for a performance is not an easy task. Imagine that you have just been selected as a cast or crew member for the school play. The director has just called the first production meeting and invited the entire company to come up with the guidelines that everyone will follow during the course of the production schedule. A great opportunity! You will work in small groups to develop your own theatre company codes of conduct.

Step One

Clarify Goals. In your small group, each individual should identify what he or she wants to get out of this theatre experience. As a group, write a short paragraph that describes your common goals. All groups should share their statement of goals. As a class, combine all the good ideas and draft a company theatre mission statement.

Step Two

Ten Guidelines. In your small group, draft a list of ten rules and regulations that you think the entire company should follow to achieve the goals you identified earlier. Arrive at a consensus within your group so that everyone is able to agree to the list. All groups should share their guidelines and note similarities. As a class, draw up a list of ten rules and regulations that the entire theatre company should accept as a code of conduct.

Step Three

Crimes and Punishments. Despite the best intentions, there will always be violations of rules and regulations. In a small group, decide on what the group will accept as appropriate "punishments" for each of your ten guidelines. Share your ideas with the class. Arrive at a consensus about how to treat violations of the rules.

Step Four

Communicate. Each individual in the theatre company should have a copy of the mission statement, ten rules, and policy for punishment. Discuss who else would need to know about your code of conduct. Teachers, school administration, coaches, parents, and employers might also need to know the expectations.

Step Five

Review. At the end of each week's production schedule, you might spend some time reviewing how well your code of conduct is working for the entire company. As a group, you might decide on procedures to change your existing code if most of you thought there was a need to modify it. You might also think of additional things to include. You might be called on to deal with extraordinary situations. Weekly reviews are good. Make a blue ribbon or certificate of appreciation to give to the member of the company who made the best effort that week.

key support for the director and require special skills for the various responsibilities they have. Their specific activities are identified, as well as some of the more elusive personality characteristics that would suit those who are selected for these jobs.

Technical Director. The **technical director** works with the director to coordinate the activities of many support people. Study the "Organizational Chart" and make a note of all the backstage people your school commonly uses. Make a list of the titles your director or school uses for the various functions that are identified.

The responsibilities of the technical director include:

1. Supervision of lighting, sound, and set construction materials and crew

2. Management of set and scene construction

3. Communication of problems and possible solutions to the director

4. Coordination of lighting and sound activities to enhance sets, movement, and acting

The director wants a lot in the technical director. Desirable qualities include solid problem-solving skills and the ability to work well with students who have different levels of skill at sound, lighting, and carpentry.

Stage Manager. The **stage manager** is the director's primary helper. His or her numerous responsibilities include:

1. General supervision of cast and crew backstage and management of all backstage activities for a production and performances

2. Scheduling for rehearsals and preparation of scenes and actors for rehearsals

3. Preparation of a promptbook that includes blocking information, cues, set changes, and lighting and sound cues

Technical director: The person responsible for overseeing design and production of the set, the lighting, and the sound and the people who work on those facets of a production.

Stage manager: The person responsible for overseeing all the backstage elements of a production.

Among the stage manager's many responsibilities is preparing a prompt-book containing all blocking information, acting cues, set changes, and lighting and sound cues.

Set designer: *The person responsible for overseeing the design, construction, and storage of sets and scenery.*

Strike: *To dismantle the set after a play and store elements for future use.*

4. Communication of information and record-keeping for attendance, cues, and prompts

5. Arrangement for props, entrances, curtain, and sound cues during performances

The stage manager needs to be well-organized, flexible, and conscientious, with good people skills and the ability to work well under pressure. Problem-solving skills are a major asset in a stage manager, as is freedom from other major time commitments, such as sports or a part-time job.

The stage manager can make or break the morale of the cast and crew. Think about the qualities you would like to see in the stage manager for your school play. Who would you nominate for this top job?

Supporting Managers and Crews

The technical director and the stage manager direct the activities of many other managers and their crews. All of the following play key roles in the backstage production of any play.

Set Designer. The **set designer** plans all sets and scenery for the production to promote the interpretation and mood of the play as the director envisions it. Responsibilities include:

1. Supervision of set design and construction, painting, and installation

2. Scheduling of construction and set-up for the first technical rehearsal

3. Maintenance of tools, safety, and clean-up throughout production process

4. Supervision of the **strike** after the show

5. Keeping records of all expenses, tools, and purchases

The qualities a director looks for in a set designer include skills in organization, carpentry, training, and time management. The set designer works closely with the director to understand the concept of the play and how the sets and scenery will be used on stage. Training others to construct parts of the set or acquire props is a major activity of the set designer, in addition to the requisite imagination and creativity.

Prop Manager. The **prop manager** has many responsibilities, including:

Prop manager: The person responsible for overseeing the acquisition, repair, and storage of stage props.

1. Acquisition of necessary props
2. Repair and storage of props for timely use on stage
3. Development of system to identify, store, and locate props for each scene
4. Organization of crew for set-up and strike of furniture and props during performances

The prop manager needs a good eye for detail and the ability to organize people and things. Imagination is also a plus. This person needs the ability to see the potential that ordinary things have to become useful in various scenes in the play.

Lighting Designer and Crew. The lighting designer interacts often with the director, set designer, and technical director. Responsibilities include:

Lighting designer: The person responsible for overseeing the design and operation of the lighting for a production.

1. Creation of light plots, gels, and focus of lighting equipment
2. Supervision of the operation of lights during rehearsals and production
3. Coordination of team to clean, check, and operate lights safely and effectively
4. Preparation of lighting prompt book with warnings and cues

Due to the technical nature of this job and the complexity of school equipment, the lighting director will work closely with school engineers and those with electrical training to insure safety throughout the production. Students on the lighting crew should be able to work well with technically trained professionals and faculty.

Sound designer:
The person responsible
for overseeing the
design and operation
of sound equipment for
a production.

Costume designer:
The person responsible
for overseeing the
design, acquisition,
creation, and storage
of costumes for a
production.

Makeup designer:
The person responsible
for overseeing the
design, application, and
clean-up of makeup for
a production.

Sound Designer and Crew. The **sound designer's** responsibilities include:

1. Creation of appropriate sound effects for the play
2. Supervision of amplification equipment, security systems, and safety procedures

The sound designer will know the qualities of the sound equipment available for the performance and make accurate judgments about amplification based on the size of the theatre and the vision of the director. Since sound equipment is expensive, security will be a major concern for the sound designer and the sound crew.

Costume Designer. The **costume designer** has many responsibilities, including:

1. Organization of costume chart to track the number and type of costumes each actor requires
2. Creation or acquisition of all costumes used in the play based on research and the director's vision of the play
3. Supervision of crew to assist actors at getting into costumes during performances
4. Record-keeping of measurements, expenses, and costume materials
5. Storage of costumes during and after performances

The costume designer will combine good design skills with the ability to sew from patterns. The choice of color and fabric to create the special "look" of each costume will be important, as well as coordinating colors from a color palette that compliments the sets and scenery. Crew members are often assigned to manage the wardrobe of specific actors.

Makeup Designer and Crew. The **makeup designer** encourages an actor's success by helping him or her achieve the "right" appearance. Responsibilities include:

1. Creation of makeup plans for each character in the play as suitable for the play's mood and blocking requirements
2. Coordination of makeup supplies, inventory, and clean-up procedures
3. Supervision and training of makeup crew

The makeup designer will help the crew practice the application of certain facial characteristics through makeup and implement secure and healthy practices in the storage of all makeup. The director will look for students with creativity and a sense of responsibility for this job.

Publicity Manager and Staff. The **publicity manager** promotes the play in many areas including:

1. Promotion of the play through press releases and media campaigns to draw audiences
2. Supervision of advertising campaign for play sponsorship and the play program
3. Creation of a poster and flyer campaign to advertise the play
4. Ticket and program preparation
5. House management of ushers, box office sales, and ticket collectors

The publicity manager needs a pleasant, yet aggressive personality to market the image of the play and promote the show. The publicity manager will need good contacts with the local business community as well as supportive parents. Business and people skills will be key qualities in developing a good publicity staff.

Publicity manager:
The person responsible for overseeing a production's promotion; the preparation of tickets and the program; and the training of ushers, box office workers, and ticket collectors.

Summary

A play requires the talents and skills of many people who work with the director backstage to coordinate the technical and managerial aspects of play production. Key assistants to the director are the technical director and the stage manager. The technical director supervises set construction, lighting, and sound for the production. The stage manager coordinates the schedules and preparation of the actors. In addition, the need for props, costumes, makeup, and publicity provides many opportunities for interested students to learn theatre skills and participate in the production process.

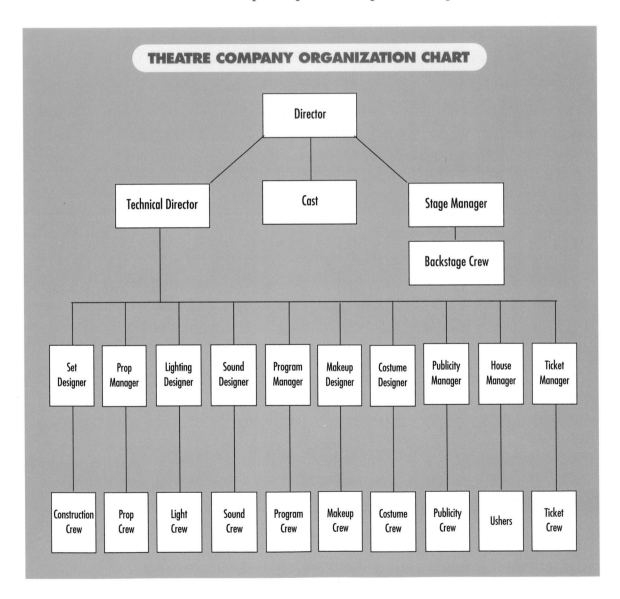

THEATRE COMPANY ORGANIZATION CHART

Awards for Technical Excellence

When you watch the Academy Awards or the Tony Awards, you are well aware that the best actors will be recognized for their outstanding performances. In addition to the awards and recognition for best actors, most professional performing groups also recognize excellence in technical fields.

Recently, the film *Jurassic Park* won Academy Awards for best sound and best visual effects. In the same year, 1993, *Mrs. Doubtfire* won the Academy Award for best makeup. Certainly, the excellence of technical achievement in those movies contributed to audience appreciation. Select one of the technical areas involved in a movie or theatre production. You could choose lighting, sound, costumes, makeup, or visual effects.

Once you have selected a technical area, complete the following:

1. Research and list for the past five years the Academy or Tony Award winners, identifying title and name of director in that area.

2. Identify five qualities that would be involved to achieve technical excellence in the area you selected.

3. Review your list of the past winners and select the one you think best represents excellence according to the criteria you identified.

4. Think of a way to demonstrate to the class that your choice represents the best technical achievement in your area. You might want to put together film clips or sound bites to demonstrate sound, lighting, or makeup. You might try to write the winner and arrange an "interview" that you tape or report on. Display or present your work for the class.

5. Hold your own technical awards night. Each of you should be prepared to nominate the best movie, play, or television program in the area of your choice. The class could designate a panel of critics or judges to determine which nominee is the winner.

Theatre Safety

Play production is a busy and chaotic time. Actors and director are blocking and rehearsing on stage. And backstage is a bee-hive of activity. In the midst of all the activity, tools, sound, and lighting equipment emerge from nooks and crannies and can create confusion and safety hazards.

A successful production relies on everybody keeping safe and healthy. Safety is everybody's responsibility.

Safety Requirements

Actors and crew members can find themselves in the midst of potentially dangerous power tools, protruding nails, paints and solvents, and a tangle of wires. Breaking a leg is not something anyone really wants to do! Consider the following guidelines for the safe and efficient use of tools and heavy equipment.

General Safety Guidelines. The director will conduct a preliminary meeting and explain to all the cast and crew the basic safety and code requirements for a safe and healthy stage production. Everyone involved in the theatre company should know the following:

1. Location of well-stocked first aid box
2. Location and operation of fire extinguishers and fire alarms
3. Location of smoke detectors, fire doors or curtains, and sprinkler systems
4. Location of emergency exits
5. School and production company smoking policy
6. Emergency phone numbers for police, fire, or medical assistance, as well as the location of a current list of emergency phone numbers for each member of the company
7. Everyone is responsible for the safety of each other

Power Tools and Safety Guidelines. Power tools are just that— very powerful; they require skill and practice for safe use. Sometimes, students think they know how to use power tools without being properly instructed. Oftentimes, tasks involving power tools look easier than they are to those who are un- trained. The use of power tools requires adult supervision.

Consider the following to ensure safety:

1. Always wear safety goggles, and consider ear plugs if the tool is noisy.

2. Always wear enclosed shoes (never sandals or bare feet) during production.

3. Do not wear fringe, loose-fitting sleeves, or dangling jewelry when operating power tools.

4. Read the directions and follow adult supervision.

5. Do not use extension cords with power tools.

6. Turn off the tool before you set it down and pick it up before you turn it on.

7. Beware of water, wet hands, or moisture when using power tools.

8. Clean up after yourself. Return tools to their proper storage area when finished with use.

9. Check equipment to make sure it is in good operating condition.

10. Know wattage of equipment before plugging it in so as not to blow fuses.

Set Construction Safety. While they may seem like just plain common sense, the following regulations for carpentry and set construction are important to review:

1. Sand all wood cuts carefully to eliminate splinters.

2. Nails and bolts should never protrude from a surface. Keep these swept off the floor.

3. Ventilate all areas when using paint or chemicals and wear a mask.

Practice safety precautions throughout play production to help maintain a hazard-free environment.

4. All sets, furniture, and props should be checked for sturdiness. Reject flimsy construction and sloppy work.

5. When covering flats, cloth should be preshrunk and fireproofed before painting on it.

6. Do not work if sleepy. Stay alert at all times.

Healthy Minds and Bodies

The additional work and stresses of play production can often contribute to colds or even minor accidents. Directors do not want actors or crew members to get sick or injured before a performance. Your responsibility to the theatre company includes staying healthy.

A Prepared Mind. Some people handle stress better than others. Play production involves frustration, problems, and deadlines. These can be a source of stress to those who are unprepared.

Try to imagine the best possible attitude you could have in the midst of delays, complaints, and problems. Visualize how to cope with stress with patience, good humor, and a spirit of cooperation. Then make it happen.

In the course of a play production, avoid those people who have a negative attitude or who complain about all the glitches that are bound to happen. It's better to associate with those who seem to cope well with the demands of play production and learn from them in the hopes that some of their patience will be contagious.

Diet, Rest, and Relaxation. The hours of practice and rehearsals often interrupt regular eating habits. Junk foods, jolts of caffeine, and sugar only jangle nerves and increase irritability. Actors and crew will find they work better, stay more alert, and are more creative when snacking on fruits and vegetables than on candy bars and potato chips. Good health is a prerequisite for performance. Maintaining your health is your personal responsibility.

Learn to take a mental or physical break regularly when working on play production. The breaks can be really simple—like yawning several times or taking a short walk by yourself down a corridor. Or bring a favorite tape and enjoy a music break when you can. Some will find that physical activity, like stretching exercises, can be a good defense against anxiety or stage fright.

The more relaxed you are, the better you can be and do. Swap relaxation techniques with another member of the cast or crew. In that way, you can add to your own collection of techniques.

Summary

Without theatre safety, there would be no performance. The director will emphasize that everyone has the responsibility of ensuring the safety of all when using power tools and constructing sets or working with technical equipment. In addition, each individual has the responsibility of maintaining personal health during the production process to give the best effort and performance possible.

Jobs To Be Had

1. **Stage Managers.** Your teacher can randomly assign some students, or ask for volunteers, to role-play the stage manager position. The scene is the first production meeting where the director introduces the stage manager to the company and the stage manager has three minutes to describe the company spirit and identify realistic expectations for the cast and crew. After the role-playing, discuss the qualities that a stage manager needs to make the production run smoothly.

2. **Apprentices.** Technical professions sometimes train young workers as apprentices to learn specific technical skills. Other professions train people as interns to give them some experience in the workforce. To get practice applying as an apprentice or as an intern, imagine that you are applying for a position as a carpenter, electrician, sound technician, dancer, or marketing assistant. Draft a letter requesting an interview or an audition. Be sure to emphasize your interest, training, and experience.

3. **Budgets.** Work in a small group that represents either set construction, lighting, costumes, or publicity. Make a list of all the expenses you think this aspect of play production would incur for producing a class play. Share your projected expenses with the entire class. Make a pie chart to represent each group's relative expenses. Then imagine that each group must reduce costs by 20 percent. In your small group, figure out your cuts.

More Backstage

4. **What's Your Color?** Everybody thinks they look good in certain colors more than others. Using a box of crayons or assorted sheets of construction paper, select the five colors you think you look best in. Then select five colors you think would work well for a partner. Share your color choices for yourselves and each other.

5 **First Aid Kits.** Imagine that an explosion just occurred backstage. You are the first to reach the first aid kit. Make a list of the ten most important items you want to find in that kit.

6. **Tardy Policy.** In a small group, discuss what you would do with a cast member who comes late to three out of five practices and keeps the rest of the cast waiting because of his or her absence. The tardy cast member is a good actor, in fact one of the stars of the show. Everybody knows that the actor has a complicated family situation and is frequently called on for family child-care responsibilities. Develop at least three options for handling this situation and share your ideas with the class.

Critic's Choice

7. **Costumes.** Stretch your imagination and design a costume for a production of *Beauty and the Beast.* Select either Belle or the Beast and research costumes used in past performances. Then be creative and draw a costume for either. Go a step further and design a makeup plot for the Beast.

The Actor's Logbook

1. ***Learning the Language.*** Technical terms can be the most confusing of all. Add at least five terms to your logbook connected with electricity, carpentry, or sound.

2. ***Technical Supplies.*** Use your local phone book as a resource to identify some of the sources for the supplies needed for set construction, costumes, and makeup. Do a phone comparison of costs for a required product. Then record the names, addresses, and phone numbers of those sources that you would want to deal with.

3. ***Communications.*** Make a list of the names and phone numbers you would need for a play production. Be sure to include this information for the director, stage manager, technical director, set designer, costume designer, and makeup crew member you would be working with.

4. ***Safety First.*** Record what you consider to be the ten most important safety regulations for your theatre company.

5. ***Letter of Agreement.*** Imagine that you have been selected for one of the backstage positions to assist the director. You have been asked to draw up a list of you responsibilities and to sign an agreement stating that you will perform your duties to the best of your ability under the supervision of the director. Draft that agreement.

Critical Thinking

6. ***Main Ideas.*** Based on the responsibilities identified in this chapter, prepare an agenda for the first meeting the director would have with the stage manager and the production crew.

7. ***Comparisons.*** Develop a list of similarities shared by all the winners of a technical achievement award, such as the costume designers for the Academy Awards. Then think of qualities that would make costume designers unique.

8. ***Safety.*** Conduct a poll in the theatre company about the most reasonable and the most absurd safety regulations that accompany power tool instructions. Discuss the liability manufacturers of power tools should have toward irresponsible users of such equipment.

Creative Thinking

9. ***Time Management.*** Everybody has the same 24 hours in every day. Still some people seem to get more done than others. Make a schedule for yourself to get the most out of the next 24 hours.

10. ***Inexpensive Costumes.*** Imagine that the director has given you a budget of $100 to put together all the costumes for your school production of *Cinderella*. Make a list of the costumes you will need and the costs of materials to make or acquire them.

CHAPTER ELEVEN

Behind the Scenes

EXPECTATIONS

After reading this chapter, you will be able to

11.1 use space creatively in relation to sets, scenery, lighting, and sound

11.2 explore play production in terms of set construction, lighting, and sound

11.3 read diagrams for set construction, sound, and lighting design

11.4 participate in individual and group theatre experiences

11.5 sketch and create simple designs for stage sets and scenery

11.6 plan lighting for a one-act play

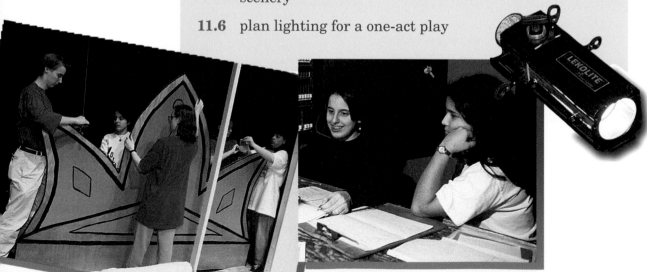

**S**tagecraft is the art and skill of transforming a limited performing space to create an environment suitable for the vision and mood of a specific play through the imaginative use of sets, lighting, and sound. What starts as an idea in a designer's imagination becomes reality through hard work and technical skills in stagecraft. Learn how sets, lighting, and sound enhance an actor's performance and the total experience of theatre.

Sets and Scenery on Stage

Some plays are performed with elaborate sets to create the atmosphere of the time and place, while other stages convey the setting using a few simple props. In either case, the stage is set, like a table, to prepare the audience for the action on stage. Actors need to learn to use the set to portray their characters effectively.

Stage Sets

The **set** is the first thing the audience sees when the curtain goes up on a performance. The set provides the physical environment in which the play takes place. The set defines the play's time, place, and mood.

The stage set also suggests something about the characters in the play and their relationships. The set provides clues about the ages of the characters and their wealth and lifestyles. The colors used will also create a mood or atmosphere for the play. There are many kinds of sets used for plays. Each has advantages and disadvantages.

Set: A physical backdrop constructed for a play that is designed to convey key elements of time, place, and mood.

Curtain Sets. Some schools have a curtain backdrop against the upstage area. This curtain is called a **cyclorama,** or cyc. A cyclorama can be used quite effectively in a couple of ways. If the backdrop is black, the stage area can be spotlighted with

Cyclorama: The background curtain that covers the back of the stage and the sides. Also referred to as cyc.

The set is the first thing an audience sees when the curtain goes up. A good set conveys much information about a play's time, place, and mood.

controlled lighting to focus audience attention on specific areas. The lighting can also change a play's mood with color variations.

Another way of using a curtain set is to create simple, free-standing set pieces to change the scene or atmosphere. These set pieces can be easily moved or changed according to the scene requirements.

Box set: A common set constructed to represent the walls of a room in which stage action is taking place.

Box Set. Using a **box set** is a common technique for creating a stage environment. The set is constructed to convey a realistic setting for the play. The box set usually has three sides and a ceiling. Doors, windows, stairs, and fireplaces are represented quite realistically for actors to use in their stage movements.

When a box set is used, the play is probably being presented as a realistic portrayal of a specific time and place. You might want to sketch a box set design to represent the realistic environment of the interior of the cottage of Cinderella and her stepfamily.

A door upstage center is usually best for an actor's entrance, but a side door is best for exits. The cottage for Cinderella needs one door. Think about the best place to locate the door in the set you draw.

Think about how you would divide a box set to represent the family room area with a table and chairs and the kitchen area. You would want to keep the two areas balanced but not of equal size. Consider the placement of windows and an interior doorway between the two rooms. Think too about how you could represent the environment of the prince's castle on stage.

Screen Sets. Often a screen, or **flat,** can be used with a cyc to develop the stage environment in greater detail. A flat consists of a wooden frame that is covered with canvas or muslin. The material covering the flat can then be painted to represent an outdoor scene, furniture, or whatever else the play calls for.

Flat: A common unit of stage scenery made from a wooden frame covered with cloth that can be painted.

Set Designer. The set designer is responsible for the design of all the sets and scenery used in a play. The set designer works closely with the technical director to create the proper atmosphere for the play and to use limited resources effectively. The set designer must also make sure that the stage area is ready for rehearsals according to the production schedule.

The construction of sets can be a complicated affair. It requires carpentry skills, artistic talent, and technical support. If electrical outlets or special effects are used during the production, these must be worked out with the set designer.

The design and construction of sets is a "behind the scenes" job. All the work and thought that goes into setting the stage influences how the actors will perform. The actors need to learn to feel comfortable in the environment created on stage.

Stage Scenery

Each **scene** in a play builds to the climax or resolution of action. Scenes will vary according to the shifts of time and place in the action of the play. The trouble is that while places may change within the play, the stage stays where it is. One of the challenges of the theatre then is to convey the shifts in

Scene: A small segment of a play, usually containing one central idea or line of action.

time and place occurring within the play easily and effectively on stage.

Shifts in Place. Think about the wonderful story *The Wizard of Oz*. The action of the play takes place in two very different locations—Kansas and the land of Oz. And within the different locations, there are different scenes. In the land of Oz, there are scenes in the field with the yellow brick road, the land of the Munchkins, and the Emerald City.

Shifts in Time. Stages often need to reflect changes in time. And if times change on stage, the actors will sometimes need to "age" on stage as well. Think about the story of Rip Van Winkle, the early American who took a nap and woke up twenty years later to find everything changed.

Fantasy Scenes. Sometimes a scene calls for a memory, dream, or flashback. These fantasy scenes require imagination for the set design and challenge an actor's skills. The audience needs to find the fantasy or dream scene believable in some way. Many plays contain dream or fantasy scenes. *The Wizard of Oz* is basically an entire dream. Think about how the movie version of *The Wizard of Oz* made the transition from the real world of Kansas to the dream world of Oz. You can think about other examples of how movies or plays create imaginative scenes for the audience.

Summary

The stage environment is both a physical place as well as a place for the imagination. Actors need to know their way around the acting area and stage. They also need to use the environment created by the stage sets and scenery to make their character feel at home. Stages can be transformed with the use of curtain and box sets as well as constructed flats. In addition, the scenery used for a play may need to represent shifts in time and place, and actors will need to show those changes in their movements as well.

Returning to *Cinderella*, let's put together a simple set for a class performance.

Step One

Set Design. Basically, the story of Cinderella uses two sets: one for Cinderella's home, especially the kitchen, and one for the prince's castle. Think of a simple way to suggest these two scenes using a simple flat, such as the one shown below. One side can suggest Cinderella's kitchen; the other side, the prince's palace. Sketch several representations. Consult with a partner or small group and ask about their preferences and suggestions.

Step Two

Scale Model. Once you have selected your best set design, draw a scale model of the set, keeping an eye on the diagram below. Study the diagram. The frame of

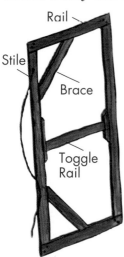

Rail

Stile

Brace

Toggle Rail

the flat consists of two vertical lengths of wood known as *stiles* and two horizontal lengths of wood called *rails*. A support is placed at the corners at 45 degrees to keep the flat from warping. This flat is then covered with canvas.

Step Three

Set Construction. If you can get an adult to help with the carpentry, construct a flat according to the dimensions of your scale model. If no adult is available to direct actual set construction, use alternate materials for your set. These materials could include a solid-colored bedsheet draped over the classroom door or posterboard taped to a door or corner of the classroom.

Step Four

Paint the Scene. Stretch prewashed canvas over the flat and staple it to the frame. You could make the flat reversible so that one side could depict Cinderella's cottage and the other side the castle. Return to your set design. Plan the colors and images used on the flat carefully. Consider how to use texture to enhance your set. Draw your scenery on your flat, sheet, or posterboard and paint carefully.

Step Five

Add Props. Consider the addition of a single prop to enhance each scene. One prop could be a stool or broom for Cinderella's scene. Another could be a fancy chair for a throne for the prince. Use your imagination and select your single prop with care. With your flat to set the scene, enjoy your classroom presentation of *Cinderella*.

Lighting Design

Stage lighting complements the sets, costumes, and props. Without it, much of the theatre experience would be lost for the audience. Lighting the stage area calls for two important skills: the first is design, the second involves the effective use of equipment.

Design Skills

Although lighting equipment is both complex and expensive, the principles that guide its use are quite simple. Stage lighting should:

1. enhance visibility
2. increase realism
3. highlight costumes, makeup, and scenery
4. contribute to the composition and design of the stage environment

These principles are presented to the audience through the position and use of special stage lights, the use of dimmers, the use of colors, and the shape and position of beams of light.

Use of Color. Color has many psychological moods. Usually light, bright colors are associated with comedy. Dark colors suggest tragedy. Pantomime is performed with bold direct light, while soft and more subtle light can heighten drama. Musicals require bright and colorful lighting. The choice of colors and intensity will be influenced in large part by the type and mood of the play being presented.

White light is used in pantomimes and musicals and to flood a large background like a cyclorama. White light is made of the three primary colors—red, green, and blue (see Figure 11.1). These are strong colors and may change how things look on a small stage. For instance, a red costume lit by red light turns a dark red on stage. But green and blue lit by red turn black. If the red costume is lit by blue light, it will turn purple. You can imagine how simply changing the color of the lights will change the whole impression of the costume and scenery.

Figure 11.1 The Primary Colors of Light **205**

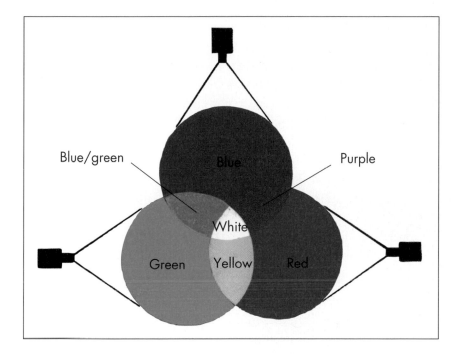

Special Effects. Rain, snow, water, moonlight, and dreams can all be suggested on stage through the simple use of lights. One of the most common ways to create special effects with lighting is to use **gels.**

Warm sunlight can be created on stage by inserting an amber gel; moonlight falls with a blue gel. Colors can also be combined by using several gels. In addition, a frost gel will diffuse and soften a beam of light on stage. In addition, a **gobo** can be cut from the gel to form a pattern that is projected on stage.

Using a painted gauze **scrim** on stage creates another lighting effect. Painted gauze when lit from the front will appear solid. When lit from behind, the gauze becomes transparent. The gauze can also be hung in front of a solid flat to give it texture and depth.

Lighting Equipment and Terms

Lighting equipment is both expensive and dangerous. All equipment needs to be checked so that it operates safely and

Gel: A very thin sheet of gelatin available in a wide range of colors that can be cut and set in front of a light to color the beam directed on stage.

Gobo: A lighting material into which a pattern such as branches or stars is cut; the pattern in inserted over a lens and the image is projected on stag; also called a cookie.

Scrim: A gauze screen that creates a variety of effects on stage when combined with light.

is properly installed and secured. The lighting designer and crew will need special instructions about fire regulations and safe working procedures. The electricity should be disconnected when lights are being set up. Cables need to be fastened and never left coiled because they generate heat.

Every school and theatre has basic lighting equipment, but the quality and quantity can vary significantly. It is important to know what is available for your use and how to use it properly.

Lighting Terms. The following are terms commonly used when using lights for the stage:

Backlighting: The use of lights above and behind performers to accent or isolate them from the background.

Border lights: A strip of lights hung from pipes above the stage.

Color frame: A metal holder that fits into a light to keep the filter or gel in place.

Fill light: Secondary light that fills in shadows created by the key light.

Floodlight: High wattage (500 to 1500 watts) instrument with the inner surface painted white or mirrored or made of polished metal used to enhance visibility. These lights have no lens.

Key light: Strong light aimed at the acting area.

Light cues: Technician's guide to all light readings and settings for acts, scenes, and all changes in lighting.

Spotlight: Lighting instrument that can be focused with lens and mirror and that has a wattage of 250 to 1500.

Wattage: The measure of electric power given to all lamps, dimmers, and fuses to identify their capacity

Types of Lanterns. Spotlights are used to create two different types of spots; one is hard-edged, the other is soft. The profile spot creates a hard edge and is usually the main source of light on a stage. Shutters can change the size and intensity of

Figure 11.2 Types of Lanterns **207**

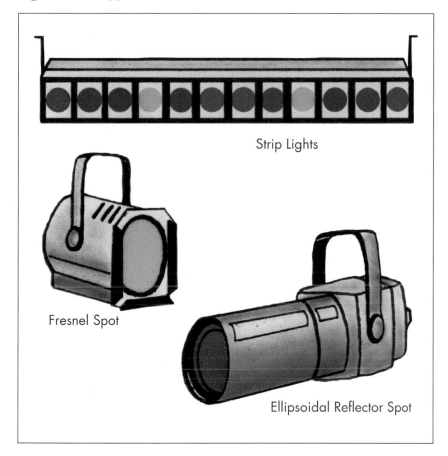

Strip Lights

Fresnel Spot

Ellipsoidal Reflector Spot

the light beam on stage. Gobos and gels can also be inserted in the profile spotlight. The Fresnel spotlight casts a diffused, soft-edged light. It produces less light than the profile, but it can illuminate larger areas on stage. (See Figure 11.2.)

Various types of lanterns can be positioned to light the upstage and the backstage areas. These are connected to the main source of electricity and controlled through a switchboard or dimmer. The best location for the switchboard on stage is on the side where the prompter is located. In that way, the prompter can also help with the lighting cue sheet.

The ellipsoidal reflector spotlight is another type of spotlight and is sometimes called a Leko light. It contains both a lens and a reflector. This type of light is used for long beams and can be focused with great precision. The beam is strong and is capable of both hard- and soft-edged light. These are usually positioned in the balcony or hung from the ceiling of the theatre.

Border Lights. In addition to the use of various lanterns, strip lights or border lights will also enhance the lighting and mood on stage. These border lights are hung from chains above the front stage curtain. Usually there are six or eight light compartments, and each has a reflector. Most schools have several border strips, and they are used to focus on lighting the upstage and backstage areas.

Figure 11.3 Light Plot

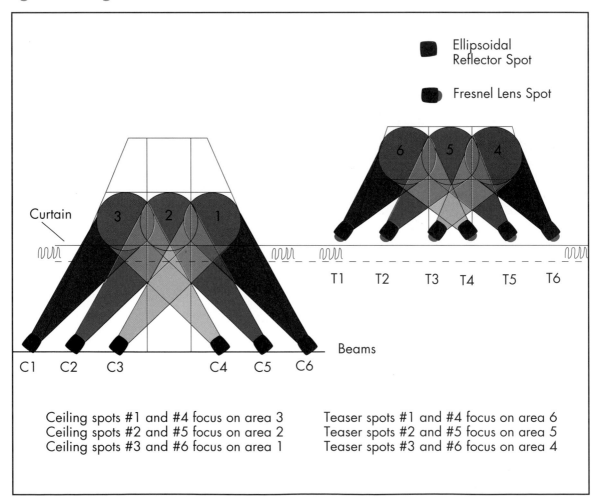

Ceiling spots #1 and #4 focus on area 3
Ceiling spots #2 and #5 focus on area 2
Ceiling spots #3 and #6 focus on area 1

Teaser spots #1 and #4 focus on area 6
Teaser spots #2 and #5 focus on area 5
Teaser spots #3 and #6 focus on area 4

Lighting Plots and Charts. Working with the director and the light designer, the lighting technician makes a **light plot.** This light plot will be used by the light crew to review the script and plan for the effective use of lights to enhance the play. (See the partial light plot in Figure 11.3.) In addition, the light director will work closely with the costume designer and prop manager to emphasize colors and accent the properties on stage.

In addition to the light plot, the light designer and crew will make a chart to number and identify important information about each of the lights available for use in a play production. (See Figure 11.4.) Then, with the light plot and chart in hand, the light cue sheet can be developed.

Light plot: A detailed plan that shows the acting area, location of light instruments, and the angles of beams of light from each instrument.

Figure 11.4 Light Chart

Instrument Schedule				
Number	Instrument Type	Wattage	Color	Dimmer
T1	Fresnel	500	#4 Pink	A4
T2	Fresnel	500	#4 Pink	A7
T3	Fresnel	500	#4 Pink	A5
T4	Fresnel	500	#17 Blue	A3
T5	Fresnel	500	#17 Blue	A2
T6	Fresnel	500	#17 Blue	A1
C1	Ellipsoidal Spot	1,000	Frost	B1
C2	Ellipsoidal Spot	1,000	Frost	B2
C3	Ellipsoidal Spot	1,000	Frost	B3
C4	Ellipsoidal Spot	1,000	Frost	B4

Summary

The use of lights can be one of the most impressive aspects of stage design. Through the understanding and application of basic light design principles, the stage can be transformed to suit the action and mood of the play. Skillful and safe use of equipment is essential to play production.

Sound Design

Sound is another essential part of theatre. An audience will quickly become annoyed if they cannot hear the actors well or if the sound equipment is faulty and conveys static or "ringing" sounds. An audience takes proper diction and adequate sound equipment for granted. But the performance of theatre is greatly enhanced through memorable sound effects, music, and, in the case of musical productions, wonderful songs and musical accompaniment.

The Role of Sound in Theatre

Theatre is both a visual and an audio experience. If you were to listen to a recording of a play or an old radio drama, you would understand the action through the spoken words. You would appreciate the role of sound effects and the ability of well-selected music to influence the mood and imagination of the listener.

Radio Theatre. You may find it hard to think about a world without television, but many people remember radio as a popular form of entertainment. While radio programs still enjoy great popularity today, these programs emphasize news, music, and information. The days of radio drama and programs like *Fibber McGee and Molly* or *The Green Hornet* are gone. Still, the influence of signature music, such the *William Tell* overture for the *Lone Ranger* series, and wonderful sound effects, such as clutter falling from McGee's crowded closet, continue to influence the experience of drama.

Critic's Choice

Lighting Effects for Drama

The theatre critic is much more aware than most audience members of the effect of lighting on the overall experience of a play. The imagination that a designer brings to the light equipment can produce spectacular results.

Look at the diagram below of the effects of lighting on an actor's face. Imagine that you are the light designer for a production of *Cinderella*. For each of the following scenes involving the prince, choose the light position, equipment, and color gel you would use to increase dramatic effects:

1. Prince introduced to the stepmother
2. Prince first sees Cinderella at the ball
3. Prince watches Cinderella dash off
4. Prince watches stepsister try on slipper
5. Prince greets Cinderella at wedding

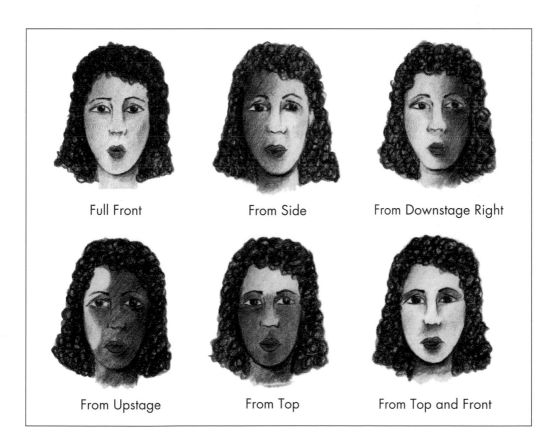

Full Front   From Side   From Downstage Right

From Upstage   From Top   From Top and Front

Sound Effects. In many cases, certain sound effects become cues for actors to enter, exit, or speak lines. In addition, sound effects are often cues for the lighting to change. These special sounds that enhance the mood or action of the play can be created live offstage or recorded on tape. In either case, timing and clarity are essential. Some "home-made" sounds do not reproduce accurately on tape, but commercial sound effect tapes are available. In some plays, recordings will be made for an offstage voice, such as the voice of God, or thoughts or memories expressed on stage.

Some sound effects can be created rather easily for the stage. The sound of thunder can be made with what is known as a thunder sheet. This sheet—a free-swinging piece of heavy sheet metal (about two feet by six feet) that is hung from a rope—will produce the sound of thunder when shaken. The sound of rain can be made by rolling dried peas across a screen frame.

The old cowboy radio programs used a simple device to create the sound of horses' hoof beats. The empty half shells of coconuts sound like horses' hooves when clapped against each other. You could practice the various gaits of a horse by watching a film of a horse walking, trotting, and running and matching the rhythm of its movement with the clapping sounds of the shells.

If you need the sound of breaking dishes, you do not want to rely on breaking something on stage. Instead, try using two metal buckets or wastebaskets offstage. In one, place some broken glass; leave the other empty. On cue, pour the broken glass from one metal container into the other.

You can have a great deal of fun identifying the sounds that might accompany any play and then imagining how to reproduce those sound effects quickly and easily to enhance your play.

Musical Effects. Music is commonly used to set the mood of a play as an audience enters the theatre, to ease the transition from one act or scene to another, and to entertain the audience during an intermission. In all cases, the music should suit the time, place, and mood of the play.

The selection and recording of musical effects takes research and technical skills. You would not want the sounds of country-western music to introduce a production of *West Side Story*. Once all the music has been chosen for the introduction, intermission, and scene transitions, the sound crew will want to record all bits of music on a single cassette. A professional sound recording studio can transfer your musical effects and music cues to one cassette.

When using music, the effect is better when music fades in and out gradually. This often demands practice and modification during the course of rehearsals.

Musical Productions. Musical performances are a favorite of many schools and often combine the interests and talents of young actors, singers, and dancers. In addition, musicals provide expanded opportunities for choreography and sound direction for vocal and instrumental music. In addition to favorite musicals such as *Oklahoma!* and *The Music Man,* some popular stories have also been adapted into musicals. Some of these include *The Velveteen Rabbit* and *Alice in Wonderland.* The choice of a musical production will depend on the available talent, stage, and local interest.

Sound Equipment

All sound equipment used in theatre serves one of three main functions:

1. to receive, or pick up, sounds necessary for the communication of words, mood, and action in the context of the play;
2. to transform, or control, these necessary sounds in terms of amplification and direction;
3. to send these sounds to the audience in an even and effective manner.

The sound designer and sound crew need to read the script and identify all sound effects and music required by the script and the director. Then they will need to secure, record, or make all sounds and music for the performance. These jobs will be related to the equipment they have available and the skills and imagination that brings sound to the audience.

Microphones. Microphones are the most common device for picking up sound. They differ in quality and location. Some microphones pick up a wide range of pitches from low to high. Others pick up only middle-range tones with accuracy. Some microphones are stationary and pick up sounds on stage from fixed, usually overhead locations. Other microphones are portable, and some can be worn as individual devices. The sound director and crew will have to learn about the type and quality of the equipment that is available for your production.

Amplification. After sound is picked up, it needs to be controlled in terms of volume and direction. Through **amplification,** the quantity of the sound can be controlled and directed to the listeners. Amplification equipment can be both simple and complex. The source of sound can be specifically located and redirected to a wider audience. For instance, an actor's voice coming specifically from downstage left can be amplified so that the entire audience can hear it clearly but distinctly coming from the specific area of the stage.

In addition to amplification, the sound director and crew will probably use a **mixer** to control the sounds the audience hears. A mixer picks up a variety of sounds and combines them into a single sound signal sent to the audience. For instance, a mixer can pick up the voices or sounds on several microphones as well as taped sound effects or music and combine everything the audience is supposed to hear simultaneously into one signal.

Speakers. After sound has been received and transformed, it needs to be sent to the listeners. This is done through speaker systems. Speaker systems also vary greatly in terms of quality and location. Most school theatres have stationary speaker systems that distribute sound adequately to the audience. Many students will be familiar with sound systems because of

Amplification:
The process of using electronic conductors to concentrate sound and change its volume and direction.

Mixer: An electronic device that receives sound signals from a variety of sources and combines them into a single sound signal for redistribution to an audience.

their interest in music. This interest and expertise will transfer very well to the stage and the various jobs of the sound crew.

Summary

Sound is an essential element of a theatre production and involves the reception and transmission of voices, sound effects, and music. Special equipment and skills deliver sounds evenly to the audience.

Set Design

1. ***The Emerald City.*** Imagine that you can transform a corner of your classroom into a set for a simple one-act production of *The Wizard of Oz.* Work in a small group and discuss the following.
   - As an actor would you rather work in a realistic or a more imaginative set?
   - What could you do to show the shift in scene from Dorothy's bedroom in Kansas to the land of Oz?
   - What three things could you do using common, inexpensive materials to create a scene for the Emerald City?
   - What props would you want to use to dress the Emerald City and the bedroom in Kansas?

   As a group, sketch or make a model of your Emerald City scene.

2. ***Curtains.*** Stretch your imagination to develop creative uses for a solid colored sheet to use as a set backdrop for *Alice in Wonderland* or *The Lion, the Witch, and the Wardrobe.* Make a list of at least three suggestions for the use of a single sheet to convey the mood, scene, and stage business for a character in one of the plays suggested.

Lighting Design

3. ***Photography.*** Gather a collection of photographs that show scenes of sets from various plays or movies. Display these photographs as an exhibit and imagine that they have been awarded first, second, and third prizes for the light and design composition. Prepare blue, red, and gold ribbons and give them to those photographs you consider to be good, better, and best.

4. ***Candles.*** Study the light cast by a candle in a dark room. Then imagine that you must recreate that look on stage. Identify the types and location of lights you would use to achieve that effect on stage.

5. ***Costumes.*** Design a costume for yourself to play the role of Cinderella or the Prince. Pay special attention to the color of your costume. After you have selected the color you would prefer for your costume, identify the colors you would want in the sets, scenery, and lights to highlight the color of your costume.

Sound Design

6. ***Equipment.*** Take a poll of students to determine the type of amplification and speaker systems they consider to be the best and the worst for listening to popular CDs. Compare results.

7. ***Budgets.*** Imagine that you have just received an unexpected gift of $100 and you want to buy new speakers for your stereo system. Make a comparison of at least three systems you could buy within your budget and compare the advantages and disadvantages of each. Indicate which system you would buy and why.

8. ***Sound Effects.*** Make a tape with at least ten different sounds you could use on stage and ask the class to guess what the sounds are.

The Actor's Logbook

1. ***Learning the Language.*** Add the technical terms that are commonly used in set construction, lighting, and sound design to your collection of specialized terms. Pay attention to the technical terms used on the next tape or CD package you purchase. You may want to add these to your list as well.

2. ***Tools of the Trade.*** In addition to the technical terms used, you might want to include an illustration of the various tools used backstage to construct sets and work with lighting and sound systems. Include labels to identify the name of the tool or the equipment and its main parts. Discuss how you plan to keep up with the many changes that occur in the technology of stage production.

3. ***Color Chart.*** Transfer a color chart showing the primary and secondary colors to your logbook. Refer to your color chart when you plan color design for sets and costumes.

4. ***Cue Sheets.*** Develop a sample cue sheet for yourself that would be suitable for your use as an actor, a member of the light or sound crew, or a prop manager. Use a play the school is currently presenting or one the class has worked on as the basis for your cue sheet.

5. ***Critic's Choice.*** Make a list of the five best movies you have seen recently. For each of the movies listed, identify the best scene, the best sound effect, and the best use of lighting. Enter this as a chart into your logbook.

Critical Thinking

6. ***Main Ideas.*** Identify the major contributions that sets and scenery, lighting, and sound make to a theatre production. Which of these three areas would you most like to gain experience in? Why?

7. ***Trends.*** Make a list of new sound equipment and technology that has become available in the past five years. Share the most imaginative use of sound equipment that you have experienced. What advances in technology do you expect to occur in your lifetime that will improve your experience of music?

8. ***Planning.*** What five guidelines would you prepare for a crew working on set construction, lighting, or sound to promote safety for the production crew?

Creative Thinking

9. ***Lighting.*** Make a list of all the movies nominated for an Academy Award for outstanding lighting design in the past year. Prepare a commercial for one of the nominees emphasizing the great lighting effects.

10. ***Sounds.*** Think of a sound that you have never heard. Write a description of that sound and then try to reproduce it.

11. ***Inventions.*** Think of a tool you could invent that would make some aspect of theatre production easier, cheaper, and more creative. Draw a sketch of your invention and give it a name.

CHAPTER TWELVE

Rehearsals

EXPECTATIONS

After reading this chapter, you will be able to

12.1 understand the role of schedules in the play production process

12.2 define and use basic theatre terms for rehearsals

12.3 demonstrate active participation in individual and team theatre activities

12.4 appreciate theatre experiences as a complex team effort

12.5 utilize time management skills to accomplish long-range tasks

rganizing the time and skills of a theatre company so that everybody is ready for opening night requires much planning and hard work. Developing a rehearsal schedule and arranging for technical and dress rehearsals is the work of the director. Actors, managers, and crews coordinate their efforts so that everyone supports and complements each other.

Production Schedule

The number of performances for a school play may be few. By contrast, the number of weeks and hours spent in the preparation for those performances is a lot larger. The school play may be given over a single weekend. The preparation time might takes from six to eight weeks. And even that might not seem like enough time to accomplish all the activities connected with putting on a performance.

Sample Rehearsal Schedule

The sample schedule in Figure 12.1 outlines the major tasks that must be completed by a variety of people for the show to open as planned. This schedule provides for six weeks of preparation and may need to be adjusted to fit your particular circumstances.

Rehearsal Time. During the first four weeks of production, actors will spend a lot of time and effort in developing their specific characters and memorizing lines. Each week, the actor will see progress in the definition of roles and the ease of movement on stage. Early in the rehearsal schedule, actors will begin to interpret the meaning of the lines as they relate to their stage characters and the central idea of the play. They will examine the issues of motivation underlying their lines and realize that the meaning of a line is related not only to the information it gives the audience, but also to the underlying intent of the character and the theme of the play.

Figure 12.1 Sample Schedule

Week	Actors	Sets	Lights	Sound	Props	Costume	Makeup	Publicity
6	Casting, reading, blocking	Plan colors	Read	Make lists	Make lists	Make lists and take measures	Plan	Make lists
5	Character analysis, blocking	Build, order supplies	Plan colors	Collect	Collect, build	Gather, order	Inventory, order	Business, plan
4	Memorize, blocking, business, motives	Build	Inventory, cues	Tape, cues	Collect, build	Sew, adjust	Design	Sponsors, media, programs
3	Business, lines, timing, cues, props	Set up	Clean	Tape	Stand-in	Sew, adjust	Practice	Tickets, training, publicity, photos
2	Polish, timing	Tech reh.	Tech reh.	Tech reh.	Tech reh.	Review costumes	Review makeup	Publicity, ticket sales
1	Dress reh., curtain calls	Dress reh.	Dress reh.	Dress reh.	Dress reh.	Dress reh.	Dress reh.	Train box office workers

OPENING NIGHT

STRIKE   Everyone in the theatre company assists in clean up, repair, return, and storage of all items.

Memorizing Lines. During the weeks of rehearsal, actors will be memorizing their lines. Each actor will find his or her own way to do this. Some pace back and forth as they memorize. Some want to recite the lines with another person. Others memorize best when they are actually on stage during rehearsals. It is never easy, but memorizing lines is always

Many essential tasks have to be completed early in the production process. As an actor, you would spend the first weeks of rehearsal reading through the play and memorizing your lines.

required. Usually, directors want the memorization to happen as quickly as possible. Aim to have lines memorized by the third week of rehearsals. After that you can concentrate on movement, timing, and use of props without the crutch of having the script in hand.

Marking the Script. In addition to memorizing lines, actors need to mark their scripts to indicate pauses, differences in tempo and tone, use of props, and stage movement that accompany any lines. These marks will also make the interpretation of character more natural on stage. Each actor will develop his or her own shorthand to mark a script indicating the desired interpretation and timing.

Team Effort. As Figure 12.1 demonstrates, all teams are busy building, collecting, blocking, and generally working on the production in one area or another. Without the efforts of one group, the show would not go one. Actors learn that without the imagination and skills of the lighting crew, they just won't look good on stage. And nobody will be happy if the publicity crew doesn't sell tickets and pack the house.

Stage Manager. The director relies on a stage manager's coordination and people skills to orchestrate the backstage efforts of the crews and actors. When problems need solutions and morale needs a boost, the stage manager steps up with suggestions and encouragement. But everyone needs to keep the big picture in mind. Everyone in the theatre company contributes some detail to the overall theatre experience.

Time Management

Everyone in the theatre company will see weekly progress in the six to eight weeks of production time. But the progress is the result of accomplishing tasks on a daily basis. The first four weeks of a production are a time when much of the preparation is going on and people have individual tasks to accomplish. At the same time, crews work to fit the many pieces of play production together.

An Actor's Week. A weekly planning calendar will be an important part of an actor's ability to keep up with the progress of the play. Every week in the production schedule should be broken into the tasks to be accomplished each day. In addition to the time spent with the rest of the actors with the blocking and timing and cues, actors will need to work by themselves or with their stage partners to polish stage business and practice difficult scenes.

A Crew Member's Week. The lighting, sound, sets, costumes, makeup, props, and publicity crews are also working individually and as a team. They, too, need to organize each week so that tasks are accomplished every day. Two weeks before opening night, the week of technical rehearsals begins. The planning, design, and construction of sets, scenery, props, and costumes must be complete. The cue sheets and prompt sheets need to be in order so that technical rehearsals go smoothly.

Imagine that your class is putting on a one-act play as a community theatre production. You have six weeks to prepare the production. Work in a small group to plan a six-week time management calendar to accomplish the tasks of your group. The groups could include: actors, sets, props, lighting, sound, costumes and makeup, and publicity.

Step One

The Tasks. Each group should list its general responsibilities. Identify the major things that need to be accomplished. Select a manager to coordinate the activities of the group and to represent your group in the coordinators' council. Hold a brief meeting of the council to share lists and identify areas that were forgotten.

Step Two

The Calendar. Make a daily calendar that covers six weeks. Identify the major tasks that have to be done each week. Also identify the details that need attention every week. You might want to develop a color code to distinguish major and minor tasks or individual responsibilities. The manager will share your group calendar with the coordinators. You might have to make adjustments based on the requirements of other groups.

Step Three

The Weeks Go By. Each person in the group should list the days of the week for each week of the production. Identify the things that you want to do each day and leave room to check off those things that you accomplish. Estimate how much time each task will take. Compare lists for each week. Discuss how you would like progress reports to be handled for the group as well as for crew members.

Step Four

The Problems. The trouble with schedules is that there are always unexpected problems. It helps to have options to pursue if problems arise. Discuss at least three things that can go wrong in each week of production. For each thing that could go wrong, think of a solution.

Step Five

Adjustments. In your group, discuss either of these hypothetical situations and come up with three suggestions for dealing with the problem. Situation A: The leading actor in the play is having trouble memorizing lines. This actor is good and well-liked but is holding up rehearsals. The director thinks the production is about four days behind schedule, and the company won't be ready for opening night. Situation B: A raging snowstorm has closed school for three days just before technical rehearsals. What can be done to make up for lost time? Share your suggestions with the whole class.

Summary

Staying on schedule is a crucial part of theatre production. Individuals and crews will see weekly progress in the accomplishment of the various responsibilities of the lighting, sound, props, sets, costumes, and publicity crews. Time management is an important skill for all.

Technical Rehearsals

As the time for technical rehearsals approaches, the pressure to get things done increases. People can easily become frustrated with delays and complications. This is a natural part of theatre production. Technical rehearsals are usually long and often tedious. While everybody needs to be there, not everyone is involved all the time. Knowing what to expect and planning how to use your "down time" effectively will help during the week of technical rehearsals.

Expectations

Sets, props, lights, and sound should be ready for use on stage when the technical rehearsals begin. This is the time when actors combine memorized lines, stage business, movement, and props to polish their timing and group interaction. This is the time when set, light, and sound crews work off cues and make adjustments in color, timing, and placement to enhance the overall impression of the play. This is a time for patience and problem-solving skills.

Getting Ready. The purpose of technical rehearsals is to coordinate the actors' actions on stage with the technical aspects of the production, including sets, lighting, and sound. While there may be group meetings prior to the technical rehearsals, most of the crews have been working according to their own calendars to prepare for this stage of the production. Preparation is now converted to actual performance. Members of the theatre company should come to the technical rehearsal armed with patience, enthusiasm, and a good dose of problem-solving skills. Having a book to read or homework assignments to do can help to pass the time when you are not actually involved with the comments and suggestions of the director and stage manager.

Stage One. The first technical rehearsal is conducted on stage without the actors. Usually, the director and technical director work with the stage manager and the lighting, set, and sound managers to run through the play act by act. The director sits in the house and takes notes about the lighting, sound, sets, and prop placement. The stage manager is backstage working with the promptbook to coordinate all cues.

The set should be in place and all scenery, furniture, and props ready for use when needed. The stage crew should have a plan for the quiet and quick movement of sets, scenery, and props so that changes do not detract from the focus on stage.

Technical rehearsals require patience and cooperation. Actors who are waiting to go on stage can pass the time by catching up on homework or reviewing their cues.

The lighting manager will try all the color and equipment combinations called for during each act. Lighting cues will be adjusted. If an adjustment in lighting is called for, this will take time. Here is an opportunity for patience and the creative use of time. If you are not on the lighting crew, you might want to take out a homework assignment; if you are an actor, you might use the time to practice and polish your lines.

The sound manager will double-check the placement and working condition of all equipment. The sound effects and music used in the play need to be available and sound adjustments made. The sound cues may also have to be adjusted. Again, this may seem like a technical delay to actors or others who are not actively involved in the sound production, but it is a good opportunity to go over your own cues.

Once the technical equipment is in place, the director will want to run through the lighting, scenes, and sounds with actual voice cues. It's time to bring on the actors.

Technical Rehearsal with Actors

When the actors work with the technical support crews, everybody needs to be clear about basic information, including who does what, when, and why. These four W's are essential to a good technical rehearsal.

Reciting Lines. During the technical rehearsal, the actors may simply be asked to recite their lines as a walk-through for the technical staff. Reciting lines serves to clarify lighting and sound cues and stage movement. The director will be taking notes. After this first run-through, the director will meet with the theatre company and tell everyone what changes or improvements need to be made. Actors and crew should come prepared to take notes and ask questions at this meeting. Actions you may have practiced for four weeks before the technical rehearsal may change as a result of this meeting. You will want to keep up with the demands of the production.

Set or Scene Changes. When actors run a line rehearsal, the change and use of sets, scenes, furniture, and props are clarified. The stage crew will learn how important timing is to the removal or change of sets and props. During a technical rehearsal, the position of scenery, furniture, and sets will be indicated on the stage area with tape. The prop manager will have a system for the use and storage of props when they are not in use. Actors need to know where things will be. Knowing the exact placement of furniture and scenery will help actors polish stage movement and their use of props.

Costume Review. During the technical rehearsal, the director and costume designer will want to check how the lighting affects the appearance of the costumes and make final adjustments. Last-minute changes will need to be made according to the requirements of the stage movement and lighting.

Sound Effects and Prompt Cues. Actors and technicians may have to make adjustments in the volume and timing of sounds during the technical rehearsal. The on-stage sound of a telephone ringing, for instance, must be coordinated with the actor's lines and movement. Also, the length of specific sound effects may need adjustment during the technical rehearsal. Actors will pay close attention to these sound effects and the effects they have on their own entrances, stage movement, and exits.

The prompter is very active during the technical rehearsal. All changes in timing, lighting, and cues need to be recorded and up-to-date. If an actor misses a line or the sound cue is off, the prompter will have to make a note to cue those involved for their performance.

Taking Notes. After the technical rehearsal, the theatre company will meet with the director, technical managers, and stage manager to review the rehearsal. Usually there will be comments about all the good things about the performance. Individuals should make mental and written notes on the positive comments about their own personal contributions as well as those directed toward the crew and the entire company. Building on positive accomplishments can reduce nervousness and make the requested changes seem more manageable.

In addition to positive comments, the director and manager will undoubtedly have comments about what still needs work.

Sometimes, these comments can seem overwhelming. Time pressures to make these last-minute changes can be a source of stress. Take each suggestion with good humor and enthusiasm and tackle each task one by one. Call on your time management skills to make the adjustments requested.

After the technical rehearsal is a time for questions and clarifications. Everybody should leave the technical rehearsal with a clear understanding of what needs to be done and the amount of time available to accomplish each task.

In addition to the suggestions for improvement, the company might be reminded of expectations for a smooth performance. Actors and crew will be reminded of the following:

1. If you forget a line, do not look at the prompter; stay in character and wait for the prompt.

2. Never peek through the main curtain to look at the audience.

3. Move quietly backstage.

4. Respect the organization of the prop, costume, and makeup crews and do not touch or remove anything without authorization.

5. Stay in character on stage. Whatever happens, do not break up and laugh out of character.

6. Reserve makeup and costumes for backstage and on stage.

7. Arrive in plenty of time for backstage preparation before all performances.

8. Stay focused on the performance, leave personal problems offstage, and give your best performance for every audience.

9. Team efforts accomplish more than any individual ones. Appreciate and express gratitude for the support and skills of everybody in the theatre company.

10. It's a play. Enjoy the fruits of your practice and skills. Take compliments and criticism graciously.

Summary

Technical rehearsals can be tedious and frustrating. Yet they are necessary to coordinate the efforts of various groups, especially the set design, lighting, and sound. The director will work with various managers to adjust lighting, sound, costumes, and actors' timing and lines during the technical rehearsal. The last minute adjustments will help polish the performance and heighten the energy of the theatre company.

Dress Rehearsals and Performances

The dress rehearsal occurs a day or two before the scheduled opening performance. The theatre company understands that this rehearsal, complete with costumes, makeup, lights, sets, and sound, is just like opening night minus the audience. There is no stopping now. The show goes on!

Preparation

It takes time to prepare lights, props, sound, costumes, and makeup for an actual performance. Usually the theatre company is called to arrive one hour before a dress rehearsal or performance. Being on time is essential for a smooth start. No one wants to make unnecessary adjustments in cast or crew because someone does not arrive on time. Everyone should be at his or her appointed place at the scheduled time before the dress rehearsal.

Stage Manager. The stage manager will check to see that everyone is accounted for. He or she will also check props with the prop manager and costumes with the costume manager. The stage manager will check his or her lists to make sure that everything and everybody is ready for the performance.

Technical Crews. The lighting and sound crews should check their equipment and controls before the audience arrives. A final review of the cue lists will help to reassure the crews

Great Plays: Making Comparisons

Great plays are great, in part, because they deal with important issues and emotions. In addition, the actors bring great skill and the director brings great imagination to the stage. Being in the audience for a really great play is truly memorable. One young actor described her first memorable play performance in terms of the impact of an effective use of a prop. She saw a performance of *Madame Butterfly* in which a bright red scarf was used to suggest blood flowing after the title character committed hari-kari. The effective use of one prop led to a lifelong commitment to theatre.

If you have not enjoyed the experience of a memorable live theatre performance, you can still appreciate great theatre through modern technology. Start your own list of the great theatre performances you have seen live or otherwise. To get yourself started, watch a video of a great play. Some suggestions include:

- *The Importance of Being Earnest*
- *St. Joan*
- *Murder in the Cathedral*
- *Death of a Salesman*
- *Romeo and Juliet*

1. As you watch the video, make a note of the following:
   • The most memorable line or gesture
   • The most memorable set
   • The most memorable costume
   • The most memorable lighting effect
   • The most memorable sound effect

2. Think about what makes the play you watched on video great. Write a paragraph defining what makes a play performance great.

3. Prepare a poster for display in the classroom that identifies the play you watched and the most memorable items you identified in the first activity.

4. After you have watched the video, either write a dramatic criticism of the play or prepare a commentary that would be suitable for including in the playbill or program.

5. If possible, attend a live performance of a professional or amateur play. Imagine you are a theatre critic and pay special attention to the skills of the actors, the vision and imagination of the director, the sets, costumes, and the music. Prepare a one-minute review of the play that would be suitable for use on a radio or television program featuring cultural events in your area.

6. Add a section to your logbook that includes short summaries of important plays. For each play, write a brief summary, or synopsis, of the action and theme and identify the characters in the play.

that everybody knows their individual responsibilities and is trained to perform them skillfully. If there is to be house music for background as the audience begins to assemble, this should start about half an hour before the scheduled beginning of the performance.

Costumes. At long last, the actors will be dressed as their characters in the play. The costume manager will assist the crew in working with each actor to check buttons, snaps, and zippers. When the actors are dressed in costume, makeup and hair styling will begin. The actors can use this preparation time to get in character while crew members are helping them look the part.

Stage Crew. While actors are getting prepared for their parts mentally and physically, the stage crew uses this preshow time to check the entire set. All scenery needs to be properly placed, all props ready for use, and the crew clear about the timing of shifts in sets and scenery.

Audience. Sometimes special audiences are invited to a dress rehearsal to give the actors and crew the sense of performing before real people. An audience heightens the energy of the theatre company, and though it may be tempting to peek out of the curtains to see who is in the audience, you should resist the temptation. Any movement behind the curtains can be detected by those sitting in the house.

Final Meeting. About ten minutes before the curtain goes up, the stage manager will call a meeting in the **greenroom.** Even if the room isn't green, actors will meet in this room backstage to hear the director's notes and comments and await their cues. At this time, there is one last check to make sure that everyone is ready for the curtain to go up. Excitement is in the air!

Greenroom: A back-stage room where actors assemble before and after performances and wait for their cues during performances.

Performance

All the work of the six-week production schedule comes together as the entire company is poised for the curtain to go up on opening night. There is no stopping, no adjustments, no delays. At the given signal and at the scheduled time, the curtain opens, and the audience enters the world you have created over the past weeks.

Stay on Schedule. There never seems to be enough preparation time, and everyone would probably like another five minutes to get in character or adjust the set. It is very important, however, that the curtain rise at the scheduled time. With the very first lines spoken on stage, the actors and crew will bring all their skills and practice to the stage to give the best performance they can.

Mistakes Do Happen. The dreaded nightmare that something might go wrong in the midst of the play is something that sometimes does happen on occasion, but the show must go on. If an actor forgets a line, the rest of the company will find a way to get around it. If an actor is truly in character and another actor forgets a line, the cue line could be repeated or stage business invented on the spot to cover up for the lapse.

Review. After the dress rehearsal and first performance, actors should get out of their costumes and makeup quickly to assemble in the greenroom to hear the director's comments. The director will encourage the company but may also make small adjustments in the timing or stage business to accentuate the impact of the play and each actor's performance. The entire cast should listen carefully and take notes to refer to after the review. Some will feel disappointed with their efforts; others will feel relieved that the dress rehearsal or opening night is over. In all cases, the company should come prepared to give its best when the curtain rises the following night.

Curtain Calls. The director will instruct the cast on the procedures for curtain calls. The curtain call should also be practiced during the dress rehearsal, even if there is no one in the audience. There are several kinds of curtain calls. In some cases, the director will want the entire cast to come on stage and take a bow as a group. In other plays, the director may decide that each actor should come on stage individually. If

Even curtain calls
should be practiced
prior to opening night.

this is the case, the order of appearance of individual actors usually proceeds from minor roles to the leading roles. Some plays, like Shakespeare's *Twelfth Night,* suggest that the curtain call could be done in the groups of actors who were on stage together—Olivia's household, Orsinio's household, and the "outsiders."

The type of curtain call is not so important as the timing of it. During the curtain call, actors receive the applause and appreciation of the audience. The clapping should be strong and sincere. The curtain should close while the clapping is still energetic.

Even on stage for the curtain call, actors should remember theatre etiquette. They should not use the curtain call to hug each other or to wave to anyone in the audience. Neither should members of the audience send flowers and other gifts on stage to any of the actors. If flowers are to be sent, they should be received backstage. Actors need to remind their families of these expectations so that everybody can act accordingly.

Summary

The dress rehearsal brings the play's performance closer to reality. Everyone will be expected to arrive an hour before the scheduled performance to get in character and double-check all equipment and cues. Actors will learn the importance of going on with the performance despite mistakes or awkward timing. The dress rehearsal will be preceded and followed by notes from the director so that last-minute adjustments can be made to polish the performance.

Active Listening

1. ***Taking Notes.*** During the technical and dress rehearsals, the director will be taking notes about the performance. You will listen to these notes in the greenroom. Prepare a note pad or a section in your logbook to organize the comments you hear. Develop headings so you can indicate the date you take the notes, positive remarks, general information or comments, criticisms, and actions you need to take.

2. ***Repeat after Me.*** After the meetings in the greenroom, work with a buddy to summarize what you thought you heard the director say. Ask your partner to summarize the director's notes. Then try to identify the three most important things you thought you heard. Compare your understanding of the three most important items with those of your partner.

Private Rehearsals

3. ***The Kiss.*** Imagine that your class is putting on a production of *Cinderella.* You and your partner have been told by the director to practice the kiss the prince gives Cinderella at the end of the play. The kiss is to last three seconds, begin in profile centerstage, and open to a full-front position holding hands with outside arms extended to include the entire stage. Practice on stage in front of the class.

4. ***The Fight.*** Imagine that your class is putting on a production of *Romeo and Juliet.* You and a partner must fight on stage, one as a Montague and the other as a Capulet in the opening scene. You and your partner must act as Benvolio and Tybalt reciting the following lines and blocking a five-second fight with swords:

> **BENVOLIO:** I do but keep the peace, put up thy sword,
> Or manage it to part these men with me.
>
> **TYBALT:** What, drawn and talk of peace? I hate the word,
> As I hate hell, all Montagues, and thee,
> Have at thee coward!

Getting in Character

5. ***Quiet Time.*** The time spent waiting while others are working out specific problems or acting on stage can become a laboratory for everyone in the theatre company. While you are waiting, you might make a list of at least ten things you could do during the in-between times.

6. ***Call Time.*** Plan how you want to use the hour before curtain to get in character emotionally and physically for the class play. Use fifteen-minute segments and think of at least three things you can do to prepare your character for stage.

The Actor's Logbook

1. ***Director's Notes.*** Add a section to your log-book to record the positive and negative comments the director makes after technical and dress rehearsals. Be sure to include a list of action items for yourself.

2. ***Personal Cues.*** Be absolutely clear about what your responsibilities are for each performance. Make a list of what is expected of you. Next to each responsibility, identify a time or cue when the activity is expected to be done.

3. ***Company Etiquette.*** You will want to impress your audience with the skills and professional approach you demonstrate during a performance. Look at the list of theatre company guidelines for a performance on page 228. What would you add to the list for you personally? What additional items would you suggest for the entire group?

4. ***Critic's Choice.*** After the dress rehearsal, write a review of the play as if you were a theatre critic. Be sure to mention the strengths of the production and identify one area you think needs work.

Critical Thinking

5. ***Main Ideas.*** Develop a daily calendar to identify the major activities for each day of the final week of production.

6. ***Compare and Contrast.*** Write a sentence or paragraph that describes the purpose and expected outcomes for the technical rehearsal as well as the dress rehearsal. Discuss how each type of rehearsal is different yet similar.

7. ***Checklists.*** Imagine you are the stage manager for your school play. Make a checklist of things you need to check during the technical rehearsal. Do the same for the dress rehearsal. Make a personal checklist for yourself so that you are mentally and physically prepared for your role in the production.

8. ***Applications.*** Think about how the time management skills you have developed during a play production can be transferred to the rest of your school year. Identify the major goals you have for each month. Develop a calendar that lists what should be done on a weekly basis to achieve your goal for a particular month.

Creative Thinking

9. ***Other Opportunities.*** To maximize the time and effort that goes into preparing a play for an audience, think of at least two additional possibilities for performances of your school play outside the school environment. Think of how this show could "go on the road" so that additional audiences could enjoy the play and the theatre company could gain additional experience.

10. ***Curtain Calls.*** Instead of a traditional curtain call where everybody bows to the audience in a line on stage, create a short "bow" for each actor in your school play or for the cast of *Cinderella*. Keep the actor "in character" for the bow and create some stage business that would be suitable for an innovative curtain call.

PART FOUR

Modern Theatre

CHAPTER THIRTEEN

Local Theatre

EXPECTATIONS

After reading this chapter, you will be able to

13.1 define the difference between amateur and professional actors

13.2 develop a plan for getting involved with community theatre

13.3 discuss the importance of theatre in current times

13.4 identify how attending the theatre will help you grow as an actor

13.5 ask critical questions about performances that you attend

lowly the lights start to dim. The people in the audience quickly stop talking and put aside their programs. The room becomes silent as the lights go to black. Everyone sits waiting expectantly. In a second, the lights will come up, the curtain will rise, and the audience will be carried away into the story played out by the characters on stage.

Community Theatre

This feeling of expectancy doesn't only happen for people in the audience of a Broadway theatre, waiting to see a production of *Cats*, *The Phantom of the Opera*, or *Guys and Dolls*. It can be felt while sitting in a church basement or a high school auditorium, on folding chairs in a small storefront theatre, or outside at a summer theatre performance. Theatre can be found almost anywhere. Whether you live in the city, the suburbs, or in more rural sections of the country, there are opportunities to attend and participate in theatre.

What Is Community Theatre?

A **community theatre** exists in most communities. It is the result of a group of nonprofessional actors coming together to pursue their love of theatre. Today, more than 6,500 community theatre groups exist around the country. There are a number of factors that make community theatre groups a very special kind of theatre group.

Community theatre: Theatre produced by an independent group within a particular community to further the artistic goals of the community.

Community Theatre Is Nonprofessional. Unlike the actors in professional theatre companies or in professional theatre performances that you may attend, most actors in community theatres are not professional actors.

Saying that an actor is not professional does not make a statement about the quality of that actor's performing ability. Being a nonprofessional means that you not making your living in the theatre. A professional actor gets paid for acting and may in fact make a living by theatre work.

*Amateur: A person
who cultivates a skill
without pursuing it for
a living.*

Community theatres attract a wide range of ability in actors. Some people may be newcomers to the stage and have had little or no experience acting. Others may have long histories of work in community theatre and may have acted in many roles. They may have taken workshops and classes in acting and theatre. Still others may be students or may have previously had professional experience in the theatre and are continuing to act, although not for pay.

What all these actors have in common is a love of theatre. Actors in community theatre can be called devoted **amateurs.**

Although the term *amateur* is sometimes connected with not being as talented, the word here is used in its highest form. An amateur actor will act and be involved in theatre even if he or she never receives any money for that work.

In many community theatre groups, no one receives any pay. Some more established community theatres may pay directors or choreographers or the business manager, but the actors themselves are usually not paid for their work.

Community Theatre Is Based in the Community. Often the plays that a community theatre group chooses to perform represent the interests and tastes of the community. Sometimes in big cities, theatre patrons complain about the plays that are presented. Some of the newer plays being performed may be offensive or not as interesting to some theatregoers. The average theatregoer wants to be entertained, amused, or stirred emotionally.

Community theatre groups may choose to present plays that are well-known and well-received by the general population. Whether it is a musical like *West Side Story* or *Godspell*, the work selected is often one with which people in the community are familiar.

Other community groups may opt to perform comedies, such as works by Neil Simon, perhaps *Barefoot in the Park* or *The Odd Couple*. Or they may decide upon classic dramatic works like *Three Sisters* by Anton Chekhov, *A Doll's House* by Henrik Ibsen, or *Our Town* by Thornton Wilder.

The choice of which play to perform is based on a desire to meet the interests and needs of the group's community and to appeal to the largest number of people possible.

Community Theatre Is a Team at Work. A community theatre depends on everybody working together to make the production a success. A theatre group may have a core of members who have been involved for a long time. These people participate in many ways to ensure quality performances.

In professional theatre, there are strict regulations about who is responsible for specific tasks. Many theatre professionals belong to unions. If you were a union actor, you wouldn't be asked to usher for a production or to run the lights. In community theatre, however, people may wear many hats.

Although there is a director or most likely an **artistic director**, most often the process of deciding on which play to produce may be part of the whole group process.

In community theatre, people may be called upon to do a variety of tasks.

Artistic director:
The person who is in charge of everything that happens on stage and gives overall creative direction to a theatre program.

Where Can You Find Theatre in Your Community?

There's probably at least one community theatre group. If you live in a very rural area, you may find a community theatre that is organized and operating somewhere in your county.

Community theatres come in all sizes and perform in all kinds of spaces. A theatre group may rehearse and perform in a church or a school auditorium. Other groups may make use of community centers. Some community theatres that have been operating for a number of years may actually rent or own their own theatre space.

In other communities, opportunities for theatre are connected with the local college or university. Regardless of whether or not the college offers a major in theatre, it may produce a series of plays during the school year.

Who Does Community Theatre?

Look into a community theatre group and you're likely to find many different people involved in performing and producing the plays the group presents to the public.

Age. Community theatre groups may have members or participants that range in age from teenagers in junior high or high school to retired people in their sixties or seventies. This age range is actually a great benefit. Plays selected for performance may call for very young actors as well as actors who are middle-aged or senior citizens. As a younger actor, you can learn about both acting and life from older performers.

Experience. In community theatre, you'll get involved with people who have all levels of theatre experience. People come to the stage for a variety of reasons. As a student, you may participate in community theatre to increase your performing experience. You might do this in junior or senior high school or as a college student studying theatre. You can choose to participate in community theatre so you can point to a wide range of experience when applying to study theatre in college or when auditioning for work in professional theatre environments.

Some people involved in community theatre studied theatre in college, or perhaps they performed in high school and college. They may have decided not to pursue the theatre as a profession, but still wish to develop their love of the stage.

Sometimes community theatre participants get involved after certain life-changing events. A mother whose last child has just left for college may suddenly realize she has time for other commitments. Or a recently retired man may decide to become involved in theatre because he's always wanted to do it.

Summary

Whether old or young, in cities or in small towns, community theatre attracts people who love theatre but do not make their living by working in the theatre. It attracts people of all ages and with all levels of experience. Programming by community theatre groups tends to represent the tastes and interests of each individual group's community.

When actors apply for work it is called an *audition*. There isn't an application form that goes along with this process, but you do need to have a performance portfolio.

Step One

You Can't Live Without It. There are two things that every professional actor will have and will take along to an audition. One is a head shot. This is a professionally produced 8 x 10 inch glossy photograph of the actor's face and upper body. This photograph usually will have the actor's name printed on the front of it. The other requirement is a résumé. This is a listing of experience and education that will illustrate the actor's performing capabilities. This will also list any special skills the actor has.

Step Two

Conduct an Interview. Select a partner and interview him or her in preparation for writing a résumé. List all the details that seem at all connected to theatre. Arrange the details in an order such as this one:

Name and address
Personal details
- include age, weight, height, color of hair

Education
- include any schools you have graduated from
- include any schools you are now attending
- include special classes you have taken that apply to theatre, such as this acting class
- include special workshops or classes
  - music lessons
  - voice lessons
  - dance lessons
  - gymnastics training
  - acting classes or workshops

Experience
List any roles you have had in productions as well as any backstage experience you have

Special skills

Step Three

Make It Look Good. If you have access to a computer, key in and print out a sample résumé. Have your partner interview you and prepare a résumé for you.

If you interviewed some successful actors who make a living by performing either on stage or in movies or on television programs, you would probably find that their interest in acting started in their childhood. Looking back in old yearbooks, you would likely find pictures of these stars in their high school plays and musicals.

Not everyone has the good fortune to attend a school that sponsors several play productions each year. In some schools, there may be no program of dramatic productions. If that's your situation, don't despair. If you're interested in developing your acting abilities, community theatre may be a good choice for you. But how do you break into a theatre group? There are a number of ways to get involved with a local community theatre group.

Attend Classes

Some community theatre groups have special programs for young people and may sponsor theatre classes and workshops. Still others plan special productions to be cast solely by young people.

Attending workshops and classes not only increases your acting skills, it's also a great way to get to know people, such as the director and other members of the community theatre group.

Volunteer to Help

Community theatres always need help. Since most or all positions are unpaid, community theatre groups depend on volunteer staff to assist with productions.

What can you do? There are a number of jobs that all theatre groups will need filled. You could volunteer to help at the **box office,** where tickets are sold. In addition, ushers are often needed. Sign up to usher and you can both see the play and get more involved with the theatre group. Ushers are responsible for tearing tickets, for handing out programs, and for showing people to their seats.

Box office: Where reservations are listed and tickets are purchased for performances.

In some larger metropolitan areas, there are organized volunteer groups that provide ushers for performances at small to medium-sized theatres. One such organization exists in Chicago and is called the Saints. Volunteer ushers in this organization show up an hour before performances, help stuff programs with special inserts if needed, and show people to their seats. At the end of the performance, these ushers will straighten the seats, pick up trash, and throw out discarded programs.

Community theatres may also require help painting sets. Stage hands may be needed to move props in between acts or scenes during performances. Working in the office is less glamorous, but community theatre groups do need office help to assist with mailings. That may mean sitting and licking stamps or applying labels to brochures. It could also mean distributing flyers and posters announcing new productions in your community.

Why would you volunteer to do some of these ordinary tasks? Volunteering will show that you are a team player. All members of the community theatre team have to do some tasks that may be rather boring but are essential for a successful production. This includes everyone from the director of a play to the person who acts as the **house manager.**

House manager: The person who is responsible for all activities related to the house and the audience.

Volunteering for a community theatre also gives the theatre group a chance to get to know you. And you will soon become a part of that close-knit group because you are there and doing things to help. This will help you advance toward what may be your real goal—being cast in a role in a production by the community theatre group. But just being there is not going to get you the part. Like anyone else interested in performing, you'll have to audition.

Try Out for a Production

If you volunteer with a community theatre group, you'll be able to find out when the auditions for the next production are being held. You may also be able to talk with the director ahead of time so you have a better idea of how to prepare for the audition.

Usually community theatre audition announcements will tell you what type of characters are needed. A call for auditions may read, "Girl, 10 to 15 years old." The director may outline specifically what a person needs to bring to an audition: "Bring a song and a contemporary monologue."

If the part is in a musical, you may be asked to sing a certain kind of song. Or you may be asked to memorize a monologue to present at the audition. Then you'll also be asked to read from a script. You may also be asked to learn a dance step, if the role calls for dancing. Then you may be given an opportunity to show how well you can execute that step in a group of actors who are also auditioning.

Make sure you prepare carefully. If you have a résumé and head shot, be sure to take these along, even if they aren't required.

Community theatre productions may not have a very long **run.** A performance may only last one weekend, or it may have an extended run that could cover weekends for a month or two.

Often a rehearsal schedule for a play may include a time of four to six weeks prior to the first performance. Rehearsals often take place on weekday evenings and weekend days.

When you audition for a community theatre production, make sure you would be able to make the rehearsal schedule.

When you audition, make sure you would be able to make this rehearsal schedule.

Make sure your behavior before and after the audition is as impressive as your actual audition. Directors are looking for young actors who are talented and who have a serious approach to performing.

There may be other opportunities to audition for parts with other theatres. You can find out about auditions for other theatre groups by:

- asking members of the local community theatre if they know of any auditions
- looking in your local newspaper for listings of auditions
- reading performing arts newspapers that list auditions

Other Opportunities to Perform

School and community theatre may not be the only avenues open to you. Other ways to get performing experience may exist in your community as well.

Think about summer opportunities. Are there summer programs offered by the park district in your community? Some communities have summer theatre classes with a big production at the end of the program.

One such example is a summer arts camp in Oak Park, Illinois, called CAST (Communication Arts, Speech and Theatre). The summer program for CAST is a six-week intensive experience of workshops and rehearsals. The program is open to young people in grades four through eight. Each year a musical is presented. If you register for the program, you can elect to be a performer or part of the stage crew or technical crew. The workshops include acting, singing, dancing, and technical theatre and are run by theatre professionals or college students who are studying theatre.

There are several performances at the end of the program. Some young people sign up for this program every summer. At the end of five years, they will have been involved in five different musicals.

Another possibility is a summer theatre camp that is a resident program. Your acting teacher may have brochures about these programs. Most often these camps are rather expensive and require an audition to be accepted. These are enjoyable opportunities and always offer some performance experience. If you have dance training, you might consider a summer dance camp as well. Many major dance companies operate summer camps for young dancers each year.

Summary

Getting involved in performances at a community theatre may best be accomplished by first letting the group get to know you. This can be done by participating in any classes the group offers, by volunteering to help with productions, and by auditioning for parts in productions. There are summer performing arts programs, either day or resident camps, that offer training and performances.

Be Involved in Theatre as an Audience Member

A real love for theatre may start on the audience side. A dancer remembers her first experience seeing a ballet. She attended *The Nutcracker* at age four and fell in love with dance. A young boy goes to a professional theatre production and sees a neighbor he knows performing on stage. He decides he is someday going to be on stage. He accomplishes that goal eventually.

Many younger and older actors credit being taken to the theatre at a young age as the reason they decided to act. Having theatre be an important part of your life means more than just studying acting. It means more than just being on stage. It means that you will want to become involved in theatre by attending theatre performances as much as possible.

The Importance of Theatre

Theatre has a long history, with roots in ancient Greece. For centuries, people have been going to the theatre and being

Let's Go to the Theatre

Imagine you have a guest from out of town. She has suggested going to the theatre. You agree but then you have the task of selecting a play you will both enjoy.

1. Your friend arrives on a Friday, so it's easy for you to grab the local paper, which lists the plays that are being performed. Look at the sample below and read over all the listings.

2. After you have read all of the listings, write down the four categories: musicals, contemporary, classical, and comedy. Can you think of any other categories you may need? Go through the listings again and write each title under one category.

3. Decide which category most appeals to you and your friend. For example, perhaps it's musicals. Look at the list and cross out any that immediately do not appeal to you. How many have you eliminated? Why did you cross these out? How many listings do you have left to consider?

4. Decide on some other criteria for choosing whether to go to a particular play and list these categories on your sheet of paper. These could include things such as price, location, or time. Now go back and look at the remaining plays in your list. Can you make a final choice from these criteria? If not, determine a way to make the final selection.

5. Discuss with your classmates the play you have chosen and why you chose that play. Listen to the choices of your classmates. Did they find the selection process easy or difficult? Talk about what other information would have made the choice easier for you to make.

Theatre this Week

"THE GLASS MENAGERIE": Tennessee Williams' poignant play about the troubles of a southern family; Northpoint Theatre, 1984 N. Bellview; 8:00 Fridays through Sundays. $14.

"HAMLET": Modernized versions of the Shakespeare classic performed by the touring troupe Shakespeare on the Road; The Auditorium, 15 W. Main St.; 8 p.m. Friday and Saturday. $12.

"MY ONE AND ONLY": Fabulous tap dancing production featuring the music of George and Ira Gershwin; Starlight Dinner Theatre, 335 County Rd.; 7:30 Fridays through Sundays. $25.

"OUR TOWN": Thornton Wilder's classic small-town story; Pembleton Players, 445 N. Clark St.; 8:00 Tuesdays through Saturdays, 2:00 and 7:00 Sundays. $16.

"SHEAR MADNESS": A mystery/comedy set in a beauty parlor; Maywood Theatre, 22 W. Main St.; 6:30 and 9:30 Fridays and Saturdays; 7:00 Sundays; 8:00 Tuesdays through Thursdays. $20.

"TRACERS": A play by John Difusco that follows a platoon from boot camp to Vietnam; Modern Repertory, 1224 S. State St., 8:00 Thursdays through Saturdays, 2:00 and 6:00 Sundays. $15.

influenced by it as they sit and watch and listen to what is happening on a stage.

Although most of us see a lot of acting, we do that mainly through watching television, movies, and videos. Too many times we miss the opportunity for a live theatre experience. What is it that is so special about going to the theatre? Why might that be different than lying on your sofa watching a video? There are a number of answers to that question.

Theatre Explores Important Issues. Live theatre can explore some important questions about life. Ibsen's *A Doll's House* was one of the first plays to ask questions about women's rights and the role of women. Thornton Wilder's *The Skin of Our Teeth* takes the audience on a rather bizarre trip through time, all the while asking what is happening to the human race.

A Doll's House was one of the first plays to ask questions about the role of women. It has been a favorite vehicle for a number of well-known actresses.

In *Glengarry Glen Ross,* a contemporary play by David Mamet, the performers make us ask questions about growing older and leading a meaningless and empty life. *Steel Magnolias* makes us look at the bonds between mother and daughter and between friends and what happens when a daughter dies. Tony Kushner's *Angels in America* examines AIDS and modern-day America.

Often the experience of live theatre is an emotional one. You may be forced to think about some important issues. But you may well find that your response is not just an intellectual one. You may shed a tear or two. You may leave angry with a character. Or you may feel a sense of hope and love as a result of what you have viewed.

Sometimes theatre can force us to look at our lives by encouraging us to laugh at the characters on the stage as well as ourselves.

Theatre Is a Shared Experience. A live theatre experience is a shared experience. Even though you may may be experiencing the performance differently than the person seated next to you, you can be influenced by the rest of the audience. Some of the audience laughs at a certain line in a play. This may have increased your appreciation for the play. You may also find yourself talking about the performance after it is over and voicing your opinions about it, sharing what you did and did not like.

Theatre Attendance Benefits the Developing Actor

As an audience member you can gain a greater understanding about life. If you are interested in theatre as a possible career, theatre attendance is also a very important activity as a learning tool.

Knowledge of the Literature of the Theatre. By attending theatre regularly, you can develop an increased exposure to dramatic literature. There are so many fine plays to know. You can read them, but nothing matches the experience of seeing the play performed on stage.

If you are going to study theatre and aim for a career on the stage, you will need to have a broad understanding of the great literature for the theatre. The more plays you see, the easier it will be when you audition for parts in some of the very same plays that you have seen.

Learning about Technique. Watching performers on stage can help you learn some more about acting techniques. You can see what other actors do with certain characters. How does that actor show when her character is scared? What does she do with her body? How does her voice reveal that she is scared?

You may notice how two actors play off of each other in their roles. What do these actors do that makes you forget they are only actors and makes you believe they are really experiencing the emotions spelled out in the script?

By going to many different theatre performances, you can compare how actors accomplish certain goals they may have.

Developing Critical Skills. Going to the theatre regularly can improve your critical skills. The more you are exposed to something and the more you learn to ask questions about what you experience, the sharper will be your ability to be critical. **Criticism** is often thought of as a negative idea. In the arts, however, the idea of criticism is a positive one.

Criticism: The art of judging the quality of a performance or a work of art.

When you attend theatre you can ask yourself questions about all aspects of the production. You can decide what you thought of the script. What about the acting ability? Who was best and why? Which actor gave the weakest performance? What did you think about the lighting and the set? How did these aspects help enhance the story that the play told? You can also think about individual performances. Did you find a character believable? What made the performance strong or weak?

By learning to ask and answer questions like this, you will increase your critical skills. And the importance to a prospective actor, director, or playwright is that you can then take that critical thinking and apply it to your own output. If you are acting in a play, you can evaluate your own performance better if you have sharpened your skills at viewing plays and asking the critical questions.

Summary

Attending live theatrical performances can help you develop a love for the theatre. Being a good audience member helps you develop an appreciation for the importance of theatre because it explores important issues and because it's a shared experience. Theatre attendance helps the young actor because it exposes him or her to dramatic literature, it helps him or her learn about acting techniques, and it develops his or her critical thinking skills.

Start from Scratch

1. ***Plan a Program.*** Pretend you have been approached by a well-established community theatre group wanting to launch a theatre group for teenagers. You have been asked to help plan what this program will be like. Meet with two or three of your classmates and develop a complete plan for this program.

2. ***What's Really Needed?*** What kind of training program is necessary for a teen theatre group? List the classes or workshops you think are needed. What content should be covered in these workshops? How long should they last? When should they be scheduled?

Try Directing

3. ***Decisions, Decisions.*** Who should be involved in choosing the plays for a teen theatre program? What kind of plays would you like to see a teen theatre program present? What specific plays would you want to include in your programming? Why? How many plays would you present each year?

4. ***Casting.*** How would casting decisions be made? What would you like to include as part of the auditioning process? How would you help young actors be prepared for the auditions? How would you advertise the auditions?

Running a Theatre Program

5. ***Staffing.*** What kind of staff would be needed to run a teen theatre program? Think about the administrative and support staff as well as the artistic staff. List all the jobs that need to be done and then determine if these jobs can be done by young people or if they need to be filled by adults. Include all aspects of production.

6. ***Evaluating Success.*** At the end of each play, what questions do you need to ask to decide if it has been successful? What will you do to improve the next performance?

Real Life

7. ***Make Some Phone Calls.*** Call up any community theatres in your area and ask if they have a program for young people. Arrange for a telephone interview with the director of the program. Ask the director questions that are similar to the questions you have had to answer above.

8. ***Make Comparisons.*** Write a description of the program. How is it like the program you planned in the first activity above? How is it different?

The Actor's Logbook

1. ***Knowing What's There.*** List the community theatre groups you are aware of in your community and surrounding communities. You may want to include the high school and college performances that are available. How many performances a year does each group undertake? What plays have they performed that you remember seeing or hearing about?

2. ***What Are Your Skills?*** Think about the ways you might be able to volunteer to help a community theatre group. List the things you know you can do. Then list the things you would like to help with or know something about.

3. ***Six Degrees of Separation.*** Who do you know that is involved in a community theatre group? Write down the names of people you know who act or participate in any way in community theatre. Decide which of these people are easiest to talk with about the group. Write a list of questions you would want to ask them about becoming involved with community theatre.

Critical Thinking

4. ***Main Ideas.*** For each of the three sections of the chapter, make a list of at least three important ideas. Try to develop an outline for this chapter.

5. ***Evaluation.*** Read a review of a theatre performance. If you can't find one in a local newspaper, then read one in *Time* or *Newsweek*. Do you think the reviewer liked the performance or not? Why? What more would you like to have known about this performance? Would you have wanted to attend this performance?

6. ***Compare and Contrast.*** Think about what is important about theatre. How are movies different than theatre?

Creative Thinking

7. ***Dramatic Literature.*** List the plays you have seen that you can remember well. After each title, list a major theme of the play. Which plays or works by which playwrights would you like to see in order to expand your knowledge of dramatic literature? Write a list.

8. ***Plan a Season.*** In a small group, decide what you would program if you were the artistic director of community theatre in your community. There will be five plays in this series. What kinds of plays would you include? List any specific titles as well that you would like to produce.

9. ***If You Wrote a Play.*** Pair up with another classmate and brainstorm ideas of what you would like to write a play about. Think about this being a play that would be produced at your school and would deal with issues that were important to you and your classmates. Write a paragraph description of what the play would be about. How would you title the play?

CHAPTER FOURTEEN

Performance Opportunities

EXPECTATIONS

After reading this chapter, you will be able to

14.1 list the kind of training available to young actors preparing for professional acting careers

14.2 discuss the differences between the three basic undergraduate degrees in theatre

14.3 pinpoint the best locations for professional theatre work

14.4 talk about professional performing opportunities outside of major professional theatres

14.5 understand ways to add professional experience to a performance résumé

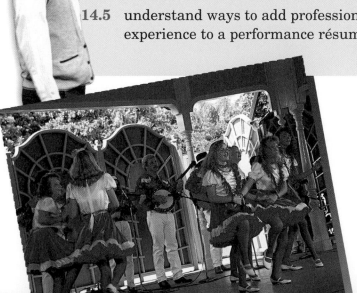

dream come true! A young boy gets to try out for a part in a major motion picture. He auditions, does a screen test, and then is chosen for the part. He goes through the filming process, the film is released, and it becomes a hit. Suddenly this boy is vaulted into the spotlight. He is offered major parts in future movies. He makes millions of dollars a year. He is a professional actor.

Preparing for an Acting Career

Not many actors get the kind of start in the acting world that Macaulay Culkin did. His performance in *Home Alone* launched him into fame and fortune. Suddenly he had a career!

The majority of working actors become professional actors after a rigorous training program. For many actors, that training starts in childhood. In fact, many young people who start acting careers as teenagers have been studying for years. First they may take dance classes and then voice and music lessons. Then come acting lessons. When the opportunity to audition for a big part comes along, they are well prepared for it.

College and University Programs

Serious theatre studies often start for actors when they enroll in college. Many colleges and universities offer programs in theatre arts. In fact, more than 1,000 colleges and universities offer four-year degrees in theatre. In addition, some 100 or more offer graduate-level degrees in theatre. These schools may have specialized programs, such as an emphasis in acting, in technical theatre, or in costume design.

Some people do break into acting without a college degree. Why should you consider going to college if all you want to do is act? One answer is that for every actor you find who hasn't pursued a college or university program, you're likely to find one or two more who have. In fact, some major names in

American theatre and film have attended very prestigious theatre programs.

Jodie Foster is an example. Although she gained success at a young age, she went on to study at Yale University's School of Drama. Another very well-recognized alumna of the Yale graduate program is Meryl Streep. Her career includes live stage performance as well as movie acting.

Why a College Program? One obvious advantage of choosing college for theatre study is that you will end up with a college degree. This can be helpful if your plans to make a living in theatre don't pan out right away. More and more people are finding it nearly impossible to get decent jobs without a degree.

Many people who study theatre will someday teach theatre. If you choose to teach, you will need a graduate degree in theatre as well. Many people in the theatre find that teaching is a good way to supplement their income.

Actors with university degrees may find themselves teaching part-time acting classes at a college. Or they may become involved in some artist-in-residence programs that place actors and other artists in elementary and high schools to work with children. Often these programs are targeted to schools where there are no specialized acting classes.

Another advantage of college programs is that they may give you a broader exposure to education. Many of the programs will have extensive **liberal arts** requirements.

Liberal arts: Courses in language, philosophy, history, and literature intended for general education.

What Kind of Degree Should You Get? Programs will vary quite a bit, depending on the school you attend. There are generally three types of degrees you can receive if studying theatre:

- **Bachelor of Arts (B.A.) in drama:** This degree gives you a broad liberal education with an emphasis in theatre; it's a good first degree if you expect to go for graduate-level training in theatre.
- **Bachelor of Science (B.S.) in theatre education:** This degree will qualify you to teach theatre classes.
- **Bachelor of Fine Arts (B.F.A.) in theatre:** This degree is considered a preprofessional degree that prepares you to work as a theatre professional.

Each of these three programs will be different. If you choose a B.A. program, you will find that some of the courses you take will be the same as students with other majors. You will have more courses in general liberal arts, which will include science, math, history, philosophy, English, and the humanities.

With a B.S. degree program, you'll have classes on teaching theory and techniques. You'll find yourself taking classes with other students who are preparing to teach other subject areas.

The B.F.A. program will give you the most intensive experience in theatre. You will take the most number of courses in acting and other theatre skills, from movement to set design. Whichever program you choose, you will find theatre study quite demanding. Although you may not have as much written homework as other students, you will find you invest many hours in memorizing lines, rehearsing scenes, and participating in performances.

Studying theatre in college can be quite demanding. As an actor, you will invest many hours in memorizing lines, rehearsing scenes, and participating in performances.

How to Choose a College. The best way to select a college or university program is to ask questions. You'll want to look at college catalogs. You can also talk with people you know who have graduated from a particular college or who are currently attending it. You may also talk to representatives from the college.

What do you want to do with your theatre degree? Answer this question and it will be easier to decide what program is best for you. You'll know which type of degree to go after. For example, if you decide you want to get a B.F.A. because you want to graduate from college and then go off to New York and launch an acting career, then you'll want to look at colleges with a B.F.A. program in theatre. Maybe you'd like to teach theatre. You'll want to track down programs that offer a B.S.

Many local libraries have collections of college catalogs. You can spend some time looking at these. You may want to start by looking at the colleges in your area or in your state that offer theatre majors.

Even though you won't be applying to colleges for several years, it's not too early to check them out. Investigate the requirements for entering the programs you like. This will help you select your precollege program of study. The ultimate decision about college will include many factors, such as the location and cost, as well as the quality of the program.

Other Programs of Study

Not all actors attend a four-year university program and receive a degree. There are other training programs that are commercial acting programs. Many of these, like the American Academy of Dramatic Arts in New York City, are intensive two-year programs. Some actors choose this approach instead of college. There are also acting classes and private teachers. Among the more well known are the Herbert Berghof Studio or the Lee Strasberg Theatrical Institute, both in New York City.

Picking out a commercial acting school or a private teacher and acting classes can be a frustrating experience. Who is a good teacher? In which situation are you truly going to get your money's worth?

Go and visit a class. Sit in on one session, if you can. Ask questions of the teacher and the students. Get a sense of how the actors interact. Then you can decide whether this group is going to work for you.

Summary

Training for actors can be found in college or university programs. The kind of degree that you receive will depend on whether you wish to pursue an acting or teaching career. Some actors receive training at special commercial acting programs or by taking classes with acting teachers. Which choice you make will be determined by your long-term goals, the money you have available, and what part of the country you wish to live in.

Professional Theatre Opportunities

When you think of acting as a career, what images come to mind? Perhaps you imagine an opening night for a Broadway play and seeing your name on the marquee. Maybe you visualize attending the Academy Awards ceremonies and waiting as the presenter tears open an envelope and announces your name as the winner of the best acting Oscar.

Maybe you know of someone who is trying to work as a professional actor. Maybe the images that come to mind include a series of auditions with no positive results or being employed as a waitress or waiter.

The second set of images is the more realistic one. Becoming a professional actor is a grueling process. Almost no one becomes an overnight success. Most actors work hard for a long time with limited success. Many actors are unemployed a good share of the time.

It takes a great deal of drive to succeed at being a professional actor. It takes persistence and self-confidence, especially when you are getting turned down week after week. Self-discipline is important, too, because the actor must stay in good physical condition and keep sharpening his or her acting abilities while trying to get work. Many struggling actors continue

Great news! You have the opportunity to audition for a new theatre company. The director has not yet announced the season but is holding general auditions. Each actor auditioning has been asked to present three monologues—one classical, one contemporary, and one comedy.

Step One
Decide. Meet in groups of three. Decide which person in your group will take which type of monologue. Discuss which monologues you want to memorize and present.

Step Two
Research. Go to the library and look at books of monologues for actors. If there are none in your school library, go to the local public library or ask if your teacher has monologue books. Each person in your group should select two or three monologues he or she likes.

Step Three
Choose. Meet in a small group and read the monologue you selected out loud to the others. Decide which monologue you prefer and then have the other two group members announce their favorite. Vote on which would be the best one for you to memorize and prepare. Why is this selection a good one for you?

Step Four
The Character. Discuss as a group the character represented by your monologue.

Write down the things you know or can figure out about this character. Discuss how you identify with the character you are playing. Talk about what you can do to get in character before delivering the monologue.

Step Five
Evaluate. After each person in your group has selected a monologue, help each other memorize the lines. After you have memorized the lines, work on a dramatic presentation of the work. Evaluate your classmates' performance by using the following:

Directions: Listen to your classmate deliver the monologue. List the name of the student being evaluated. Then rate the student's skills, using the following symbols:

+ = excellent
o = adequate
– = needs improvement

Finally, make specific comments about the student's skills in each area.

Skill
Rating
Comments
Knowledge of Character
Body Movements
Development of Character's Voice
Relationship of Character to Audience

to take acting classes while trying to get work. This helps them improve their skills and make connections for future jobs.

Although all of these things may sound negative, people do make a living in the theatre. There are several things you can do to improve your chances for success.

Live in a City

There's no way to get around it. If you want to work in professional theatre, you will need to live in or near a major metropolitan area. The reason? Only larger cities have a lot of professional acting possibilities.

New York is where many aspiring actors go to get their start because there are so many opportunities. There are many professional theatres in New York.

Chicago has been labeled the "Second City." That label may not be appropriate any longer when it comes to theatre opportunities. Chicago has a vibrant theatre community and many professional theatres with new plays being developed all the time. Some actors you may know of got their start in Chicago, including Jim Belushi, John Malkovitch, and John Mahoney. David Mamet, a playwright and director of both plays and films, spent his early days in theatre in the Chicago area.

Los Angeles is a third big city with many opportunities for the actor. Although most people think of the movie industry when they think of Los Angeles, there are also many live theatre performing opportunities in that city as well.

Are those the only cities in which one can make a living as an actor? No, but those are the cities in which there are the greatest number of possibilities. You stand a better chance of making a living as an actor in one of these cities.

Who Employs Actors?

Theatres do, of course. That question is answered easily. But there are many levels in that answer. In Chapter 15, we will discuss performing opportunities in film and television. For now, we are going to look at live theatre performance.

In New York City, there are different levels of theatres. Broadway theatres are the largest theatres in New York City.

This doesn't mean that all Broadway theatres actually have addresses on Broadway Avenue. This is actually a distinction related to size or number of seats in the house. These theatres are clustered in the theatre district around Broadway, from 44th to 52nd streets.

In New York, there are also off-Broadway theatres. These are smaller professional theatres. They may be either near the Broadway theatre district or farther away. Off-off Broadway theatres are found in more distant neighborhoods and are generally rather small.

Another important distinction among these three has to do with pay scales. The Broadway productions are the most elaborate and costly productions, and the actors and other theatre professionals receive the highest pay. Off-Broadway plays have a lower pay scale. The amount actors in off-off Broadway receive ranges from little to nothing.

Other cities, such as Chicago, have similar distinctions based on size of the house. In Chicago, there are Loop and off-Loop theatres.

Regional Theatres. Not all opportunities exist in Manhattan. Actors can make a living and get valuable experience in what is known as regional theatre. These are smaller professional theatres that exist outside of New York City that may not have national reputations.

Regional theatre includes theatre opportunities on the East Coast outside of New York City, such as the New Haven, Connecticut, or the Boston area. Milwaukee and Minneapolis have active theatre communities. Seattle is another exciting smaller city with a booming theatre community.

The opportunities in these regions may not be as numerous, but the competition is not as fierce.

Touring Companies. When plays and musicals succeed on Broadway, they are often taken on tour to other major cities throughout the country. The casts of these touring companies are often different from the original Broadway cast. A tour of a major musical might be booked for many months in another city, or it might have a smaller engagement of a few weeks before traveling on to a different city.

Plays and musicals that are successful on Broadway often go on tour with different casts. A touring company may spend many months in a large city or several days in a small city before moving on.

When the tour originates from New York, the casting is done there. Exceptions might be when a play or musical calls for a child actor. That role will be filled by a young actor from the city where the play is running. An example of that is *Les Miserables* and the character of the child Cosette.

Dinner Theatre. In many cities and in some suburban communities surrounding major cities, there are dinner theatre companies. These combine a restaurant with a theatre performance. The plays produced in such theatres are usually musicals or comedies. These theatres provide work for both seasoned actors and younger performers. The audience is seated at tables, so the layout is different than a usual theatre. Even though the dinner is served prior to the show, attention may be less focused on the stage.

Children's Theatre. Don't forget children's theatre! This may include things like puppet theatre. This opportunity may not appeal to some actors, but there is a chance to make money from theatre and gain more confidence and experience. Some children's theatre companies may tour and do many performances in schools.

How Actors Get Work in Professional Theatre

To get work you have to audition. There's no getting around the often disheartening experience of getting up in front of a director and showing your stuff and then being told to go home.

Opportunities don't just drop in your lap if you're an actor. You have to make them happen. Besides tracking down auditions and going to them, the actor has to continually make connections in the theatre world.

Contacts can mean work in the future. For example, a young actor in New York may choose to work with a young director on an off-off Broadway production for little pay, hoping that when the director graduates to off-Broadway productions, he or she will be remember the young actor. Actors may also participate in staged **readings** of new plays for no pay, hoping that if the play is produced, their work in developing the role will be rewarded by being cast in that role.

Reading: *A staged or unstaged performance of a play that actors do without memorizing the script.*

Summary

There are many performing opportunities in professional theatre, but these are found primarily in large cities. New York is the city with the largest number of professional theatres, but Chicago and Los Angeles have many opportunities as well. Regional theatres can be found in other large cities. Some actors find work in touring companies of Broadway productions. To succeed, actors must work hard at developing acting skills, must audition regularly, and must develop contacts in the theatre community.

Other Performing Opportunities

More opportunities await the actor who is willing to think past New York City and a large theatre. In fact, young actors can take advantage of other chances to build a performance history.

Summer stock: *Semiprofessional theatre companies that produce plays throughout the United States and other countries for a whole summer.*

Repertory: *A sequence of plays done over a period of time.*

Summer Stock

Many actors and directors got their start in **summer stock** theatre companies. They may produce a **repertory** of plays

Critic's Choice

You Decide

Imagine that you are looking over the catalog for a well-regarded college theatre program.

1. Shown below is a partial listing of theatre classes offered. Read over the description of each course. Write down why you think each course is important for the theatre student to take. Which courses do you think should be requirements for all theatre majors? Which courses should be electives?

Theatre 201 Acting I: Basic Skills
An introduction to the basic skills needed by an actor. The course will involve physical, vocal, and improvisational exercises. Students will learn and perform short scenes and monologues to gain awareness of their own and others' needs on stage.

Theatre 210 Body Movement for the Actor I
An introduction to the development of the proper flexibility and strength needed by an actor on stage. Students will work on developing their own movements and learn how to modify their natural movements to fit the needs of characters they may portray.

Theatre 212 Stage Combat
An introduction to the safe acting of unarmed combat (including the use of slaps, punches, kicks, falls, and rolls) and the use of swords and daggers.

Theatre 214 Accents and Dialects
An introduction to the eight most commonly used English and foreign language dialects and accents actors need for the stage. Emphasis is on the technical aspects of the dialects and accents, including vowel and consonant pronunciation, rhythm, and vocabulary.

Theatre 215 Production Techniques I: Sets and Lights
An introduction to the set and light crew jobs for a theatrical production. Students gain practical experience working as members of a production crew for a season production.

Theatre 225 Stage Makeup
An introduction to makeup techniques, including face casting, bald caps, mold making, prosthetics, and teeth casting.

2. The college offering these classes is nearby. It has just started a new summer program offering theatre classes to young people. These are the same classes that are taught during the year at the college. Young students may take the summer classes and receive college credit if they receive a grade of B or above.

   You will be able to take one class this summer. Which class would you choose to take first? Why? If you could take two classes the following summer, which two would you select? Why?

3. Make a list of other classes you think a theatre student should take in order to have a complete theatre education. Should these be required courses? Discuss with your classmates which courses you think every theatre student should take. Why?

over several days, weeks, or months. These theatres usually open in June and close at the end of August. Summer stock offers both amateur and professional actors a wide range of experiences.

The pay scale of summer stock depends on many things. Apprentices usually receive little or no money. Hours are long, and the work is exhausting. But if you are an apprentice, you receive valuable experience working with professional directors, actors, and technicians.

Summer stock is an intense experience. Even if the company only produces one play, this must be done as quickly as possible. Lines must be learned quickly. Scenery is built on the spot. Costumes are prepared and ready right away. Rehearsals run all day but usually for no more than a week. Then the play is performed.

If the company is producing plays in repertory, then the actor may have a schedule of rehearsing one play during the day and performing a different one at night. This "pressure cooker" environment creates invaluable experience for the young or student actor. Such training prepares the actor for the demands of other professional theatre.

Theme Parks and Cruise Ships

Have you been to Great America, Opryland, Busch Gardens, or Disney World? These amusement parks offer exciting employment opportunities for young performers. Many of these theme parks have shows that run several times a day. They hire young actors, dancers, and singers to perform throughout the park. Generally, performers must be at least eighteen years of age. Large amusement parks will hold auditions in several major cities to hire summer staff.

The work is often grueling. Not only do performers have to run shows many times a day, but they also have to withstand the heat of summer. The pay is good for young performers, but the hours are long with little time off. Nonetheless, it is an exciting opportunity for young actors who are determining whether they want a life in the theatre. Summer work performing in a theme park is another line for your performing résumé.

Performing at theme parks is often quite exhausting. Performers and crew generally have to run shows many times a day. Nevertheless, working in a theme park show is good experience for young actors.

Much like summer amusement park jobs, performing on a cruise ship seems glamorous. In reality, the job demands hard work, long hours, and long stretches of time away from home. But if the actor can stomach those demands, this is professional work. This further develops performing skills and experience.

And Not Just Adults

Young actors are needed for professional productions. There are a number of live performing opportunities that some actors your age have taken advantage of. These opportunities for young actors include:

- **Opera Companies:** Supernuminaries, often called supers, are walk-on roles in large opera productions. The scene may be a street scene or a family scene in which children and young people are needed. The actors do not sing and are rather like extras on a movie set.

- **Dance Companies:** Every Christmas, big productions of *The Nutcracker* are presented in cities all over the country. There are many roles for children and young people. Performers must, of course, have experience in dance. Competition for these roles may be quite stiff.

- **Touring Companies:** Large musical productions that start out in New York and then tour may hire young actors locally. In other words, if there are parts for children and young people, these performers will be hired in each city in which the production is running.

- **Seasonal Plays:** A play version of Charles Dickens's *A Christmas Carol* may be a standard performance in some cities. Every year, a theatre will perform this work. There are several roles for young people of various ages in this play.

It helps to be small! That may not be the case if you are trying out for the basketball team, but if you are auditioning for a role of a ten-year-old, it may come in handy. Teenagers who are on the small side may be hired for children's roles.

Special abilities can make you more appealing as a performer. For example, dance training can open up opportunities, such as the dance company or opera company possibilities mentioned earlier. If you are a gymnast and can do flips, if you can juggle or if you can ride a unicycle, you may be able to add that skill to your acting talent to open up performing opportunities.

A Word about the Union

Ultimately, most professional actors will join the union. The Actor's Equity Association includes all professional performers in legitimate theatre in the United States and Canada. This covers Broadway and off-Broadway productions, touring companies, repertory theatres, dinner theatres, and children's theatres.

Joining the union isn't an automatic thing. You have to earn a place in the union with an Equity contract. This places you in a different pay scale from nonunion actors and eliminates certain performing opportunities. Some places do not hire Equity actors. Young actors may find more opportunities available by not joining the union.

Being in the union offers some advantages and benefits. It doesn't assure you work, although it may give you more information on what jobs are available. You also receive free advice and seminars, plus an assured pay rate, if you are hired.

Summary

Opportunities for performers include summer stock theatre, theme parks, cruise ships, dinner theatre, and children's theatre. All of these can provide a young actor with important experience as well as income. Other performance opportunities may be with opera or dance companies, with seasonal productions, and with touring plays. Professional actors may eventually join a union, but this may eliminate some opportunities for the struggling actor.

Interviewing

1. *Imagine the Situation.* Choose a partner. Imagine you are in an interview involving a high school student and the head of a college theatre department. If you are playing the student, assume that you have already done well in an audition and that the department chairperson is making the final selection of students.

2. *If You Were There.* Plan an interview. If you are the interviewer, write out the questions you would ask the student. If you play the student role, list the things you would want to tell the interviewer.

3. *Now Do It.* Role play the interview. Discuss how both students felt in their roles and make suggestions for improvement.

Making Connections

4. *Think about Auditions.* Make a list of audition opportunities. This list can come from a local newspaper, a regional acting newsletter or magazine, or a national listing. Pretend you are a twenty-five-year-old actor with a college degree and a small amount of professional acting experience. Which productions would you choose to audition for? Why?

5. *Networking.* You have just moved to town. You are a young actor looking for performing opportunities. You don't know anyone in the local theatre community. How would you attempt to make connections with people in the theatre world? What would you do to meet directors and other actors?

Be an Apprentice

6. *Think about Your Skills.* A new summer stock company will launch its first season next summer near your community. Because there are limited funds, the director has announced that there will be a number of apprenticeships for students. The company will be performing one musical and one comedy. Think about the experiences and skills that you have that would make the director interested in you as an apprentice. Make a list of them.

7. *Apply.* Write a letter to the director applying for an apprentice position in a summer stock theatre program. Explain in the letter why you would be an asset to the program.

Acting Out

8. *Audition.* You are going to an audition for the role of a twelve-year-old in a small professional production. You have prepared your monologue well, but you are very nervous waiting for the audition to happen. You have a few minutes before you will be called into the audition. As a class, decide what exercises or activities you can do to reduce your nervousness.

9. *Get Rid of Those Nerves.* Take turns leading the class in some exercises to reduce nervousness before auditions. How do you feel after doing the exercises?

The Actor's Logbook

1. ***Learning the Language.*** Add each of the words and terms in boldface in this chapter to the appropriate page in the glossary section of your logbook.

2. ***How Did They Get There?*** List all the people you know personally who have worked professionally in the theatre. If you don't know any personally, do you have friends or acquaintances who know professional actors? List these people. Come up with a list of questions you would like to ask professional actors about their training and their early experiences.

3. ***Look at Those Bios.*** Collect several programs from professional theatre productions. If you haven't attended any yourself, ask family, friends, and neighbors for programs. Read over the biographies of the actors and list their education. What schools are mentioned? What other training is included in these biographies?

Critical Thinking

4. ***Main Ideas.*** For each of the three sections of the chapter, make a list of at least three important ideas. Try to develop an outline for this chapter.

5. ***Evaluation.*** Read a newspaper or magazine article about a famous actor. Think about what kind of training the actor has and what experiences he or she first had as a professional actor. How do you think this training influenced the kind of work the actor is doing today?

6. ***Comparison.*** Why is live theatre performance important to an actor who wants to act for film and television? What skills would an actor develop on stage that would help on camera? What skills would not be important for on-camera work?

Creative Thinking

7. ***You Be the Director.*** Imagine you are the director of a new professional production of a play in a regional theatre. You have announced auditions and are listening to monologues. In addition to the way the actor presents the monologue, what other things might you notice about the actor? How would these other factors influence your attitude toward this actor?

8. ***How to Get There.*** Think about what you would like your life to be like fifteen years from now. What theatre experiences would you like to have under your belt by that time? Draw a timeline for the next fifteen years. List the goal(s) you think are achievable for each year that will get you closer to your long-term goal of being a professional actor. Include educational plans, volunteer opportunities, and performance experience.

9. ***Applications.*** Work in small groups. Choose a play you would like to produce. Then write up audition notices. Include what kind of monologue(s) you would like the actors to prepare. Discuss what kind of experience you would like the actors to have.

CHAPTER FIFTEEN

Film and Television Acting

EXPECTATIONS

After reading this chapter, you will be able to

15.1 list some of the challenges of acting in front of a camera that are different from acting on a stage

15.2 briefly explain how a film is shot

15.3 demonstrate various points of attention actors use

15.4 identify different types of shots used in motion pictures

15.5 understand the process by which actors can gain skill in on-camera techniques

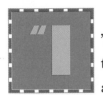'm going to be there one day. It's my name they're going to be calling!" Many aspiring actors sit each year and watch the Academy Awards presentation. And each year they promise themselves that one day they will reach this goal. Having that Oscar to set on your mantle takes more than wishing and dreaming. It means a lot of hard work.

Film Is Different than Being on Stage

Acting in a film or in a dramatic television production is quite different than acting on stage. And at the same time, there are a lot of similarities in the two forms.

The Basics Are Still There

Acting is still acting, whether it's in front of a live audience or in front of a camera. Many of the basic acting skills that you have learned in this class are important for the movie or television actor as well as for the stage actor.

A film actor needs to understand characterization. If you are acting in a movie, you will still need to work to know the character you are playing very well. You will need to get in character and stay that way when you are being filmed.

Daniel Day-Lewis, playing the role of Christy Brown in *My Left Foot*, had a very demanding role to play. Christy Brown was severely handicapped by cerebral palsy; the only part of his body that he could really control was his left foot. Reports are that, while filming the movie, Lewis stayed in character even when off the **set.** He did this in order to maintain the intensity and believability of the character he was playing.

The use of the body is important on camera as well as on stage. In fact, in a film it may be more critical. The camera is unforgiving. You may have heard of actors gaining fifty pounds for a particular role. An actor will do this in order to look the part he or she is playing better. Because the camera may often show the actor close up, it is even more important

Set: The physical setting where the movie scene is being filmed.

Film and television actors have to work just as hard as stage actors to
make a character believable. To realistically portray Christy Brown,
Daniel Day-Lewis had to put himself in the character of a man severely
handicapped by cerebral palsy.

to have the body look right for the part. Even though you don't
see all that is happening in a scene in a movie, an actor still
must be able to use his or her body in the same way that he or
she would on stage.

Vocal training is just as important for television and film
acting as it is for stage acting. If you are working on camera,
you obviously don't have to worry about saying your lines loud
enough for the back row to hear. Still, all the voice training
that an actor receives for stage work can come in handy in
film as well.

The Differences

Acting on camera is easier, you might say. If you're acting in a
movie you don't have to memorize all your lines at one time.
Nor do you have to remember them all at the same time.

While this is true, there are a number of ways in which working on camera is more demanding than working on stage.

Working on Camera Is More Intense. Have you ever seen a production of a play and then later seen the filmed version of the play? Actually, this happens often. Some examples of successful plays that have had a further life as a movie include *Steel Magnolias, Six Degrees of Separation*, and *Children of a Lesser God*. Many classic works of theatre have been made into movies. Shakespearean plays, for example, have been made into movies. Kenneth Brannagh, an English actor and director, is noted for his work both on stage and in filming Shakespeare.

What's the difference? If you have ever seen two versions of a work, you will probably recall some scenes in the movie that weren't in the play at all. A work on stage is confined to the stage and to the specific time and place set for that particular scene. Often, other times and scenes or other characters are referred to in the dialog but the real action is rather static.

In a movie, the **screenwriter** can actually take you to the place referred to. For example, in the staged version of *Steel Magnolias*, M'Lynn Eatenton, the mother, recalls all that happens during her daughter's death by talking about it at the beauty shop. In the film, you see hospital scenes. In the film, the characters respond to each other and the death by interacting at the cemetery after the funeral. This scene is not in the play.

Screenwriter: The person who writes a television or movie script.

Location. Films may require you as an actor to go on location to some very distant places. In a play like *Miss Saigon*, some of the scenes are set in Saigon during the Vietnam War. The set is created to look like Saigon.

If this play were made into a movie, it would probably be filmed in Vietnam or another country nearby that looked like Vietnam. Being on location can be quite challenging physically to the actor. If you were cast in a movie production filming in Vietnam, you'd have to endure the weather and possibly some of the discomforts of being out in the countryside. That might mean dealing with heat or insects. The actor on stage doesn't have to face any of these elements.

If a movie shows a winter scene, that means the actors had to be outside in the winter. If it's a scene of white-water rafting down a river, the actors were there.

Working on Camera Is More Physical. The actual physical demands placed on a film or television actor may be much greater. When you think of movies you have seen at a theatre or on television, you probably remember many action scenes. These scenes may involve fights between characters or car-chase scenes.

Sometimes the actual scenes are filmed with stunt men or women. These are actors who are specially trained to do these action scenes without getting hurt. In the movie, the character doing the stunt will be substituted for the real actor at certain points in a scene.

Stunt men and women are frequently used as stand-ins for actors involved in dangerous stunts in movies. Performing stunts requires a great deal of training, attention to safety, and perfect physical fitness.

Some actors, however, choose to do some or all of their own stunts. This may mean they have to learn some new skills for a movie. Let's say there is a movie where the character rides a horse and is thrown by the horse. The actor must learn to ride a horse and be comfortable around horses. In addition, the actor may need to learn how to be thrown from a horse.

The long, grueling hours of filming place a physical demand on an actor as well. If you're performing on stage, you have two hours of performance. If you do a matinee and an evening performance, you may have four hours on stage. But with film work, you may spend long hours on set day after day while the director is shooting scenes you are in.

How Films Are Made

A stage production is quite simple. You start at the beginning and go right through to the end without stopping, other than for scene changes or an intermission. The play is broken up into different acts and different scenes. Usually a play has two or three acts and may have several scenes in each act.

With a film, the screenplay is broken down into many small scenes. The **screenplay** includes descriptions of the scenes, the characters and their actions, and camera angles, as well as the dialog.

Screenplay: *A play that is written to be filmed.*

When a director sits down with a screenplay, he or she does not decide to start filming at the beginning and go straight through to the end. The director chooses what scenes to shoot and in what order. For example, if there are eight scenes where a character is on a farm, these eight scenes will all be shot together, even though they appear at different times in the movie.

The director then breaks down the scene into a series of short shots. Each shot may be filmed many times and at different angles and different distances. Every time the shot is filmed, all of the details must be perfect because the camera records everything.

Obviously this is very tedious work. You, as an actor, are required to be in character and act suddenly and for a very short period of time. You may be asked to do a shot again and again until the director is satisfied.

Summary

Working as an actor in a film or dramatic television performance requires many of the same skills that a stage performer needs. But the process is quite different. Film work may be physically more demanding and require more work to stay in character while the movie is filmed.

On-camera Techniques

Just as you need to study and practice to develop skills to be a good stage performer, you also need to develop some skills that are unique to acting for the camera. If you are unfamiliar with camera techniques, you may be so conscious of the technical parts of acting in front of the camera that you will actually give a poor performance.

The Camera

It's important to have the right attitude about the camera. While the camera isn't really a substitute for a person or an audience, as an actor, you need to think of the camera as a person.

Point of attention: *Someone or something to look at.*

When you are working with a camera, just as when you are acting on stage, there are three **points of attention.** The points of attention are:

- One actor looking directly at another. This is the most common shot.
- An actor looking to the side. This is used when an actor is talking about or thinking about other people or things.
- An actor looking down. This is used when an actor is thinking or talking about himself or herself.

When working with a camera, you will look directly at the camera when your point of attention is your partner. As an actor, you will use the second and third points of attention while listening to your partner's lines and during your lines. Directing your attention to the camera may happen either during your lines or your partner's lines.

Young actors who have mostly stage experience often find it beneficial to practice the different points of attention that are needed for on-camera work. Take this opportunity to practice for your big break in films.

Step One
Read the Story. Read through the following short script, trying to decide what point of attention would work best in each segment:

ASHLEY: Do you believe how much homework we have for history tonight?

JEAN: I don't know how I'm going to get it done. I have basketball practice after school.

ASHLEY: I have to baby-sit. The kids are crazy. I can't get any homework done when I'm with them.

JEAN: At least it's money.

ASHLEY: I only get $4.50 an hour and it's for two kids.

JEAN: I have to baby-sit my brother sometimes but I don't get paid anything.

ASHLEY: Your parents don't pay you anything!

SANDY: Are you going to the play auditions after school tonight?

JEAN: I have basketball practice. They're tomorrow after school too.

SANDY: No, that's just call-backs. You have to show up today if you want to be in it.

ASHLEY: Darn. I can't get out of baby-sitting!

JEAN: (*at the same time*) If I skip basketball practice, coach is going to really be mad. I missed one practice last week.

SANDY: Well, I don't mind a little less competition. I'm going to get one of the main roles anyhow, so you won't have to waste your time trying out.

Sandy leaves. Ashley sticks a tongue out at Sandy's back.

ASHLEY: Do you have a quarter and a dime? I think I'm going to call Mrs. Rose and see if I can get out of baby-sitting.

Jean hands Ashley money.

JEAN: Good luck.

Step Two
Practice in Front of the Class. Take turns reading these parts in front of the class. Discuss what your points of attention were. Discuss as a class how you would shoot this if you were filming this scene. What shots would you use? If you have access to a video camera, take turns videotaping this scene. Give everyone a chance to be on-camera. Discuss the problems with acting this scene.

When making gestures or movements in front of the camera, it's important to slow down your movements a bit. Remember not to overact for the camera. Don't use too many gestures or expressions. But at the same time, don't let your performance be dull by having very static expressions.

Some Camera Shots to Master

Once you have remembered where your point of attention needs to be and are conscious of how your facial expressions and movements may look on film, you need to learn a few more camera tricks that will help you to be comfortable.

The Standing or Seated Two Shot. This shot occurs in a scene in which two actors are sitting or standing side by side. In real life, you would see only the profile of the two people. But this isn't good for film, because you can't really see their eyes and mouth, which means you can't see their expressions.

In this type of scene, you will generally use a 45-degree-angle head position, so your eyes and mouth can be seen at least partially. This may seem a bit awkward, because you won't be able to really see and react to your partner's expressions and actions, but it is the best angle for the camera.

The Walking Two Shot. With this shot, the two actors need to use the same head position as with the seated two shot, but there are a few more rules to follow:

- Walk close to each other and stay side by side.
- Once the director says to start, wait two seconds, or two beats, before you start walking.
- Do not walk and talk at the same time; instead, start saying a word or two before you start walking.
- Make sure you and your partner start walking at the same time and use the 45-degree angle throughout.

Reversal: When two characters are located in opposite directions and face each other.

Reversal. Whenever you and another actor are located in opposite directions and face each other, this is called a **reversal.** In a filmed scene, you may have a reversal in which one actor

In a standing or sitting two shot, the actors stand or sit at a 45-degree angle so the camera can see their facial expressions.

is put in front of the camera and the other one is next to the camera. If you are the actor facing the camera, the camera then becomes your partner.

You may also have a reversal with a walking two shot when you and the other actor stop and turn to face each other. In this situation, it's important not to speak your lines and look into your partner's eyes; instead, focus on your partner's ear that is closest to the camera. Sounds weird, doesn't it? But it will appear as if you are looking at your partner on film and give the camera a view of your facial expressions.

Sometimes you will have a **reaction shot.** This is when the camera focuses on you while you are listening to your partner speak. When you are doing a reaction shot, make sure you are really thinking about what your partner is saying. When you are responding to your partner, let two beats go by (two seconds) before you answer. This seemingly dead time is needed for editing the scene later.

The Basic Shots. A close-up shot shows the actor's head and shoulders. A medium shot reveals the actor from the head down to the waist. A three-quarter shot shows an actor from head to knees. A full shot displays all of an actor's body.

Reaction shot: When the camera focuses on the character who is listening to another character talk or act.

Marks: Marks on the floor to show an actor where to move or stand.

Two more shots are important to know. A pan shot is where an actor crosses as the camera pans, or moves, with him or her. A walk-in shot occurs when one actor is in front of the camera speaking while the other actor enters the scene from off-camera.

It's fun and helpful to watch movies and think about the shots that are being used and the points of attention the actors are depending on. This is a good way to become more familiar with these techniques.

Marks. If you've performed on stage, you may have needed to pay attention to certain little tape **marks** on the stage that showed where things were to happen or where props were to be set. Similarly, in filming, the actors have marks that show them where they are supposed to be.

Floor marks are actual chalk or tape marks on the floor. An actor is expected to be right on the mark at specific points in the dialog and/or action. As an actor, you must remember that precision is very important. You must be right on the mark, not close to it. The camera is counting on you.

Peripheral marks are specific objects that an actor can see out of the corner of his or her eye. These might be a tree, a piece of furniture, or some kind of architectural prop. You may be told that, when you are in line with this mark, you will need to do something—either start moving or stop moving.

Following marks may feel a little awkward in the beginning because you will be asked to walk and talk and be at the right place all at the same time. With practice, using marks will become more comfortable for you and give you the confidence you need to perform on-camera.

Summary

When working on-camera, it's important to remember points of attention, whether you are talking to your partner, thinking or talking about yourself, or thinking or talking about someone else. Actors should know the seated or standing two shot, the walking two shot, and the reversal. The correct use of these techniques allows the audience to see more of an actor's expressions and gestures. The basic shots range from close-ups

Critic's Choice

Be Siskel and Ebert

Choose a movie you would like to review. This may be a movie you have recently seen or a movie that is now in theatres that you would like to see. Find someone else in the class who wants to review the same movie.

Before you go and see the movie or start working on a movie review, work either in small groups or as a class to decide what criteria you are going to use for deciding the quality of the film. Look back over some of the acting skills you have studied. Then also think about what is important in a movie production that is different than a play. Come up with a list or a chart that will help you make some decisions about how good the movie is.

1. Go to see the movie. Or, if it's out on video, rent the video and watch it. Take your chart with you while watching

and make some notes. Take some time to look over your notes and then arrange your notes in an outline form.

2. Write a one- or two-page review of the movie, making use of the points in the chart that seem important. Remember, in a review you want to tell something about the story, but not too much. In addition, you will evaluate the performances and the production and make a recommendation for the prospective viewer.

3. You and the classmate who watched the same film should discuss it in front of the class, much like Roger Ebert and Gene Siskel discuss the movies they review. See if you can agree on the movie. What rating would you give the movie: one, two, three, or four stars? Why? Would you send people to see it? Don't read your review but use it as a basis for your discussion.

4. Look up a review of the film you chose to review. You may need to find a review in a national magazine like *Newsweek* or *Time* if you can't find one from your local newspaper. Did your review agree with the other reviewer's? How was it similar? Discuss with your classmate how reading this other review changed your opinion of the movie.

to full body shots and can include pan shots and walk-in shots. Marks are indicators that give actors directions on where they need to be at a specific point in the script.

How Does Anyone Ever Get a Job?

If you want to make it in the movies or in television you will probably have to go either to New York or to Los Angeles. However, movie companies are increasingly selecting other locations, such as Chicago and Seattle, for filming movies.

It Takes Lots of People to Make a Movie

Everyone wants a lead role. Competition for these roles is fierce and usually only well-known actors are considered for the major roles. And these actors are represented by an agent. But there are a number of other acting possibilities in the making of a film.

Day players are actors who may just have one line in the film. These actors, as well as the featured actors, are cast by the casting director.

Stunt players may do anything from falling off a building to fighting. These actors are well-trained in stunts and also well-paid, although they usually go nameless as far as the general public is concerned. Even though they have been trained to do these stunts, there is always a risk of getting hurt.

It's not very glamorous, but the job of **stand-in** is an important one. The stand-in is the person who stands in for the main actor. Actors are selected who are approximately the same size and coloring of the stars. These people stand in place for the featured actors while a scene is being set up. When it is time to actually shoot, the real actor comes out and takes the place the stand-in has been occupying. A stand-in is never seen on camera.

Extras are the people who are seen but not heard in the movies. They may be the people walking down the street in a street scene, the other people in the elevator, or the crowd in the stadium. Working as an extra can be tedious and boring.

Day players: Actors who generally have very small roles and may be hired on a daily basis.

Stunt players: Specially trained actors who do dangerous stunts in movies.

Stand-in: An actor who stands in place for a major actor while a scene is being prepared for shooting.

Extras: Actors who have no lines and essentially serve as background in scenes that involve extra people.

Movie extras are the people who appear as background characters in a scene but have no lines. Doing extra work can be a fun and productive way to learn more about the filming process.

Extras are hired through special agencies and through the Screen Extras Union. Extras are hired by the day.

When you work as an extra, you may find yourself sitting around for many hours until it is finally time to film the scene that you and other extras are needed for. Even though it is boring and the pay is not much, working as an extra can give you an insider's view of what the movie-making business is like.

Occasionally a movie needs young actors. In some cases, a casting director will conduct a national search, looking for just the right person. This search may be advertised in metropolitan newspapers and sometimes on radio stations. Young people are encouraged to audition, usually by appointment. After several rounds of auditions, a director may decide to run a screen test for the most likely prospects.

*Screen test: A filmed
audition to determine
what an actor looks like
on film.*

The Screen Test

A casting director may like how you look and sound or how you move. But the director needs to see how you will appear on-camera. A **screen test** gives the director additional help in selecting actors.

For a screen test, you will generally be asked to appear three hours before the actual filming. You will be sent to have your makeup and hair done, and you will be provided with a costume. Then you will be directed to the set where the action of the scene will be blocked for you and another actor, who may have already been selected for the cast. After that comes a run-through of the scene. Then the scene is filmed or taped.

Screen tests can be daunting for a young actor, but they are a necessary part of the casting process. It's important for an actor who wants to work in film to prepare as much as possible for a screen test by getting experience in front of the camera.

How to Get On-camera Experience

There are classes for everything. Learning to act in front of the camera is no exception. Commercial acting schools may offer classes in on-camera techniques. There are classes in film and television acting that are conducted with the use of video equipment or closed-circuit television. These classes may be quite expensive. If you choose this route, you will want to investigate the classes and get recommendations from students who have completed the class.

Another way to get experience in front of the camera is by volunteering. Wherever there are film students, there are opportunities to appear in student film productions. Independent filmmakers may also use actors who are willing to work for free on their projects.

This opportunity may present itself to you when you reach college. If you are serious about acting in film, you should audition for these productions and get as much on-camera experience as possible. You will be building your résumé and increasing your confidence in front of the camera.

In order to break into television or film acting, you will need an agent, but you probably won't be able to get an agent without some track record. So it's important to get as many performing opportunities as possible, whether they are live theatre performances or film productions.

There are two main unions that actors who work in film may join. The American Federation of Television and Radio Artists obviously deals with television actors. The Screen Actors Guild represents actors on film projects, either for television or for motion pictures.

A Note about Soap Operas

Soap operas have long been a good opportunity for inexperienced actors to develop and to be noticed for other more challenging work. If you have ever watched a soap opera, you may think that the actors are not very good. In reality, the actors who perform on daytime dramatic television shows may be very talented actors. Often the scripts are not well-done and the characters and plots not well-developed, leaving actors and directors little to work with.

Competition for regular character roles on soap operas is keen. A young actor looking for television experience may find that extra work and smaller roles on daytime television are both good ways to get a start in the business. To find these opportunities, an actor must live in either Los Angeles or New York.

The experience of acting in one of these shows can be compared to the repertory company in live theatre. The actor must be flexible and will have long and regular hours of rehearsing and performing. It can be a good base from which to build strong acting skills.

Summary

Even though major roles in movies are hard to get, many actors find work in smaller capacities in motion pictures. The screen test is a way for a director to determine how an actor will look on-camera. This is not the only way to get experience on-camera. Actors can take classes in working on-camera and can audition to appear in film productions by students and independent filmmakers. If an actor is in New York or Los Angeles, work in daytime television can provide good on-camera experience.

If You Were to Audition

1. ***Look for Opportunities.*** Find an audition announcement for a motion picture production. You may need to look in a national trade magazine or in local acting audition newsletters.
2. ***Now Prepare.*** Decide how you would prepare for the audition. What would you take to the audition? How would you look and act at the audition?

Find a Screenplay

3. ***Look at a Screenplay.*** Go to your library or a bookstore and find a copy of a screenplay (a shooting script if possible). Or if you know someone who writes screenplays, ask the writer for a copy of a screenplay. Read through the screenplay.
4. ***Think about Differences.*** Discuss with your classmates how a screenplay is different from a play. What did you find most surprising about the form of the screenplay? Can you visualize how the movie will be shot from the instructions built into the screenplay?

Develop Your Eye

5. ***Think before You Watch.*** Watch a movie or television show on video. This may be an individual activity or one that your teacher asks you to do in class. Prepare to list the shots you see by writing headings for each of the three points of attention, the basic shots discussed on pages 283–284, variations of the two shot, reversals, and reaction shots.
6. ***Watch a Video.*** Watch the first thirty seconds or one minute of the video, then put it on pause. Check off on your list the differ-

ent points of attention you noticed and the different shots. Start the video again and watch another very small segment. Then check off from your list again the things that you saw.
7. ***Evaluate.*** If you are working as a class or a small group, discuss whether the shots were effective. Do you think a different shot would have been more effective? Go to a different section in the video and repeat this exercise.

You Call the Shots

8. ***Write a Script.*** Take one or two pages from a play that you like. Make a photocopy of those pages. Break it down into a shooting script, indicating what kind of shot you would use and what actor(s) you would be focusing on. If you need to, cut apart the lines from the photocopy and paste them on another sheet of paper so you have space to write out the camera directions.
9. ***Think It Over.*** What is most difficult about making these decisions?

Acting Out

10. ***Look at Yourself.*** Pick a one-minute monologue to memorize. You may use a monologue you have already memorized. Arrange to have a classmate or a family member videotape you delivering this monologue.
11. ***Be Your Own Critic.*** Look at the videotape of your performance and list the good things about how you came across on camera. Then list the areas where you could improve. Tape the monologue again. Have you improved?

The Actor's Logbook

1. *Learning the Language.* Add each of the words and terms in bold type in this chapter to the appropriate page in the glossary section of your logbook.

2. *Whom Do You Admire?* Make a list of your favorite actors from either television or movie performances. Select three of these actors and find out as much about them as you can. Read articles about these actors and find out how they made it into television or motion pictures. You may need to look up articles about these actors in the *Reader's Guide to Periodical Literature* or by using InfoTrak, an on-line database of periodicals. For each actor, make a note of what kind of training he or she had and how he or she got the first movie roles.

Critical Thinking

3. *Main Ideas.* Write a two-paragraph summary of the main points of this chapter.

4. *Compare and Contrast.* How is working as a motion picture or television actor similar to being a live theatre performer? How is it different? Which would be harder: to start as a live theatre performer and switch to movies or to have been a movie actor and then switch to the stage? Why do you think that?

5. *Evaluation.* What opportunities are available to you to prepare you for a career in movies or television acting? What can you do to gain experience with on-camera techniques and to be-come more comfortable in front of a camera?

Creative Thinking

6. *Adapt a Play.* Pick a play you are quite familiar with. Think about what scenes you would be able to add to a movie version that do not exist in the stage version. Write down all the extra scenes that you would put in the screenplay if you were to write it.

7. *No Couch Potato.* Watch your favor-ite television program. Notice the interactions between the characters. Pretend you are behind the camera. What different shots would you choose to communicate a differ-ent feeling about the scene? Take notes. After you have watched the show, write up your plan to alter the filming of the show, explaining why you would want to do what you plan to do and what specific changes you would introduce.

8. *Where Is Your Attention?* Select three conversations to monitor. One conversation should be at home, one at school, and one in another setting. You should be able to hear these conversations, but you should not be involved in them. Notice the points of attention in the conversation. When one person speaks to another, does he or she look at the other person? When that person talks about himself or herself, where does he or she look? Does this person ever look down or to the side? Think about how you would film the conversation to reveal what the character is thinking about. How would this character have to behave differently to show up well on-camera?

CHAPTER SIXTEEN

Elements of Style

EXPECTATIONS

After reading this chapter, you will be able to

16.1   define what is meant by *theatrical style*

16.2   discuss style differences in various historical periods

16.3   list elements that are part of theatrical style

16.4   give examples of theatrical styles

16.5   identify how setting a classical play in a different period might increase audience understanding of the play

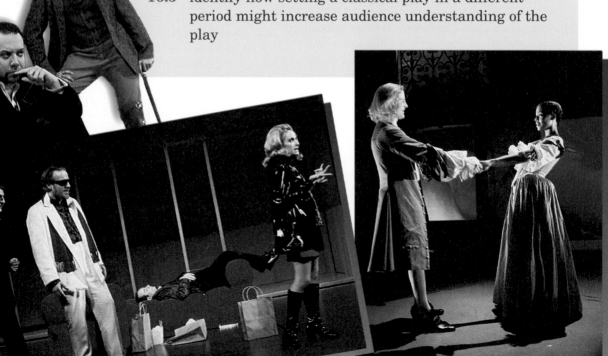

I t is the 1920s. The men are gangsters, small-time crooks. Their big concern is where to find a big crap game so they can gamble. The women they date are attempting to look glamorous. It's Prohibition, a time in U.S. history when alcohol could not be produced or sold. In spite of this, these characters know where to get a drink. Into this somewhat seamy world marches a female Salvation Army officer who is trying to get reprobates to reform. This is the setting for a musical by Frank Loesser called *Guys and Dolls*, and when the lights come up on the Broadway production, it is soon very clear that the show is set in the 1920s.

Style Is What You See and Hear

When you think of the word **style,** you may think of fashion. In theatre, style refers to how a play is written and what time period it's connected to. When you see a production of *Grease,* you can quickly tell that it is set in the 1950s.

In understanding theatrical style, you must first study the culture and values of the people living in a particular time period. You can take on the style of a particular period by saturating yourself in the study of the period. Study the country, the people, the theatre, and the playwright of a historical play, and you will begin to understand it.

As an actor, your main concern is to present the character in a play in a truthful and believable manner. This can't be done simply by studying the time in which the play takes place. You must get close to and develop an affinity for the character as well.

Style: The manner in which a play was written and the period to which it relates.

Style Is a Complex Issue

Simply knowing that a play is historical is not always a sure indicator of the acting style necessary for the play. In fact, sometimes we make assumptions about plays from certain time periods—assumptions that may or may not be appropriate.

An example of a difference in required acting styles can best be seen by contrasting plays from two different time periods. We'll look at a fifth-century (B.C.) Greek play by Sophocles and a seventeenth-century play by the French playwright Molière.

In *Oedipus*, the acting style is that of the ancient Greeks. They used formalized verse, large, overstated movements, and large masks. Costuming wasn't important, nor were human or personal details.

Molière's *Les Prècieuses Ridicules* ("The Pretentious Ladies") is on the other end of the style spectrum. This play is about aristocratic ladies and gentlemen in the reign of Louis XIV of France. The actors in this play need to pay attention to some personal characteristics. Such things as drinking tea and using fans are critical elements to the proper presentation of the play.

Sometimes, however, old is not necessarily stuffy and formalized; nor is contemporary equivalent with a very realistic acting style.

Some of the Elements of Style

Just what exactly do you look for in a play? What are those elements that make up style?

Use of the Body. How actors use their bodies is an important element of style. In some styles, bodily movements are overstated, even larger than life. Some historical styles call for very stiff and proper carriage of the body. Still others would be seen as more realistic or natural.

Costuming. How elaborate is the costuming of a play? Do the characters wear wigs or do they have natural-looking hair? Are the costumes large and involved or is the clothing worn by the actors simple and basic? The answers to these questions tell us something about the time period the play is set in. They also give the actors insight into the characters of the people in the play.

The style of a play is usually reflected in the costumes of the actors. In
turn, the cut of the costumes can have an impact on the movements of the
actors.

The costumes of a period have an impact on the movement
of the actors as well. If an actor is wearing a simple tunic for a
Greek play, his or her movement will be less restricted than
the movement of an actor in a play from the seventeenth century, when the gentlemen wore high-heeled shoes with buck-
les, long square-cut coats with lace at the cuffs, and breeches
below the knee.

Mannerisms. Today, on greeting a friend you might wave or
give them a high-five greeting. A century or two ago, it was

the custom to bow and curtsey as a way to greet each other. In the past, the use of a snuff box was a part of social custom. In fact, using snuff was a rather elaborate affair; there was a proper way to use one's fingers and to shake any snuff particles off of one's clothing.

Acting Style. The style of acting an actor may use ranges from a rather formal and stiff style to a more natural and realistic style. An actor may use a highly exaggerated style of acting for one time period, but for another would develop a style that doesn't call attention to the body or voice or mannerisms. This style would be called a realistic acting style.

Historical Periods

Several periods in history have had a special impact on acting. These periods have very distinctive styles connected to them. Your challenge as an actor is to understand the style by understanding the period.

You should learn the characteristics of each historical period—the political, social, economic, philosophical, literary, and dramatic movements of the time. The following periods are those most often encountered when performing in the theatre:

Greek period
Roman period
Medieval and Tudor periods
Elizabethan period
Seventeenth-century neoclassical period
English Restoration and the eighteenth century
Napoleonic period
Romantic period
Victorian and Edwardian periods
Realistic Period

An Example of Style

One of the well-known and classic works of theatre is *The Three Sisters* by Anton Chekhov. This play is set in 1901 in Russia and shows the rather meaningless and decaying lifestyle of upper-class Russian families.

Natasha, a character in the play, is an interesting example of the use of style to make a point. She is a peasant girl who has luckily married into an upper-class family. She tries valiantly to imitate the sophistication of this family but fails. For example, she tries to imitate the custom of using French phrases in conversation and sometimes interrupts her native tongue to speak in French.

The character as written by Chekhov does not realize that her attempts at sophistication are pretentious. She simply is not sophisticated. This is amusing to the other characters and gives them an opportunity to make fun of her.

If you were playing the role of Natasha, you would need to know these facts. You would need to overplay the part, to exaggerate the upper-class behavior, in order to communicate what is happening in this play. Failure to play this role correctly would take away significantly from what the playwright is trying to say.

To play the role of Natasha in *The Three Sisters*, an actor needs to know the background of the play (Russia in 1901) and to understand that Natasha is essentially a peasant girl trying to fit into sophisticated, upper-class society.

Summary

It's important for you as an actor to understand theatrical style. A particular style will depend on the historical period and will involve such things as body movements and mannerisms, ways of speaking, and costuming. Studying the history and customs of a period can give you information on how to play a character in a historical play.

History and Style

Studying the different historical periods most often found in theatre can be fascinating. What follows will be an overview of the most common periods in which plays were written or are set.

Greek Period

Greek actors performed in large amphitheaters, so actors needed to have strong voices. Audiences were often separated from the stage by as much as a hundred yards. Stage movements had to be clear and meaningful, so actors used sweeping gestures.

Costumes in early Greek theatre were very simple, straight-line garments. In the latter part of the Greek period, the costumes became much more elaborate. They were large, heavy, and colorful so the audience could see them. The themes in Greek dramas centered on rulers and gods. Because of this, the actors needed to seem larger than life. Main actors wore high headdresses and masks. At times, masks were not made to fit the face but were placed over the head to make the actor appear taller. If the emotions of the actor changed within the role, the actor often changed masks. These masks helped create a larger-than-life quality.

Greek acting was highly stylized. It did not mimic the way the ordinary person behaved or spoke. This was primarily because the focus of Greek drama was heroes. Audiences came to the theatre to see heroes perform great and horrible deeds. The highly exaggerated acting style underscored the Greek belief in a universe of gods who participated in the lives of heroes and kings.

You can do what directors do and experiment with setting a play in a different historical time period than the one in which it was written. Remember this is an experiment. Have fun with it.

Step One
Pick the Style. Choose three different historical periods that interest you. Work with two or three other classmates. Write down the name of the period. Write down everything you know about that period.

Step Two
Find a Scene. Pick a scene from a play that you especially like. This can be a scene involving two or more characters. It doesn't need to be a long scene, perhaps only two or three minutes. It should be a fairly dramatic scene.

Step Three
Research. Now do some library research about the three historical periods you have chosen. With your classmates, find out what you can about the costuming of each period, the acting style, mannerisms, use of movement, and the use of voice. Take notes from your research.

Step Four
Plan Your Scene. Discuss the scene you have chosen with your classmates. What do you think the playwright is trying to say? Write down the main idea in two or three sentences. Then look at the three different historical periods you have

chosen and decide what the acting style would be for each.

Step Five
Practice. With your other group members, develop the characters in the scene to fit the different historical periods. You don't need to memorize the scene, but do rehearse the scene using a different acting style for each period.

Step Six
Costuming. Determine what kind of costumes you would use for these characters in the scene you are working on for each of the periods. Either draw some costumes or make photocopies of similar costuming from a book on historical costumes. What would the set be like? What kind of props would you need?

Step Seven
The Presentation. Present the three versions of your scene to another small group or in front of the whole class. Explain the setting and the costumes you would use.

Step Eight
Evaluate. In your small group, discuss the following questions: What did you learn about the scene by doing it in different historical periods? Did it help you understand the periods any better? Which periods were hardest to do? Why? Which of the periods most closely fit the scene you had chosen? Why?

Elizabethan Period

This is the period we usually associate with William Shakespeare. His plays dominated the theatre in the last part of the sixteenth century and the first part of the seventeenth century. The heroes of Shakespeare's tragic plays perform great deeds, suffer for their misdeeds, love heroically, and fight valiantly.

The people who went to see Shakespeare's plays represented a cross-section of life, from royalty and wealthy landowners to middle-class merchants to poor working-class people. These were not quiet audiences, and they were likely to eat, drink, smoke, and talk during performances.

Shakespeare wrote historical plays, tragedies, and comedies. He often borrowed stories from history or folklore.

If you have ever read a play by Shakespeare, you know that he wrote in blank verse, or unrhymed iambic pentameter. This is very different from everyday speech. The language of his plays is very important. The lines must be delivered with exceptionally clear diction. Attention to movement or mannerisms may not be as important as delivery of the lines.

If you play a Shakespearean role, you will need to develop your character primarily by studying the play and the dialogue. You will also need to concentrate on proper delivery of the lines, so that the meaning of the words and the dramatic impact of them is clear.

Playing a Shakespearean character requires exceptionally clear diction and attention to the language of the play.

Seventeenth-Century Neoclassical Period

Molière is the chief representative of this historical period. His plays are noted for their exciting characters, comic situations, and bright language. In his plays, Molière made fun of the aristocracy's extravagance and hypocrisy. Using humor, he tried to point out their foolish behavior and false values.

An actor in a Molière play must take his or her role seriously. It is the seriousness of the actor that makes the audience laugh. In such a role, an actor also needs to use his or her body to help interpret the character. For example, a very erect posture or an expression of earnestness can make a character appear ridiculous in certain situations.

The costumes and customs are important in Molière's work. Gentlemen wore wigs and perfume, carried lace handkerchiefs, and bowed frequently. Ladies would carry a fan, move with grace and ease, and flirt outrageously. All of the Molière characters are to be played with zest and enthusiasm for life. This will make the action and dialogue move rapidly. These plays are known for their wit, intelligence, and enthusiasm.

Romantic Period

The term *romantic period* doesn't really have anything to do with what we usually think of when using the word *romantic*. The Romantic period lasted from about 1800 to 1850. It was known for its emotionalism rather than reason. It was also characterized by social unrest, creativity, individualism, freedom, and an emphasis on the basic rights of people.

Some of the well-known poets of that time were Blake, Wordsworth, Shelley, Keats, and Coleridge. In the theatre, works by Goethe and Schiller were part of the Romantic movement.

The theatre of this period emphasized well-tailored and richly detailed costumes. Dresses were full-length, heavy, and colorful. Men wore suits with full-length trousers, handsome coats, and matching accessories.

The acting style for this period requires skill in movement, dance, song, and pantomime. Actors in Romantic plays use large, sweepings gestures. The action should be accompanied by flourishes. Speech in plays from this period calls for a rather loud, sweeping, and grand voice.

Realistic Period

Realism emerged near the end of the nineteenth century. The realistic movement brought with it everyday dialogue, detailed stage directions, authentic settings, complex and psychologically deep characters, and the common person.

One of the most important individuals in realistic theatre was Andre Antoine who had a theatre in Paris called The Free Theater. He produced plays that were about everyday subjects. His actors moved naturally and believably and spoke like common people.

The realistic movement soon spread to other countries. Stanislavksi, known for his method of realistic acting, had a big impact on the spread of this movement. He emphasized both acting and stagecraft that was realistic.

Realistic playwrights such as Ibsen, Chekhov, Shaw, and O'Neill wrote many plays calling for an acting technique that looks into the hidden depths of the characters and the values of society. Characters in realistic plays resemble ordinary people. They speak and act simply. When audiences view these plays, they can see certain parts of themselves or of people they know in the characters playing on the stage.

If you are doing a realistic drama, you need to concentrate on using your body, your voice, your mind, and your emotions to develop a believable character.

Summary

Some of the different historical periods include the Greek period, which emphasized grand, larger-than-life heroes and gods with grand costumes, movements, and voices. Shakespeare is representative of the Elizabethan period; he wrote historical plays, tragedies, and comedies. The language of his plays is of utmost importance. Molière represents the seventeenth century. He made fun of the aristocracy by showing their ostentatious and hypocritical lifestyles. The Romantic movement was characterized by high emotion, and the costumes were rich in detailed and well-tailored. Realism came at the end of the nineteenth century and featured common people and real language and movement.

A New Look at Shakespeare

Shakespeare may be the playwright with whom directors most often try new settings and time periods in productions. Imagine you are a director and you have the option of setting a play in any time period in history.

The most important part of the process is to pick the Shakespearean play you find most interesting. You may not have time to read whole plays. Instead, read the synopses of the plays in the book by Charles and Mary Lamb called *Tales of Shakespeare*. Decide on the play you will produce.

Reread the story of the play you have chosen. Make sure you understand it well. Try to describe what the play is about in three or four sentences. If you are having trouble with this summary of the story, show your teacher what you have written down and ask for feedback or help. Then answer the following questions:

1. What historical time period do you think the play was intended to be performed in? What time periods in history might be interesting substitutes for the playwright's intentions? For example, if the play is about a war, think about what other wars you could use as a setting. It could be the Revolutionary War, the War of 1812, the Civil War, World War I, World War II, the Vietnam War, or the Persian Gulf War. When you have selected another time period, decide why this new time frame will help the audience understand what the story is about better than the originally intended historical period. What about this new time period may distract the audience or take away from a better understanding?

2. What will the set be like for this production? Either write out what it will be like or make sketches. How will this set demonstrate what historical period this play will be in?

3. What will the costumes for the main characters be like? If you can draw, make a sketch of these costumes. If you are uncomfortable with that, then photocopy samples of costume styles that would fit the time period.

4. As director of this new production of Shakespeare, what kind of acting style would you try to get your actors to develop? How would this acting style connect with and support the historical time period you have selected for this play?

Using Style

Sometimes directors will choose to set a play in a period other than what the playwright originally intended. The director may do this with a well-known play to help the audience gain a deeper understanding of what the playwright was trying to say. In these situations, an actor needs to understand both the original setting of the play and the newly chosen setting.

Hedda Gabbler in the 1950s

A recent production of *Hedda Gabbler* was set in the South in the 1950s. Written by Ibsen, the story is of a woman who is restrained by the values of her society, which keep her from having a fulfilling life. Ibsen set the play in the late 1800s.

The Broadway production of this play had as a heroine a 1950s wife in a southern town. The production explored how she is not able to grow as a human being because of the rigid role she plays. This version of the play also explored racial tensions.

Many reviewers and audience members did not find this new interpretation of the play believable. It did not have a very long run.

Shakespeare and the Video Camera

Many of Shakespeare's plays have been set in time periods other than what he intended. A recent production of the *Merchant of Venice* by director Peter Brooks was set in the

Nontraditional casting can often help an audience to understand more clearly the message of a play. For instance, casting an African American actor to play the Jewish character Shylock in *The Merchant of Venice* allows modern audiences to comprehend the racial tensions and prejudices underlying Shakespeare's story.

1990s. The costumes were all contemporary. The language of the play was not changed, but it was spoken differently than in usual Shakespearean productions. The delivery of the lines was sometimes slower. Some speeches were delivered in a "rap" style.

Many of the speeches were videotaped by some of the minor characters, so actors could be seen on stage as well as on video screens. The character of Shylock was played by an African-American actor. The character of Shylock is a Jew who is despised by other characters in the play. This choice to use an African-American actor in the modern version helped audiences understand better the kind of racial tensions and prejudice that Shakespeare was addressing with his play.

A Play within a Play

A production by the Stratford Festival in Ontario provides an example of how another director tried to make an older work more understandable for today's audiences. The work was Gilbert and Sullivan's opera *The Pirates of Penzance*. The story is a simple one of a ship of pirates at sea and some of their adventures. The story is set in the 1800s and is usually performed in a rather romantic style.

The director at the Stratford production took some liberties and created a little play that surrounded the actual Gilbert and Sullivan work. The production starts with a band of actors coming on stage along with a somewhat demanding and eccentric movie director. He is filming *The Pirates of Penzance*. Periodically throughout the production, the action goes back to the filming and the problems with the movie company. Then it cuts back to the actual opera in performance.

This approach gives audiences a new view of a well-known work. The characters of the actors playing the roles create another storyline that adds interest to the story of the opera.

Summary

Some directors choose to set well-known and classic plays in different time periods than those in which they were written. They do this to give their audiences a new understanding of what the play is about.

Analyze

1. **Ask Questions.** Take a play from both a historical and a contemporary period. Do a play analysis and compare them by considering the following questions: What are the differences in the types of characters and the ways in which an actor would have to approach studying them? What is different about the language in each of these plays? How would this affect an actor? What about the setting? Customs? Clothes? Family relationships? Political relationships? Views on religion, sex, marriage, families? What about racial implications? Record your findings. Discuss these with others in your acting class.

2. **Find a Video.** Watch a video or movie of a Shakespearean play. Think about the main characters. Describe the acting style used in the performance. How well do the actors handle the language of Shakespeare?

You Be the Playwright

3. **Find Your Text.** Choose a familiar quotation from a Shakespearean play. Make sure it is a passage that you understand. It could be a famous line from Lady Macbeth or Hamlet's soliloquy. Read it many times until you are quite comfortable with it and think you understand it well.

4. **Get Your Pen Out.** Rewrite the quotation to fit a 1990s setting. Choose two other historical time periods and rewrite the quotation to fit the language and spirit of those periods. How important is the actual language?

A Notebook of History

5. **Ancient.** Make a notebook of samples of clothing or accessories from both the Greek and the Roman periods.

6. **Closer to Now.** Now add to your notebook. Find photographs or drawings for the following periods: Elizabethan period; English Restoration and the Eighteenth Century; Napoleonic period; and Romantic period.

Acting Out

7. **Research Your Role.** Imagine you have just had the good fortune of getting a part in George Bernard Shaw's *Saint Joan*. You will be playing the role of Joan of Arc. How will you begin to research your role? What do you need to know about the time period in which Joan of Arc lived? How can you get more biographical information about her?

8. **Think about the Playwright.** What is important for you to know about Shaw and the time in which he lived? Do you think Shaw was simply writing a historical play or was he making a statement about his time as well? What kind of character do you think Joan should be? What kind of acting style would you use?

The Actor's Logbook

1. ***Learning the Language.*** Study the historical time periods listed on page 296. Write down those that were not described in the text. Research a little bit about each time period. In your logbook, write a brief description of each period.

2. ***Acting Styles.*** Read on pages 294–296 what the elements of style are for the actor. Write down the different elements and, after each, write a description of the style for the mid-1990s. What factors would make it easy for an audience to know the time period?

3. ***Training.*** Refer to the list of elements of style you have listed in **2.** What training can you get as an actor to help you be prepared to develop the widest range of acting styles?

4. ***Masks.*** Find some examples of masks that were worn in Greek theatre. Make photocopies of these masks. Collect any other pictures of masks that were used in other theatrical periods or styles. Paste these in your logbook. Notice how the masks are similar or different.

Critical Thinking

5. ***Main Ideas.*** Write out a summary of each of the historical periods described in the text.

6. ***Compare and Contrast.*** How would a performer in a Greek tragedy differ from a performer in a work by Molière? How would the actor look different? Sound different? Act different? Use his or her body differently? In what ways might these two roles be similar?

7. ***What's Missing?*** What more would you want to know about the historical time periods briefly described on pages 298 to 302? Write down the other things you would like to know. How would you find this information?

Creative Thinking

8. ***Out of Time.*** Select your favorite actor from your favorite television show. Describe that person's acting style. Now imagine that the program was set during the Civil War. How would the story be different? How would the acting style be different? Could you tell the story of this program in that historical period? Why or why not?

9. ***What Comes to Mind?*** Make a list in your notebook of each decade for this century (1900, 1910, 1920, and so on). Next to each decade, list words that are characteristic of that time. These words could describe the clothing of the time, events of the decade, music, or language used during that decade. Write as much as you can. If you were to set a play in these decades, which elements might be most important to include?

GLOSSARY

A

Adaptation: A change on the spur of the moment due to unforeseen circumstances, usually used in relation to improvisation.

Amateur: A person who cultivates a skill without pursuing it for a living.

Amplification: The process of using electronic conductors to concentrate sound and change its volume and direction.

Antagonist: The character or situation working against the protagonist.

Antipathetic forces: Those forces working in opposition to the protagonist.

Arena stage: A stage that is entirely surrounded by members of the audience. This is sometimes called a "theatre in the round."

Articulation: The clear and concise pronunciation of words and sounds.

Artistic director: The person who is in charge of everything that happens on stage and gives overall creative direction to a theatre program.

Audition: An opportunity to try out for a part in a play.

Auguste clown: A traditional clown type often paired with the whiteface clown as the silly, bumbling sidekick; these clowns rely on pale facial makeup and exaggerated facial features to create the clown character.

B

Backstage: The area behind the set or backdrop that is not seen by the audience.

Bit: A character with very few lines in a play.

Blocking: Planning the actors' movements and the positions of sets for a play production.

Box office: Where reservations are listed and tickets are purchased for performances.

Box set: A common set constructed to represent the walls of a room in which stage action is taking place.

Callback: Asking selected actors to audition for a second or third time for a part in a play.

Cast by character: The situation in which actors portray traits that are outside their personal experience.

Cast by type: The situation in which actors are selected for parts that are very similar to their own personalities.

Casting: The process of choosing actors for the particular roles in a play.

Catharsis: The feeling of emotional release during a play when the tensions and conflicts in the characters have been revealed and resolved.

Character: A role played by an actor on stage.

Character makeup: Makeup that changes the appearance of an actor into that of the character being portrayed.

Character role: A role in which the actor and the character do not share many traits. The actor takes on a role that is very different from his or her own personality.

Characterization: The art and skill of putting together all the aspects of a character to make that role believable and realistic on stage.

Clowns: Actors who entertain an audience through the use of exaggerated facial expressions, gestures, and pantomime.

Coloring: Creating shades of meaning by inflecting or changing the pitch of the voice.

Comedy: A play with a happy ending and humorous treatment of characters and situations.

Communication: The exchange of ideas through speech or other forms of interchange.

Community theatre: Theatre produced by an independent group within a particular community to further the artistic goals of the community.

Costume: Clothing that is used to further the portrayal of a particular character on stage.

Costume designer: The person responsible for overseeing the design, acquisition, creation, and storage of costumes for a production.

Costume silhouette: The outline of a costume worn by an actor on stage.

Countercross: An actor's movement in the opposite direction of the cross made by another actor.

Criticism: The art of judging the quality of a performance or a work of art.

Cross: An actor's movement from one area of the stage to another while in character.

Cue: A signal for an actor to speak or move on stage, often the last word or action of another character.

Cyclorama: The background curtain that covers the back of the stage and the sides. Also referred to as *cyc.*

Day players: Actors who generally have very small roles and may be hired on a daily basis.

Diaphragmatic breathing: The special kind of deep breathing, using the muscle between the abdomen and rib cage, that is necessary to produce a strong voice.

Director: The person in charge of bringing a theatrical production together by coordinating the acting, technical requirements, and business functions.

Discourse: The formal combination of words into meaningful patterns.

Discovery: The finding out of important information within a play that was previously unknown.

Downstage: The area of the stage that is closest to the audience.

Drama: A play that considers serious issues and suggests solutions.

E

Emotion memory: The replacement of an actor's feelings for a character's feelings.

Empathy: The flowing of emotion from the actor to the audience and its return.

Emphasis: The stress placed upon a syllable, word, group of words, or portion of a speech.

Exposition: The part of a play that provides important information to the audience.

Extras: Actors who have no lines and essentially serve as background in scenes that involve extra people.

F

Flat: A common unit of stage scenery made from a wooden frame covered with cloth that can be painted.

Full back: The position in which an actor stands with his or her back to the audience.

Full front: The position in which an actor faces the audience directly, usually in a standing position.

G

Gel: A very thin sheet of gelatin available in a wide range of colors that can be cut and set in front of a light to color the beam directed on stage.

Gobo: A lighting material into which a pattern such as branches or stars is cut; the pattern is inserted over a lens and the image is projected on stage; also called a *cookie*.

Greasepaint: Oil-based stage makeup.

Greenroom: A backstage room where actors assemble before and after performances and wait for their cues during performances.

H

House: The auditorium or seating area from which the audience views the performance.

House manager: The person who is responsible for all activities related to the house and the audience.

I

Identification: Taking experiences from an actor's life and, for motivation, relating them to a character.

Illusion: Making the audience believe the actions on stage within the framework of the play.

Imitation: Reproducing the appearance and actions of a character in order to create a believable portrayal.

Improvisation: Creating a brief acting scene on the spur of the moment with little preparation.

Inflection: The voice's rise and fall in pitch.

Intensity: The use of vocal variation to produce a feeling of power and control in the voice.

Intuition: Immediate knowing or insight without going through a logical process.

L

Liberal arts: Courses in language, philosophy, history, and literature intended for general education.

Light plot: A detailed plan that shows the acting area, location of light instruments, and the angles of beams of light from each instrument.

Lighting designer: The person responsible for overseeing the design and operation of the lighting for a production.

M

Makeup: Color or lines applied to the face and features of an actor to aid in creating a character.

Makeup designer: The person responsible for overseeing the design, application, and clean-up of makeup for a production.

Mannerisms: The unique gestures and idiosyncrasies that make each person different. Identifying a character's mannerisms is very helpful in creating a natural and believable character for the stage.

Marks: Marks on the floor to show an actor where to move or stand.

Method acting: An acting technique in which an actor tries to identify with the character emotionally in order to create a realistic performance.

Mixer: An electronic device that receives sound signals from a variety of sources and combines them into a single sound signal for redistribution to an audience.

Musical: A type of play that contains both song and dance.

Mystery: A type of play that focuses on a crime or situation that requires the use of clues to figure out the solution.

N

Nonverbal communication: Any communication that does not involve speech. This could include gestures, body language, and facial expressions.

O

Offstage: The parts of the stage not visible to the audience.

One-quarter: The position in which an actor stands a quarter turn from the audience.

P

Pancake makeup: Water-based makeup.

Pantomime: A sequence of facial expressions, gestures, body positions, and movements that convey a story or character without words.

Pathos: The feeling of pity or sympathy the audience has for a character.

Pause: A brief suspension or hesitation of the voice.

Period play: A play set in a particular historical period with the speech patterns, manners, and costumes of that time.

Pitch: The relative highness or lowness of a person's natural speaking voice.

Play: A story told in dialogue form by actors on stage for an audience.

Plot: The events of a story organized by a playwright to achieve a dramatic effect.

Point of attention: Someone or something to look at.

Profile: The position in which actors face each other directly so the audience sees their profiles.

Projection: Controlling the volume and clearness of the voice so that it can be heard by the audience.

Prop manager: The person responsible for overseeing the acquisition, repair, and storage of stage props.

Props: Stage properties. Objects used for a performance, including hand props, objects carried on stage by an actor, and set props, which are large items placed on stage, such as furniture.

Proscenium stage: A conventional stage where the audience views the play through a permanent framed opening that is usually curtained.

Protagonist: The main character in a play.

Publicity manager: The person responsible for overseeing a production's promotion; the preparation of tickets and the program; and the training of ushers, box office workers, and ticket collectors.

R

Range: The distance in pitch between the highest and lowest tones a person can make without straining the voice.

Rate: The speed of speaking.

Reaction shot: When the camera focuses on the character who is listening to another character talk or act.

Reading: A staged or unstaged performance of a play that actors do without memorizing the script.

Repertory: A sequence of plays done over a period of time.

Resonance: The vibrating quality of the voice that amplifies and enriches the tone.

Resonators: The spaces in the head and chest, along with the nose, throat, and mouth, that play a part in voice production.

Resource: Something that is useful and can be called upon when needed.

Reversal: A change of flow of the action within a play; or when two characters are located in opposite directions and face each other.

Rhythm: The alternation of silence, sound, strength, and weakness in speech.

Royalty: The payment made to a playwright for permission to perform his or her play.

Run: The continuous series of performances of a play.

S

Scene: A small segment of a play, usually containing one central idea or line of action.

Screen test: A filmed audition to determine what an actor looks like on film.

Screenplay: A play that is written to be filmed.

Screenwriter: The person who writes a television or movie script.

Scrim: A gauze screen that creates a variety of effects on stage when combined with light.

Script audition: An audition in which an actor reads an actual scene that involves the character the actor would like to play.

Set designer: The person responsible for overseeing the design, construction, and storage of sets and scenery.

Set: A physical backdrop constructed for a play that is designed to convey key elements of time, place, and mood; or the physical setting where a movie scene is filmed.

Setting: The time and place of a play.

Sound designer: The person responsible for overseeing the design and operation of sound equipment for a production.

Stage: The place where actors create performances.

Stage business: The actions performed by an actor on stage that involve the use of props.

Stage fright: The feeling of nervousness before a theatre performance.

Stage manager: The person responsible for overseeing all the backstage elements of a production.

Stage movement: The movement of an actor from one position on stage to another.

Standard American English: American English spoken without a regional accent.

Stand-in: An actor who stands in place for a major actor while a scene is being prepared for shooting.

Steal the scene: To divert attention away from the actor on stage who should be the center of attention.

Stimulus: Anything that starts the thinking process or that awakens one of the senses.

Straight makeup: Makeup that enhances the features of the actor without changing his or her appearance.

Straight role: A role in which the actor and the character are similar. The actor makes only slight changes to portray the character in the play.

Strike: To dismantle the set after a play and store elements for future use.

Stunt players: Specially trained actors who do dangerous stunts in movies.

Style: The manner in which a play was written and the period to which it relates.

Subordinate: A character or position that is of less importance than another character or position on stage.

Substitution: The use of one of an actor's experiences to relate to the experiences of a character within the play.

Subtext: The foundation of character traits, and perhaps actions, not specifically outlined in the action of a play.

Suffering: Undergoing or experiencing any emotion or feeling within a character.

Summer stock: Semiprofessional theatre companies that produce plays throughout the United States and other countries for a whole summer.

Sympathetic forces: Those forces working for the good of the protagonist.

Sympathy: An emotional understanding between two people.

T

Technical director: The person responsible for overseeing design and production of the set, the lighting, and the sound and the people who work on those facets of a production.

Text: The words of a play.

Three-quarter: The position in which an actor turns away from the audience so that only a portion of his or her head and shoulder can be seen by the audience.

Thrust stage: A stage that is surrounded on three sides by the audience.

Timbre: The natural tone of the voice that makes it sound different from other voices.

Tragedy: A play in which the main character has a major flaw or is caught in circumstances that must be overcome, or the flaw or circumstances will destroy the character's life.

U

Upstage: The area of the stage that is farthest from the audience.

V

Volume: The force of air that determines how loudly or softly a person speaks.

W

Walk-on: A small part for an actor that does not include speaking lines on stage.

Whiteface clown: A traditional clown type that uses white facial makeup with black and red painted features and dresses in a loose jumpsuit to play tricks on others.

Wings: The offstage area to the right and to the left of the acting area. The wings are usually curtained so as not to be visible to the audience.

CREDITS

Cover
Top center: Jennifer W. Lester; **top right:** Jeff Ellis; **center left:** Jeff Ellis; **center right:** June Rothman; **bottom left:** Jeff Ellis; **bottom center:** Ophelia M. Chambliss; **bottom right:** Jeff Ellis

Chapter 1
1: Jeff Ellis; **2 left:** Jeff Ellis; **2 center and right:** Bradley Wilson; **4:** Northwestern University, National High School Institute; **8:** Jeff Ellis; **9:** Jeff Ellis; **11:** Jeff Ellis; **13:** Fritz Curzon/Performing Arts Library; **16:** Scott Mc Kiernan/Zuma

Chapter 2
20 left: Bradley Wilson; **20 right:** Jeff Ellis; **22:** Jeff Ellis; **23** Jeff Ellis; **27:** Jeff Ellis; **31:** A.M.P.A.S.; **34:** Bradley Wilson

Chapter 3
38 left and right: T. Charles Erickson; **38 center:** Bradley Wilson; **40:** Publishing Services Group; **41:** Publishing Services Group; **42:** Publishing Services Group; **43:** Publishing Services Group; **46:** Publishing Services Group; **47:** Jeff Ellis; **49:** Joan Marcus/Performing Arts Library; **53:** Northwestern University, National High School Institute; **54:** Publishing Services Group

Chapter 4
58 left: Jane Mont/Performing Arts Library; **58 center and right:** Scott Mc Kiernan/Zuma; **61:** Jeff Ellis; **62:** Northwestern University, National High School Institute; **67:** Scott Mc Kiernan/Zuma; **68:** Scott Mc Kiernan/Zuma; **69:** UPI/Bettmann; **73:** Scott Mc Kiernan/Zuma

Chapter 5
81: Jeff Ellis; **82:** Jeff Ellis; **84:** T. Charles Erickson; **88:** Ophelia M. Chambliss; **89:** T. Charles Erickson; **90:** June Rothman; **91:** June Rothman; **92:** June Rothman; **93:** June Rothman; **94:** Phillip Caruso/Motion Picture & Television Archive; **97:** Bradley Wilson; **99:** Ophelia M. Chambliss; **100:** Jeff Ellis; **101:** Ophelia M. Chambliss

Chapter 6
104: Bradley Wilson; **106:** June Rothman; **109:** June Rothman; **112:** Clive Barda/Performing Arts Library; **113:** Bradley Wilson; **118:** Bradley Wilson

Chapter 7
122 left: Jeff Ellis; **122 center and right:** Bradley Wilson; **125:** Jeff Ellis; **131:** Jeff Ellis; **133:** Jeff Ellis

Chapter 8
138 left and center: Jeff Ellis; **138 right:** Bradley Wilson; **141:** Michelle Bridwell/Photo Edit; **145:** Northwestern University, National High School Institute; **149:** Bill Richert/The Second City; **150:** Bradley Wilson

Chapter 9
157: Jeff Ellis; **158 left and right:** Jeff Ellis; **158 center:** Northwestern University, National High School Institute; **160:** Bradley Wilson; **166:** Bradley Wilson; **169:** Bradley Wilson; **170:** Gerry Goodstein

Chapter 10
178: Jeff Ellis; **180:** Jeff Ellis; **183:** Bradley Wilson; **186:** Jeff Ellis; **191:** Motion Picture & Television Archive; **194:** Jeff Ellis

Chapter 11
198: Jeff Ellis; **200:** Jeff Ellis; **203:** Publishing Services Group; **205:** June Rothman; **207:** June Rothman; **208:** Paula Weber; **211:** Ophelia M. Chambliss

Chapter 12
218: Jeff Ellis; **221:** Jeff Ellis; **225:** Jeff Ellis; **233:** Jeff Ellis

Chapter 13
237: T. Charles Erickson; **238 left:** Bonnie Kamin/Photo Edit; **238 center:** The Sheboygan Theatre Company; **238 right:** Gerry Goodstein; **241:** The Sheboygan Theatre Company; **243:** Susanne Johnson Talent Agency, Ltd.; **246:** Michael Newman/Photo Edit; **250:** T. Charles Erickson

Chapter 14
256 left: Irish Studios/The Sheboygan Theatre Company; **256 center:** John Neubauer/Photo Edit; **256 right:** T. Charles Erickson; **259:** Morton College Theatre; **265:** Joan Marcus; **269:** John Neubauer/Photo Edit

Chapter 15
274 left: Mark Richards/Photo Edit; **274 center:** David James/Motion Picture & Television Archive; **274 right:** Murray Close/Motion Picture & Television Archive; **276:** J. Hession/Shooting Star; **278:** Michael Montfort/Shooting Star; **281:** Jeff Ellis; **283:** Motion Picture & Television Archive; **285:** Buena Vista Television/Motion Picture & Television Archive; **287:** Phillip Caruso/Motion Picture & Television Archive

Chapter 16
292: T. Charles Erickson; **295:** T. Charles Erickson; **297:** T. Charles Erickson; **300:** T. Charles Erickson; **303:** T. Charles Erickson; **304:** Jennifer W. Lester

INDEX